PATTERNS OF POLICY

PATTERNS OF POLICY

Comparative and Longitudinal Studies of Population Events

Edited by
John D. Montgomery
Harold D. Lasswell
Joel S. Migdal

Transaction Books
New Brunswick, New Jersey

In Memoriam

Harold D. Lasswell (1909-1979) died while this book was still in press. As one of the seminal thinkers in this century, he had created new patterns of thinking about politics and pioneered one new field after another, including the policy sciences. He will be missed by all those who learned from his innovative ideas about civic life but most of all by those who also experienced his great personal warmth.

John D. Montgomery
and
Joel S. Migdal

Copyright © 1979 by Transaction, Inc.
New Brunswick, New Jersey 08903

Library of Congress Catalog Number: 77-94305
ISBN: 0-87855-269-3 (cloth)
Printed in the United States of America

Library of Congress Cataloging in Publication Data
Main entry under title:

Patterns of policy.

   Includes bibliographical references and index.
   1. Population policy—Addresses, essays, lectures. I. Montgomery, John Dickey, 1920-920-   II. Lasswell, Harold Dwight, 1902-   III. Migdal, Joel S.
HB885.P38   301.31   77-94305
ISBN 0-87855-269-3

CONTENTS

PART III: POLICY AS PROJECTION

INTRODUCTION

THINKING ABOUT POLICIES IN PATTERNS: CONTEXTS AND SEQUENCES

Harold D. Lasswell, John D. Montgomery, and Joel S. Migdal

Can recurrent patterns be observed in the policies of different countries that attempt to deal with major social problems? The essays in this volume present both evidence and implications that such patterns can be discussed and that it is possible to think about policy in terms of fruitful, comparative analysis.

The search for patterns of policy begins with the growing range and numbers of governmental interventions intended to affect the natural increase and the movement of people. Population concerns have become a distinct and rapidly enlarging sphere of political activity. In one way or another, governments have long intervened in the civic order hoping to influence the size, quality, or location of their populations; such interventions are not exclusively modern phenomena. What is different about current population policies is that many of the formerly "indirect" interventions (that is, policies that had

1

unintended population effects) are now being scrutinized and turned into "direct" public policies because of these by-products. Governments are recognizing the significance of population changes as a constraint on nearly all of their activities. Schooling, housing, urban development, land tenure, taxation: these are only a few areas of public policy that are now seen as population-related activities. Because the issues involved in these policies are inherently important, and because they have already been the subject of substantial research, population policies are an especially inviting target for comparative and longitudinal analyses.

The search for patterns of population policy centers about three related dimensions that correspond to the three parts of this book: forms of internal dynamics in the policy experience in different countries, or in single countries over time; the types of relations between policies and their social and political context; and anticipated dimensions of future interactions between a policy and the social order.

THE INNER DYNAMICS OF POLICY EXPERIENCE

Studying policy experiences themselves to identify recurrent patterns requires extensive use of case histories, especially those in which the events are recorded in a form that permits the observer to extract their essence for purposes of comparative analysis.

One of the paradoxes of this inquiry has been the scarcity of such histories in the face of so much experience. Considering the importance of population issues and the extensive research devoted to them during the past decade, it is surprising that social scientists have been unable as yet to utilize actual policy experience as a guide to those who are attempting to use public resources to influence family decisions. Analyses abound with hypotheses about relationships between social circumstances and family size and location, but little is known about efforts to use such circumstances as a basis for government interventions.

The strategy followed in these studies of policy dynamics has been to make use of existing histories, standardizing the arrangement and presentation of experience just enough to permit us to accumulate comparative data without distorting the events as originally observed. The principles of standardization adopted in this volume include two elements, those involving "sequences" and "actors." In this context, the scenario of sequences is said to begin with circumstances leading decision makers to their first definition of the problem and delineation of its dimensions. It continues with the processes of policy promotion and proclamation, and the assignment and use of resources in policy implementation, and it concludes with various transitional and terminal phases of decision making. The terms used to describe these functions and phases have not been standardized in these essays although the concepts themselves are familiar to students of the policy sciences and readers of an earlier volume on the subject.[1]

The second common element in these case studies is the attempt to characterize the actors who took part in these processes of decision making. Such generalizations have been based on either the participant's status (religious leader, and international organization, or a government minister), or his function (opposition or supporting coalition). They, too, permit the reader to perceive common patterns of interaction that might not have been evident, even to the actors themselves, during the events described.

Three types of case histories are presented here: the single country study, the comparative analysis of a few country experiences, and a more comprehensive conspectus stemming from examination of large numbers of individual policy histories. Each of these three approaches presents its own paradigms of policy analysis, illustrated respectively in these pages by Ickis, Korten and Korten, and Montgomery.

The country study obviously presents the most intimate or personalized view of the actors. It may introduce comparative or institutional dimensions, as in Ickis's use of organization theory to explain the behavior of individual participants in policymaking. But insofar as it transcends immediate experience at all, its primary usefulness in the current search for patterns of policy lies in its cumulative properties, that is, its potential utility for structuring data for subsequent analysis.

The comparative case studies in this volume focus on the behavior and characteristics of institutions, especially those engaged in various aspects of policy implementation. The Kortens' study of policies in El Salvador, Costa Rica, and Nicaragua, for example, highlights comparative patterns and variations in the events leading to national population policy. Similarly, the Warwick essay on population policy in the Philippines, Egypt, Mexico, and Kenya offers new insights into the interaction between the inner dynamics of policy and the dimension examined in Part II, the larger context, within which policy is framed. Comparative case studies are essential for generating hypotheses about the relation of policy dynamics to their specific institutional and normative settings.

The most all-inclusive conspectus of policymaking is illustrated by Montgomery's essay, which attempts to identify categories of experience in such a way that frequencies of probabilities can emerge from the analysis. Thus, for example, he identifies the most frequent pattern of coalition-building during the process of promoting family planning policies: the private physician and volunteer social service leaders, working with political leaders (a coalition that led to the prescriptive adoption of an antinatalist policy in nine of the twenty-four countries he consulted). His study of the procedures used in appraising family planning also permits the reader to identify the hypothesized social relationships that are most frequently invoked in evaluations of program success or failure.

These three perspectives are not, of course, mutually exclusive, but each calls for a different focus of attention and achieves a different level of abstraction. The challenge of the individual case study is providing the detail required for vitality as well as contextual accuracy; that of the comparative study is exploring the interaction of the internal dynamics of policy with the settings in which policymaking takes place; and that of the multicountry conspectus is producing generalizations that are inductively defensible.

Population policies, unlike foreign policies or agricultural policies, are not standard functions in the public sector. They do not define the jurisdictional reach of a single career bureaucracy; they have no history. Indeed, they have only recently been recognized as distinctive aspects of public policy. And the few systematic studies of population policy that are now available are limited in scope, tending to concentrate on family planning or family allowances, which are not necessarily the most important instruments available for public action. But they do permit policy scientists to examine the inner dynamics of country experiences in initiating, organizing, implementing, and evaluating population interventions. Population policies provide, even in this limited context, an excellent laboratory for comparative and longtitudinal analysis.

THE CONTEXT OF POLICY

The inner dynamics of population policies—the actors and sequences involved—give us only part of the history of these policies. Patterns can also be discerned in the contexts within which population issues arise. Those searching out contextual patterns want to know: When does population become an issue for direct policymaking? Which internal and international conditions facilitate governmental concern, or else inhibit the issue from ever reaching the agenda? What are the effects of cultural factors, levels of development, public opinion, and the structure of institutions on the policy-making process and on the ultimate input of the policy? Contexts affect the urgency governments feel to deal directly with the population question and the content and effectiveness of their responses once they decide to act.

Historically, "direct" policies have probably had much less impact on population behavior than programs undertaken for other purposes that incidentally influence birth or migration rates. As political leaders become more concerned with population densities, movements, and locations, therefore, these "indirect" consequences of public policy are beginning to enter into the calculus of national and local planning. Even so apparently remote a concern as land reform can be treated (as F. Iqbal does in this volume) as a population issue. Population policies are a growing sector of conscious public action partly because they are beginning to incorporate the indirect effects of previous government actions. The period between 1960 and 1974 seems to have been critical, not only because of the far-reaching demographic changes that occurred then, but also because that was a turning point in directing the attention of governments to possible effects their actions may have on population issues. In 1960 there were only three countries with population policies and only one offering family planning services, but by 1975 an estimated 93 percent of the developing world's population lived in countries that espoused such policies or offered such services.

Three major factors have contributed to this rising awareness of the importance of "indirect" population policies and their transition to "direct" policies: the increasing scope of national interdependency, the rediscovery of demographic variables as influences on human welfare, and changing perceptions of the role of government in societal affairs.

Since the sixteenth century various parts of the globe have entered into an interacting world-system.[2] Diverse and isolated peoples have engaged in economic relations contributing to their individual welfare but leading increasingly to their mutual dependence. Events in distant areas now routinely affect the size, composition, and movements of population in other areas.

These continuing population changes, starting with colonial expansion and yielding in the end to economic interdependence, were both an effect of the world-system and a prerequisite to its continued development. Population changes responded to the world-system's increasing interdependence: the unprecedented rates of natural increase after the colonial era began to affect whole continents simultaneously, and new forms and rates of internal and international migration have continued to emphasize the global nature of population behavior. Their potential effect on the continued growth of the world-system has summoned widely differing proposals. In the past, some argued for intervening in population movements and social structures to achieve a worldwide division of labor, including plantation economies and slave trading.[3] More recently, others have argued for the need for growing and more mobile labor forces.[4]

In the course of the past generation, the international concerns over population changes have become formally institutionalized. Growing numbers of international agencies, both within the United Nations and within regional groupings, have begun to deal with population issues. A year devoted to concern with the question of population was capped in August 1974 by the World Population Plan of Action, issued by the United Nations World Population Conference held in Bucharest. Simultaneously, the World Bank and the Agency for International Development have increasingly tied their lending to responsiveness on the population issue by borrower countries.

A second strand leading to a change in the sense of urgency is a growing awareness of the rapidity of population change. In part, this awareness stems from new and more reliable demographic data outlining the dimensions of the situation. China's census in 1953, for example, established that there were already more than half a billion people in that country, a finding that had important policy repercussions in subsequent years.

Other objective criteria also lent to the sense of urgency. In Mexico, where there was a complete turnabout from pronatalist to antinatalist policies in 1972, officials were facing a school population that was growing by more than half a million students each year. Countries throughout Asia, Africa, and Latin America have experienced the mushrooming of squatter settlements and shantytowns. Such changes result in an increasing demand for everything from assured supplies of food to sewage facilities.[5]

A third source of the present sense of urgency is the changed public perception of the role of governments in affecting social behavior. The dominant, overarching political values of the modern era have been state sovereignty and national integration. The acceptance of these goals has meant that in recent times the very nature of society has become a direct object of political concern. Social structure itself is increasingly viewed as a political issue; the state's role in affecting class and status is activist. Although throughout history governments have intervened in population matters, the scope and level of involvement have been growing exponentially during the last generation. Population issues have become part of the political domain as never before.

Yet once governments abandon their positions of neutrality on population issues, their purposes may still vary widely. Historically, most interventions have favored population growth to insure the survival of the group (whether family, tribe, or nation). Only in very recent times have these concerns generally receded, bringing qualitative issues to the fore.

The concern with population growth historically could be seen in population policies which have attempted to: (1) replace populations lost through famine and war; (2) enlarge military or labor force potentials; (3) settle remote or barren areas; and (4) maintain the vigor and ethnic purity of the "race." The reasons that have induced governments to adopt antigrowth policies have been equally varied: (1) to conserve food and water; (2) to maintain economies of scale in farm units; (3) to improve the quality of services available to the community; (4) to maintain ethnic homogeneity; and (5) to weed out weaker members of the race by tests of survival (in ancient times).

Modern governments have continued to vary markedly from one another in their population goals. Policies oriented toward population growth still dominate the field. Some of these efforts to foster a large population are analyzed in Nancy Lubin's chapter on population policies in the Soviet Union since the October Revolution. Even when governments try to be neutral on family decisions, the consequences tend to be pronatalist in most societies where social traditions favor children and protect those engaged in childrearing. Espousing growth is politically easier for most governments than discouraging it because pronatalist policies continue to support longstanding trends that have insured survival. The possibility that group survival may no longer be a pure function of numbers and fecundity is hard to assimilate. While fertility policies, on balance, seem to favor growth, governments have become increasingly restrictive in policies of growth through interstate migration. Phillip Clark's chapter on Australia and Ellie Glaessel-Brown's paper on the Dominican Republic point to the continuation of harsh restrictions on immigration even when there are clearly perceived needs for the functions immigrants can perform.

Espoused antinatalist policies (or promigration policies) are more interesting to policy scientists than pronatalist (or restrictive migration) policies because they arise out of a dawning recognition that so-called "natural forces" are somehow failing to serve human needs. But governments prefer not to interfere with such "natural forces"; even modest policies aimed at reversing the benefits that society normally bestows upon childhood and parenthood require strong convictions on the part of political and social leaders, and they almost invariably encounter resistance from other social forces. Thus such policies enter the political arena, and the struggle that follows takes on a predictable pattern. The family itself becomes a political issue, and "baby politics" divides society along lines that can be identified as clearly as the interest groups associated with labor, religions, ethnicity, or capital gains taxes. Eventually, the political struggle ends and the arena changes to administration where new participants emerge. The cycle is complete when social processes respond to the population policies, creating a new round of problems for the political arena.

The essence of family planning in its earliest stages was the assumption that individuals will act in the public interest if they are sufficiently conscious of the implications of their actions. But this assumption is no longer tenable; it runs contrary to too many aspects of human behavior. Family planning enthusiasts no longer rest their case on the proposition that because mankind as a whole would benefit from population control, each family will automatically set limits to its own size. Population policies now present the incentives at family level; family planners no longer simply equate the public good and the private good. The logic of social action rejects the hope that if one wants his neighbor to have fewer children, it automatically means that he wants fewer of his own. Similarly, with the burdens posed by rapid urban growth, governments have increasingly become aware that exhortations and restrictions are inadequate. The incentives to move or not to move must change the very calculus for action at the individual and family level. These contrary value preferences become even sharper when they involve the behavior of competing ethnic groups or social or economic classes. Myron Weiner's essay highlights the clash of such value preferences and the policy responses in an Indian state.

In the same manner, a decision to have an extra child (assuming it to be rational at all in any meaningful sense) arises out of a calculus that incorporates many private and collective values. Parents may desire a larger family because it becomes a source of self-protection, since it would increase the resources available to defend the household against intruders (a common condition in Ethiopia and Nepal, for example). Or it could add to its wealth, improve its sense of well-being, protect an inherited trade, provide added pleasure in the parents' private lives, enhance the parents' social status, or conform to their perceptions of their religious obligations—or perhaps, in various degrees, advance all of these values. In each instance the private gain might well encumber a public loss. These considerations help explain why family planning so often begins with an official denial that the state has any legitimate concern over fertility decisions, and ends up as an active communications program designed to change existing family-size preferences.

In short, as leaders have developed more articulated, detailed, and complex preferences for defining the quality of life in their societies—and indeed the nature of the societies themselves—they have greatly increased their concern with social processes. But as Migdal's paper demonstrates, social processes are less easily manipulated than political relationships. Among the elements of the context within which governments try to adopt and implement policies are (1) the levels of economic and social development, (2) the configurations of social structure and popular opinion, (3) the legacy of previous governmental decisions, and (4) the nature of political institutions. These four elements provide a basis for exploring comparative patterns of the wider context inhibiting or facilitating the government's efforts through policies in various problem areas.

Population processes have fluctuated greatly through history, and a combination of contextual elements have made them difficult for leaders to manipulate consciously. Thus it becomes increasingly important to identify the patterns of social and political contexts and of reinforcing and conflicting policies that affect population.

In effect, any attempt to gain control over the population process forces us to look at several analytic levels simultaneously and hypothesize about the interactions among them. These levels include (1) aggregate changes in population, (2) public policies (both those directly dealing with population changes and those having unintended effects on population), and (3) civic policies (individual or family actions) having an effect on population changes. Focusing on these three levels enables us to note the effects that varying contexts have on policies. For example, we might ask what effect varying institutional contexts (e.g., level of institutionalization or regime type) might have on population policies. Or, alternatively, one might ask, as Donald Warwick does in his essay, how particular cultural elements and historical patterns have led to widely different impacts for family planning programs.

Diagrams A-F

A	B	C
Population changes: fertility composition, movement	Public policies with intended effects: continued, terminated, introduced	Public policies with unintended or indirect effects: continued, terminated, introduced

D	E	F
Civic policies with intended or unintended effects (besides compliance)	Population changes: impacts on quality of life	Proposed public policies

Diagrams A,B,C,D,E, and F indicate the principal subdivisions of the projection and the recommended sequence of preparation. The subdivisions will not be completed "once and for all" at any one time. They will affect each other, and as data begin to feed back during future years, further changes will be made.

Diagram A, dealing with demographic data, suggests the projection is expected to include changes in *fertility rates, composition,* and *movement* of the population.

Diagram B calls attention to the probable future of *public policies* with *intended* effects on family planning and fertility, population composition, and movement. The problem is to estimate which policies will be *continued* (with modifications), *terminated,* or *introduced.* In addition, the problem is to estimate what population changes can be attributed to these policies. Clark's study of migration in Australia is essentially an exploration of Diagram B.

Diagram C refers to the probable future of public policies with *unintended* or *indirect* effects on population. Changes in land ownership and rights, educational services, and labor legislation are examples of public measures that may be enacted with other than population consequences in mind but which affect family planning and fertility, population composition, and movement in varying degrees. Iqbal's article, for example, attempts to guage some of the effects of land reform on fertility by considering a number of critical intervening variables. Part of the projection calls for estimates to be made of the probable impact of these policies on population.

The public policies mentioned in diagrams B and C are part of the public (official) order of the country under study. They are decisions of the institutions specialized to government, law, and politics. Obviously, they have consequences for the civic (private) order. In fact, the principal impact of public order decisions is usually on civic choices. The formation and execution of public policy in these instances aims to affect the result of policy formation and execution in the civic order (in the family, for example).

The estimates that are made of the public policies referred to in diagrams B and C will have evaluated the conformity of civic policy to public decisions. This leaves entirely uncovered, or covered only by implication, the large volume of civic policy that is in opposition to public policy, or that deals with matters outside the scope of public authority. In the future, tribal customs may continue to exert an effective veto on official regulations. Customary prescriptions may supplement as well as supplant any governmental decisions having population impacts. As diagrams D and E suggest, projections should include policies within the civic order (except compliance choices) that influence population change. What policy changes are anticipated? What impacts are they likely to have on population? Civic policies are also divisible into the categories of *intended* and *unintended* (or *indirect*) effects.

The impact of public policy on social processes, as is discussed in Migdal's paper, depends very much on the strength of the state (the degree of political centralization which gives the state the autonomy and coherence to implement a broad range of measures) and the structure of the society. Western societies have been characterized by strong centers, a consensus of values and beliefs that gives the basis for an integration of elites and organization from diverse sectors. Third World societies, on the other hand, often display their strength, not in centers, but in the numerous interdependent ties dispersed throughout the society (for example, kinship ties, local village ties, and patron-client ties). Such societies may be much more difficult to change through public policy, not only because of their dependence on traditional structures, but also because of the relative inefficacy of public policy. Thus we can hypothesize that they will exhibit a much weaker relationship between changes in public policy and similarly directed changes in civic policy. By the same token, we can anticipate the need for great sensitivity to changes in the civic order that affect the capacity and will of the government.

The patterns of policy identified in this exploratory volume are sufficiently numerous and far reaching to warrant the conclusion that the investigation is a promising direction for scholarly and planning efforts to follow. A further implication is that the making, implementation, and study of social policies, both public and civic, will become more effective as they become more repetitive and cumulative in future years.

POLICY AS PROJECTION

Policies both anticipate future events and attempt to change the course of future events. Whether explicitly or not, policy planning is a form of social projection. An important step in the task of relating a policy scientist to a particular country (or to any other context) is to develop a preliminary projection of population changes, public policies, and their interconnections.

The chosen context of policymaking may be a single country, an area within a country, or a transnational region or group of countries. Most policies occur at the national level where political leaders attempt to come to grips with the interaction between population changes and public policies. Though this level of policy analysis may seem an obvious starting point, the recent Club of Rome works indicate that global problems are also a basis for analyzing the need for solutions even when the opportunities for creating effective public policies for the world are minimal.[6] It is not yet even feasible to project a policy model applicable to all countries since important bodies of needed data are missing. But it is now possible to suggest a framework on the basis of which desired data can be obtained and made available for future use. The flow of data during the years to come will make it possible to revise scientific models as well as future projections and descriptions of past trends. Moreover, these revisions will stimulate modifications in goals and strategies in the policy process. The initial projection undergoes constant, progressive change.

Once it is recognized that projections are an inherent part of policymaking and of the role of the policy scientist, it becomes imperative to try to gain as much control over the processes as possible so that implications of planning are carefully examined. The basic objective is not forecasting; it is control. Such a conception emphasizes the role of creative imagination in designing strategies by which generalized goals can become realized objectives. Control means bringing as much rigor as possible into the process of forecasting despite the difficulty of forecasting social change. Even such an elusive subject as the consequences of increased human longevity can be projected, as Gaither Bynum's chapter demonstrates.

Such an effort at projection would involve three steps. The first step for each public policy is to examine trends and estimate future developments *at each level of authority* for each outcome phase. As these operations proceed, data and judgments are accumulating about both internal and external factors that condition the policy process and its impacts. The last step in the sequence in policy analysis is evaluation, both of the policymaking process and of the eventual impacts on society.

NOTES

1. Warren F. Ilchman, Harold D. Lasswell, John D. Montgomery, and Myron Weiner, *Policy Sciences and Population* (Lexington, Mass.: D.C. Heath, 1975).

2. See Immanuel Wallerstein, *The Modern World-System* (New York: Academic Press, 1974).

3. On the complex relationship among slavery, capitalism, and the expansion of commercialism, see Eugene D. Genovese, *Roll, Jordan, Roll* (New York: Pantheon Books, 1974), pp. 44-47. On plantation economy and forced and cheap labor, see Clifford Geertz, *Agricultural Involution* (Berkeley: University of California Press, 1971), pp. 110-11; and Ramiro Guerra y Sánchez, *Sugar and Society In The Caribbean* (New Haven: Yale University Press, 1964) p. 19.

4. See, for example, Clark Kerr et al., *Industrialism and Industrial Man* (Cambridge, Mass.: Harvard University Press, 1960).

5. John D. Montgomery, "Planning to Cope," in Ilchman et al.; John E. Jackson, ed., *Public Needs and Private Behavior in Metropolitan Areas* (Cambridge, Mass: Ballinger, 1975).

6. Donella H. Meadows, et al., *The Limits to Growth* (2nd ed.: New York: University Books, 1975): and Mesarovic, et al., *Mankind at the Turning Point* (1974).

PART I
INNER DYNAMICS OF POLICY

1

POPULATION POLICIES AS SOCIAL EXPERIMENTS

John D. Montgomery

Decision makers concerned with the impact of public policies on social behavior are beginning to consult the policy sciences in the hope of finding better ways to learn from experience. Like other prudent managers, government officials want to avoid experimenting with public policies if they believe they can find guidance by analyzing successes and failures elsewhere. But comparative policy analysis[1] takes place on many levels. It examines decrees, statutes,[2] technological decisions,[3] organizational structures,[4] effectiveness in delivering benefits, budget and program dimensions,[5] and historical processes[6] in various comparative contexts. But which approach offers the best prospects for appraising experience and converting the knowledge thus gained into a basis for action? This chapter will suggest a procedure for examining patterns of policymaking that will permit the observer to locate his immediate experience in relation to other comparable situations. Examples are drawn from population policies, but the approach is applicable to all forms of social intervention. The fact that nearly all countries have now experimented with various forms of direct population policies and programs has created a vast reservoir of untreated experience in that area. The continuing urgency of the problem and the diminishing effectiveness of tradi-

17

tional population policies make it timely to consider how best to convert that experience into data.

POLICY SEQUENCES AND PATTERNS

Population policies have evolved in sufficiently similar contexts to permit comparison among emergent sequences and patterns in all parts of the world. The actors involved in initiating, influencing, deciding, implementing, and opposing policies have also played roles that can be compared even in quite different settings. As yet, however, the basic patterns of policy interaction are as ill-defined as Rohrschach ink blots. There are still too few policy histories available to fill in the details. Moreover, what is known about policy experience is derived primarily from the work of population specialists rather than policy analysts. It is not structured to aid decision makers. For example, the demographic facts that might require a decision to intervene in population issues are well documented; but little is written about how they were perceived, or about the coalition-building processes that occurred once the public sector became engaged. What laws were passed, and what agencies were organized to implement them, are public knowledge. But much less is known systematically about the administrative processes and policy transitions that followed. And the procedures that have been used to evaluate their effects are now a subject of intense debate among demographers and other social scientists.[7] The first step to reduce these uncertainties is to see if there are sequential patterns in which decision-making functions have occurred and policy actors have influenced events.

Recognition of the Problem: The "Intelligence" Function

Like most other government actions, family planning programs usually start as a result of a series of decisions taken privately in reaction to social changes of public importance. They tend to begin unofficially, tentatively, and outside the government's jurisdiction altogether. Family planning is characteristically a service that is provided wholly by private physicians until government or civic leaders become aware that a demand or need for it is of public concern.

Civic leaders do not perceive such a demand by direct observation. They may be personally aware of growing queues and crowded streets long before recognizing the existence of a "population problem." But their private awareness provides no basis for policymaking until systematic disruptions or dissatisfactions appear in public functions or until demographers and planners have performed the "intelligence" function of gathering, interpreting, and applying general data about population change. This process converts vague personal observations into the definition of a social condition.

Demography, the professional intelligence arm of population policy, is a highly developed art form. But relying upon it for policy guidance is both costly and politically risky. Regular census-taking has not been a tradition in most countries where the population is growing rapidly. Even countries that do take a national census sometimes produce data that are too "fragile" to serve policy needs. Indeed, only in exceptional cases have such data proven decisive in producing government interventions. (India is one such case: in formulating the first five-year plan in 1951, the official spur to action in family planning was the fact that the census had just demonstrated what officials considered an "astonishing" rate of growth.) In countries where economic planners dominate public policy, demographic projections can provide rigorous and convincing evidence of the need for action. But most countries have edged toward strong population policies in response to political, not demographic, data; action has usually preceded planning.

Factors Limiting the Actual Use of the "Intelligence Function"

Three factors have limited the use of scientific intelligence data in the establishment of population policies: cost, resentment over the invasion of privacy, and ideology.

The sheer cost of census-taking is sufficiently massive to discourage frequent surveys even in rapidly changing and wealthy countries like Switzerland and the United States, the two countries that have conducted a continuous census since the eighteenth century. Census-taking in Africa now costs about twenty-five cents per head; the 1980 census will use standardized reporting systems that require no coding before the data is processed, but it will nevertheless cost at least fifty cents per capita.

The cost factor can, of course, be reduced by the interim use of other data-gathering devices, such as scientific sampling taken at annual or five-year periods. Even so, most population intelligence still comes from improvisations and makeshift estimates. China, whose population policies have the reputation of determined target-setting, performed the intelligence function by mobilizing two and a half million officials, students, and party cadre members to tabulate the entire population in the single twenty-four–hour period of June 30, 1953. In actually counting 582,603,417 Chinese, they claimed to have produced the most "comprehensive and useful census" in a century. Challenged as it has been in detail and methodology, this exercise proved to be seminally important in subsequent population policy-making.[8] Israel used the army to take a one-day census in the occupied territories after the 1967 war—an operation that was considered a military necessity. India's 1971 census used free enumeration and tabulation by school teachers, and most of the other labor required was available free or below marginal cost. But the census still cost five cents per head, largely because so many extra supplies—3,000 metric tons of paper, among other items—had to be purchased.[9]

A second limitation on demographic intelligence is the inhospitable cultural environment in most countries for scientific inquisitiveness about private matters. Even if a family's size as such is not investigated too closely, its mere location can be a difficult and sensitive issue. Migration is a persistent reality; migrants and nomadic peoples are hard to track down for purposes of census-taking in much of Africa, Asia, and the Middle East. Because of limited resources, Ghana's census of 1948 resorted to enumerating the population in different areas on different dates, an approach that made it impossible to generate migration statistics or avoid double counting and undercounting. Moreover, in using the family and household as a unit, despite wide variance in different countries and regions, the census did not permit statistical analyses of individual relationships that are so important in Western census data.[10]

Widespread illiteracy and the resulting carelessness in reporting also make census-taking difficult in these conditions. In Bangladesh, a demographer noted that when asked how many children they had, mothers tended to report only the number of sons.[11] Often parents do not keep track of their children's ages. To compensate for this difficulty, both in 1960 and 1970 the census takers in Ghana attempted to get women to estimate the age of their children by relating their births to important national events they recalled. By chance, however, both of these censuses occurred three years after a major event (independence in 1957 and overthrow of the civilian government in 1967). As a result an unusually high number of children were reported as three years old in both 1960 and 1970. Other "lumps" in the age cohort tables were noted at the nearest five- or ten-year cohort.[12]

In many countries, stillbirths and deceased children are not reported, which means that fertility behavior cannot be studied accurately. Capping these technical and cultural difficulties is the desire for privacy on the part of both rural and urban poor, especially those who distrust official visitors (often assumed to be inspectors or tax collectors). Many subgroups in the population have never had any favorable outcome from interviews with government officials, and have no reason to expect any benefit to emerge from telling the truth to a census taker.

A third major constraint on the development and use of population intelligence is ideology. Politicians are suspicious of any numbers that might discredit preferred dogma. Three types of countries are particularly vulnerable to ideological considerations affecting population policies: those with ethnically homogeneous regions, Marxist regimes, and aid-receiving countries that fear outside manipulation.

A special form of ideological concern is the desire to suppress data that might appear threatening to specified ethnic groups. Rwanda, for example, had a competent resident demographer who was never invited to supply data for planning purposes because of the ethnic instability of the country. Especially where communal rivalry is severe, officials are often unwilling to risk the consequences of announcing uneven ethnic growth, since it might be interpreted to mean that some groups are engaged in slowly "usurping" the rights of others. In such cases, population problems have to be diagnosed and treated indirectly, for example, by noting the increasing length of the queues lining up for government services.[13]

In some Marxist countries, the productivity of human resources is regarded as a function of a properly regulated economy, which makes anti-Malthusianism all but obligatory. Data do not always support that proposition, however, and leaders in these countries often feel constrained to suppress evidence that numbers are becoming excessive until they have found an acceptable explanation. Ideological distrust of demography has spread into the international arena because so many political leaders have the impression that aid donors discriminate against rapidly growing countries. The suspicion that the "imperialist" countries are attempting to substitute population control for economic justice is often reinforced by casual statements and deeds on the part of aid donors, such as the U.S. Congress's desire to cut aid to countries without family planning programs regardless of their demographic condition.

Because of such constraints, population intelligence often consists of surrogate data. Malaysia, which is sensitive to communal differences, supplemented the 1950 and 1960 census with agricultural productivity surveys (mostly among ethnic Malays) to give planners a more accurate focus on population relationships. In Lebanon, where for reasons of ethnic rivalry exact censuses have not been taken for many years, the government used the labor force count as a basis for identifying and predicting population change even though the data excluded unpaid family workers and wives.[14] Even in China, for want of data the Ministry of Public Health had to anticipate the results of the 1953 enumeration by consulting land-use reports, which showed that the rural population was much greater than official data had suggested. Without waiting for census returns, it ordered its staff to make birth-control facilities available on request, thus silently reversing the Maoist-socialist doctrine against such interventions.[15]

Countries have also used sample village data as surrogates for a national census. Such surrogates pose problems of their own, however. The Ghana census reports of 1960 showed many quirks of reporting (the population of Kwahu and Knepi were reported as 500,000 in 1891, although the census of 1911 had reported only 58,525). Still other anomalies appear in in-depth census reports that have made it almost impossible to identify trends and make projections in that country.[16]

Interpreting population intelligence requires special professional care where analysts are forced to use unconventional procedures, a condition that is common where political circumstances make it impossible to collect objective demographic data. This requirement poses an especially serious problem for policymakers because those are usually the very countries where the population is undergoing the most rapid change. Thus the population intelligence function, though highly technical, is rarely divorced from politics. Demographic studies emerging from census bureaus do not really define the population problems faced by politicians, though politicians cannot interpret the problems without their aid. Nor can population intelligence be perceived as a preliminary stage of decision making, to be set aside like a completed census. It cannot be superceded or displaced by other functions in the policy process. Population policies are in a state of constant interaction with social forces; both the procedures and the substantive outcomes of population intelligence are likely to change in response to the needs of policymakers.

Building Coalitions for Action: The "Promotion" Function

A vigorous political process is placed in motion after a major population problem has been identified and leaders have obtained substantial information about it. Political leaders soon discover that

Table 1
Structure and Process of Coalition-Building in Family Planning Policies

COUNTRY	INITIATING ACTOR AND DATE	PRINCIPAL COALITION PARTNER AND DATE	COALITION-BUILDING TIME	SOURCE OF INTERNATIONAL INTERVENTION	SOURCE OF OPPOSITION
Bangladesh	C (1953)	A (1972)	C-A	19	$ B (1965)	E
Chile	A (1938)	B (1965)	A-B	27	A (1962)	F
China (old)	A ( )	A (1933*)?				
Columbia	A (1959)	D (1965)	A-D	6	$ A (1965)	F
Costa Rica	A (1962)	B (1963*)	A-B	1	A (1966)	F
Egypt	C (1953)	A (1955)	C-A	2	$ A (1967)	H
Fiji	C (1949)	A (1951)	C-A	2	$ C 1957	H
India	A (1925)	D (1935)	A-D	10	A 1940	I
Indonesia	A (1957)	D (1963*)	A-D	6	A 1963	E
Iran	C (1960)	B (1966)?	C-B	6?	$ C (1957)	I
Japan	A (1923*)	D (1948)	A-D	25	A 1922	E, (G)
Korea	A (1953*)	D (1963*)	A-D	10	A (1962)	H
Malaysia	A (1933*)	C (1955)	A-C	12	$ A (1959)	F
Mauritius	D (1950)	A (1958)	D-A	8	$ A 1963	F
Mexico	A (1959)	B (1961)	A-B	2		E, (G)
Morocco	C (1965)	D (1966)	C-D	1	$ C (1965)	E?
Pakistan	A (1947)	C (1958)	A-C	11	$ A (1954)	
People's Republic Of China	C (1949)	D (1953*)	C-D	4		H
Philippines	A (1933*)	D (1953*)	A-D	20	$ A (1953*)	F
Singapore	A (1949)	D (1959)	A-D	10	$ A (?)	F
Sri Landa	B (1949)	A (1953)	B-A	4	$ B (1953)	F
Sweden	A (1923*)	D (1929)	A-D	5		H
Uganda	A (1957)	C (1962)	A-C	1	$ A (1966)	E, (F)

ACTORS: A, Private physicians, volunteer social service leaders. B, Officials in Health Ministry. C, Civil or military bureaucracy. D, Political leaders or media. E, Nationalist movement. F, Religious leaders. G, Socialist leaders. H, No public opposition.

VOTES: *Date estimated. ?Information doubtful or uncertain. $Important international intervention, including financial operating support. –Unknown.

SOURCE: Population Council and AUFS Country Studies.

important interests are at stake and it is they who have to identify the likely consequences of alternative solutions. The coalition-building process that ensues involves a search for partners in persuasion. The practices known as log-rolling or interest articulation begin to press for a formal, authoritative decision about future courses of action. The intelligence function has been described as professionalism tinged with politics; what follows is quintessentially political.

Table 1 is based on policy histories of twenty-three countries. It identifies the principal "actors" in initiating, supporting, and opposing family planning policies. Since the processes of policy promotion and coalition building in these countries took place over many years and in many different circumstances, the roles and tactics of these actors varied considerably. There is nevertheless enough experience in common to permit us to draw a few broad conclusions about the initiators, supporting coalitions, and opponents of the resultant policy.

The initiative for introducing family planning services has come predominantly from private physicians and voluntary welfare leaders even in states that strongly prefer using the public sector as the chosen instrument of change and "modernization." International support has often been a decisive influence on the final decision, building upon a momentum developed internally. In all twenty-three of these countries, family planning is now financially supported as an official public policy, and fifteen of them adopted that decision after strong private leadership and promotion. Technical and bureaucratic forces, either civilian or military, took the lead in six more. Official public health and medical ministries led the way in only one country, and political leaders in one more.

Where the private service sector was not the initiating actor, it figured almost as significantly as the principal coalition partner: in five countries they performed this constituency-building role. Thus in twenty of the twenty-three countries in this sample, private actors dominated the promotional phases of policymaking. Only in Morocco, the People's Republic of China, and Iran were the efforts of private physicians and social service volunteers found insignificant in the policy histories compiled for this study of policymaking coalitions.

Countries in which the promotion of family planning started in the public sector were led predominantly by the bureaucracy (civil or military), not by politicians. The bureaucracy served as the principal coalition partner in three countries, and political leaders in ten.

The most important coalition-building links, as might be expected, were between the private sector and the political leadership—but these links took the longest time to forge (six years in Colombia, ten in India, six in Indonesia, twenty-five in Japan, ten in Korea, twenty in the Philippines, ten in Singapore, five in Sweden, five in Uganda: an average of eleven years). Nor was the route easier from private sector to the public bureaucracy (Malaysia in twelve years and Pakistan in eleven years). A more efficient link led from the private sector to the ministry of public health (except for Chile which started long before most governments were officially concerned with family planning).

The reverse link, from the ministry to the private medical sector, was also efficient when the initiative flowed in that direction. And when the initiative developed within the bureaucracy, the links were usually forged quickly with the private sector (except for a nineteen-year period in Bangladesh).

The quickest means of reaching the political leadership was provided by the bureaucracy, often acting in response to international pressures. (As indicated earlier, intensity of international lobbying on behalf of family planning is not reflected in this analysis of domestic coalitions, but the link to action was usually the bureaucracy.)

It would not be appropriate to measure or compare the effectiveness of these links by recording the time that elapsed between the initiation of family planning activity and agitation and the adoption of an official program of support. Such policies are so recent in most of the world that only countries that had no family planning movement at all until the 1960s would display efficient coalition-building strategies if the time dimension were taken as the test of efficiency. The same consideration weakens any conclusions one might draw about the coalition-building process where bureaucracies or political leaders are involved. A more important question is the extent to which the different coalition-building strategies contributed to long-term program impact. The fastest route to success in getting a program adopted—linking the concerned bureaucracy with the political leadership—was followed in countries that did not achieve notable success in the family planning program itself. It was the countries that followed the slower strategy of building alliances between private sector activists and the political leadership that had the greatest acceptor rates and the most marked program impact (see Table 2). Speed in getting family planning programs adopted by the government is not necessarily correlated with success in getting family planning accepted by the public.

The same caution should accompany analysis of the processes by which international assistance is involved. But the linkages estab-

Table 2
Acceptors (in thousands) of All Program Methods, Government Expenditure (thousands of U.S. dollars) and Total Per Capita Expenditure (in U.S. cents) on Family Planning in Sixteen Countries, 1971-75

	1971			1972			1973		
	Acceptors	Gov't Exp.	Total Per Capita Exp.	Acceptors	Gov't Exp.	Total Per Capita Exp.	Acceptors	Gov't Exp.	Total Per Capita Exp.
1. COSTA RICA	25.4	40	17	26.7	49	20	34.5	52	22
2. DOMINICAN REP.	19.7	270	10.6	18.7	179	6.2	24.3	159	5.1
3. GHANA	22.7	733	11	30.5	391	7	29.8	653	9
4. HONG KONG	28.9	140	9.2	30.3	249	11.1	31.4	292	16.9
5. INDONESIA	519	3725	6.3	1079	5663	8.6	1345	6024	11.8
6. IRAN	385	4186	24	445	9000	35	470	13,000	41
7. KOREA	671	2800	18	614	3470	17	677	4061	17
8. MALAYSIA[a]	54.8	695	7.4	56.4	827	8.5	57.3	1136	11.4
9. MAURITIUS[b]	10	82	26	7.9	97	37	15.4	211	74
10. NEPAL	39.3	185	6.3	50.6	185	4.5	72.9	214	5
11. PHILIPPINES	408.8	56	13.4	621.9	1259	21.6	737.9	4008	27.1
12. SINGAPORE	25.1	290	15	27.6	389	18	33.7	491	26
13. TAIWAN	206.1	642	6.0	272.3	800	6.8	260.8	1146	9.0
14. THAILAND	363.8	120	6.4	403.2	604	9.3	378.7	550	8.7
15. TUNISIA	34.8	129	18.8	37.9	143	19.3	43.8	295	21.4
16. TURKEY[c]	53.7	1383	4.1	51.8	1763	5.0	58.7	1855	5.1
Total number of acceptors (thousands)	2955.10			3773.80			4271.20		
Total gov't exp. (thousands of $)		15,476			25,068			34,147	
Average per capita exp. (US cents)			12.46			14.68			19.40

Table 2
(cont'd.)

			1 9 7 4			1 9 7 5	
		Acceptors	Gov't. Exp.	Total Per Capita Exp.	Acceptors	Gov't. Exp.	Total Per Capita Exp.
1.	COSTA RICA	25.7	326	60	31.0	643	86
2.	DOMINICAN REP.	38.1	454	20.7	70.8	823	39.9
3.	GHANA	34.2	1036	12	31.2	1226	16
4.	HONG KONG	28.3	353	17	22.4	340	14.3
5.	INDONESIA	1593	9165	17.3	1758	13,436	21.6
6.	IRAN	481	19,830	60	506	28.000	85
7.	KOREA[a]	678	4350	21	686	4500	19
8.	MALAYSIA[b]	6.17	1229	12.0	69.3	1642	15.6
9.	MAURITIUS	13.6	353	100	13.5	650	128
10.	NEPAL	104.4	435	8.3	104.7	1138	11.5
11.	PHILIPPINES	752.5	8755	41.0	750.8	8517	41.7
12.	SINGAPORE	35	657	31	38.3	921	42
13.	TAIWAN	283.7	1418	10.4	298.7	1352	10.9
14.	THAILAND	445	625	12.3	513.3	935	8.8
15.	TUNISIA	50.9	747	40.9	58.1	834	48.4
16.	TURKEY[c]	66.6	2339	6.3	66.6	2000	6.3

	1974	1975
Total number of acceptors (thousands)	4691.70	5018.70
Total gov't. exp. (thousands of $)	52,072	66,957
Average per capita exp. (US cents)	29.38	37.18

Sources: Dorothy Nortman and Ellen Hofstatter, "Population and Family Planning Programs: A Fact-look" Reports on Population/Family Planning, Number Two (Seventh Edition - October 1975 and Eight Edition - October 1976), Population Council, New York. The original source should be consulted by readers interested in limitations of this data base.

The number of acceptors, expressed in thousands, represent the clients of government-supported family planning services by all program methods. Government expenditure figures, in thousands of US dollars, represent government budget for the year. The per-capita total expenditure figures, in US cents, represent the annual per-capita expenditure of government and non-government agencies such as international agencies, foreign governments, and private organizations.

Notes:
  a The acceptors figures for Korea are compiled by adding up figures of acceptors of different methods. These figures may overstate the total.
  b. The expenditure figures for Malaysia represent expenditures by government and non-government agencies. Government expenditure figures are not available separately.
  c. For the year 1975, the figures for acceptors and total per capita expenditure are not available; 1974 figures are repeated for that year.

lished in these processes are significant. Given the availability of international funds for family planning in recent years, it comes as no surprise that invitations from either public or private advocates are sufficient to bring about such involvement. Clearly the greatest prospects for substantial financial aid are when the channels are official and such assistance can be used in support of public programs.

Opposition to family planning comes more often from religious sources (twelve countries)[17] than from nationalist sources (six countries)[18] or from those espousing Marxist ideologies (four countries).[19] This fact may be associated with the origins of the movement itself, which so frequently developed out of concerns for family welfare and maternal health or, in nearly all other cases, at the "technobureaucratic" level, which also tends to be relatively free of ideological overtones. Politicization comes later, after support has been built up internally and internationally. Making family planning a political issue turns out to be an unrewarding enterprise for the opposition once public leaders and private preferences have been enlisted in its favor.

International interventions not only enlarged the resources available to the coalitions supporting family planning, but they also raised the stakes and heightened the tensions among disputants. Opposition forces found it hard to justify an antifamily planning position when the objectives were those of maternal health and ecological benefit, but they found a more familiar target for their propaganda and agitation after international aid began: foreign agents and the public fear of dependence and powerlessness. The conservative opposition to family planning in El Salvador was confined to vague newspaper attacks on its possible future effects on the wealth and power of the state; it was not until international support changed the dimensions of the program that it became feasible for left-wing doctors to condemn the university family planning service (1965) and even threaten to suspend participating physicians if they continued the practice (1966). In Kenya the Catholic church's opposition—the major institutional restraint on public action—was fairly muted until 1967 when Odinga was able to raise the racial theme and suggest that motives of genocide had inspired the family planning movement and its international supporters. The clamor of the opposition rose even higher when the conservatives joined to condemn family planning as an alien force that "promoted adultery."

The ethnic or racial theme is frequently introduced at later stages of opposition coalition building, especially when international proposals for family planning interventions become too heavy handed. World Population Year, the UN's effort to assist coalition building in behalf of family planning in the Third World, was countered by anti-Malthusian claims that rich countries were trying to weaken poor ones by reducing their principal base of power.[20] There is a hidden agenda of racism in many of these protests on the international as well as national level, though charges of genocide are refuted by experience in the few countries where family planning is officially supported and accurate demographic records exist to measure population changes by ethnic groups.[21]

COALITION-BUILDING SEQUENCES AND THEIR RELEVANCE TO POLICYMAKERS

Coalition-building processes can be observed in any issue of social policy. The pattern observed in family planning policies may or may not be typical, but it appears to follow a logical sequence. (1) The movement starts with concerns in the private sector, expressing by practicing physicians (public or private) over the effects of excessive childbearing on maternal health and family welfare, especially among the poor. (2) As the movement gains in momentum, public or private leaders seek support from international sources which provide both finance and prestige but at the same time create a highly visible target. (3) Reaction in opposition to such programs now becomes more vigorous, resulting in compromised official declarations and a retreat from all-out commitment, combined with a larger public understanding of the issues. (4) There follows a small beginning of official activity through clinical services attached to maternal and child-health centers.

Identifying the processes of coalition building through such standardized zones of influence can serve a useful purpose to policymakers since it permits participants to classify the interests involved in family planning proposals and the tactics used to advance them. Decision makers cannot be satisfied with the passage of a law or the enactment of an administrative decree. What is required is not the "minimum winning coalition" to get a program adopted, but a large enough consensus to generate continuous support and neutralize the manifold ways of subsequently sabotaging a program that may have gained only nominal acceptance.

The Action Phases: Prescription, Invocation, and Application

Once the decision to undertake a family planning program is authoritatively made, action moves successively away from the zones of political authority that announced the decision, through the administrative hierarchy that will conduct its own battles over organization and resources, and into the geographic localities in which the routines are finally to be established. Implementation is a process that establishes its own rules. The successive negotiations in this phase follow patterns different from those created by the coalitions that reached the original consensus. But the original coalitions are not as yet politically obsolete; they retire from the struggle only at the risk of imperiling their program. Premature satisfaction based on the issuance of a law or decree is only an invitation to new forms of opposition. If political leaders turn their attention elsewhere, their nominal subordinates can begin to renegotiate substance while they are establishing the procedures of the program. Donald Warwick's chapter in this volume explores this phenomenon in detail.

Such relaxation of pressure is said to have been the cause of the setback family planning suffered in Kenya after it had become official policy. The action phases became a bureaucratic quicksand in which the program began to sink, leaving behind scarcely a trace of the struggle. Such events are as much the result of inertia and indifference as of active opposition (though the two causes are not easy to distinguish so far as results are concerned).

The prescription of family planning as an official solution of population pressures is usually an aggregate of events, not a single action. In most countries, the government as a first step unofficially tolerates family planning activities carried out by private physicians. Policy continues to emerge as the ministry of health begins to allocate resources to supplement the private effort. This gradual incremental approach to policymaking reaches public notice through references to population problems in the national plan, trial balloon speeches by health officials and political leaders, small but growing budgets allocated to family planning, and perhaps a major parliamentary address referring to the tensions introduced by population growth. Such episodes indicate that family planning is edging toward national policy. Laws, proclamations, presidential speeches, and other official statements accumulate the authority of a prescribed policy. Sometimes it is an international signal—such as a statement prepared for a UN meeting, a summary submitted to an unofficial annual review of family planning programs, or a speech by a delegate to a world congress on demography—rather than an internal document that most succinctly and authoritatively defines the national position.

The vagueness of this incremental process is masked by an appearance of decisiveness created by reports from the Population Council or a UN agency that a given policy was "adopted" on a certain date.

Such announcements, often designed to satisfy international pressures, sound more like a definite commitment than they often turn out to be. Indeed, the bargaining that led to the original consensus was usually achieved in the first place by increasing the vagueness of purposes to be served by the program that was to be undertaken. It is only at later stages, after opposition has become politically ineffective, that negotiations turn to specifics. The politics of consensus that produces a policy prescription then yields to the bureaucratic politics needed to produce a program.

The objectives of bureaucratic politics differ considerably from those of coalition building. They relate to the allocation of resources more than to policy prescription, and thus involve maneuvers replayed on an annual basis. They usually take place outside the glare of publicity, and the parties to the bargaining process represent hierarchies rather than constituencies. Redefinitions of purposes and programs require the participation of the careerists to whom new roles are assigned. There is a reverse flow of doubts upward and within the administration system, calling forth new bargains that assign responsibility among agencies, choose areas and sequences in which services are to be offered, work out staffing and personnel patterns, determine budgetary limitations and allocations, and in general transmit and divide up the authority required for program implementation.

In the case of Kenya, the official announcement of family planning occurred in specific enough terms in the development plan for 1966-1970, conveying, indeed, a deceptive impression of commitment. A family planning council was to be established to coordinate public and private agencies; there was to be an education program, along with an evaluation of its effectiveness; personnel were to be trained in government agencies; and family planning clinics were to be established in government hospitals and health centers. The government was to render assistance to the Family Planning Association of Kenya in the procurement of supplies and materials, and the assignment of technical assistants in demography, administrative training, and public education was a further indication of the government's official commitment to family planning. Next, within a few months of the publication of the development plan in 1966 appeared a circular distributed by the Ministry of Health, advising its staff of the plan to establish a national family planning program and the intent to provide information and services. In May 1967 a local press release indicated the purpose of the family planning program. The occasion for the release was a World Health Organization assembly meeting, when the Kenya delegate announced the new plans, stressing the purpose as family and child well-being rather than population control. Early in 1968 a pilot area (Central Province) was designated. By December 1969, before the results of the pilot project were known, the Second Development Plan described the high rate of current unemployment as an effect of population growth: an early hint that national interests beyond concern over family and maternal welfare were to be served by family planning. At the same time, the government doubled the number of clinics to be supplied with family planning services, indicated that local district medical officers were to be trained to replace expatriate physicians, and increased the amount of Kenya government support to the program in order to reduce its reliance on foreign aid. Each stage of programming called for greater detail, more specific indications of commitment and changed rationales to accommodate isolated but troublesome political resistance. Policymaking continued to call for important decisions even after family planning had become official and the administrative efforts had begun.

The transmission of the new action norms to public health officials is often accompanied by rising dissonance within the operating system. Policy statements can be transmitted faithfully from the center to local regions, and from the national hierarchy to subordinate units, and still meet with resistance from implementing officials. Apart from the continuing lateral negotiations among elements of the administrative community to divide responsibility for designated operations, a distinct and independent pattern of "holdout resistance" usually leads to uneven observance of new instructions.

Clinicians who are unsympathetic to the change can often impose a silent veto upon it. In some cases, compliance with the policy at operating levels can actually be an off-duty and even surreptitious affair, involving some risk on the part of subordinates in the community health centers and hospitals who are observing a new policy against the wishes of their supervisors.

Once these participants have been won over by the program, they may succumb to the temptation of excessive routinization. This signal of acceptance raises new risks: the establishment of intermediate goals as ends in themselves. In family planning the assigning of acceptor rates as targets has often introduced a kind of brutal inhumanity into the program. The commitment to these intermediate targets was strongly reinforced by international agencies in the early years of foreign assistance to population programs.

Officials who measure program success by increased numbers of registered contraceptive users soon discover that enlarging the number of family planning clinics does not produce a continuous rise in the use of contraceptives. Additional resources allocated to family planning begin to produce diminishing returns after a few years. This plateau of acceptance permits skeptics to argue that the unofficial private clinics that had preceded official involvement were more effective than the new and costly public programs. Up to this point, the resources devoted to family planning activities have tended to increase incrementally year after year. For example, in a group of sixteen countries[22] for which continuous and comparable data are available for the five-year period 1971-75, the total government expenditure increased more than fourfold from $15.5 million in 1971 to $81.5 million in 1975, whereas the total number of "acceptors" in these sixteen countries barely doubled from 2.9 million in 1971 to 5 million in 1975. The average total per-capita expenditure for these sixteen countries, including government and nongovernment funding, showed an increase from 12.46 cents in 1971 to 37.18 cents in 1975.[23] (see Table 3). These figures also illustrate another trend in family planning expenditures in most developing countries: each year larger proportions of the family planning budget have been devoted to salaries and other personnel costs, evidently the amount of funds that can be profitably utilized for contraceptive supplies is limited by the number of "acceptors" that can be reached. Thus, the familiar plateau effect occurs, (at least in respect to the group of countries for which data are available). The leveling of acceptance rates, coupled with steadily rising costs, can be interpreted only as a decline in cost effectiveness within a few years after large-scale activity begins (see Figure 1).

There are many reasons for these diminishing returns. One is that the early clinics were able to exploit a public demand that already existed, merely providing more effective methods of contraception to those who wanted them. Each new facility added thereafter has to reach successively less informed or more resistant clients. The second reason is motivational: some clients are more resistant to using public than private facilities for such personal and intimate services. Some observers have noted that public clinics tend to be more crowded, more impersonal, and slower than their private forerunners. A third reason is administrative: a small-scale pilot project often operates with better leadership, a more dedicated staff, and a more flexible procedural style than a routine, large-scale bureaucra-

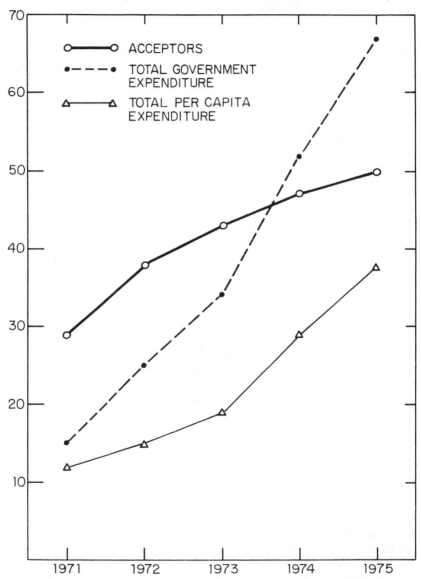

Figure 1

Growth Rates in Total and Per Capita Expenditures and Family Planning
Acceptors in Sixteen Countries, 1971-75

Note: On the vertical axis, the number of "acceptors" is measured in hundred
thousands, the total government expenditure in hundred thousand US dollars and
the total per-capita expenditure in US cents. For details please see Table 2.

tic service can sustain. Private clinics can offer a more client-oriented approach than public health centers and generate a correspondingly more favorable response from the intended beneficiaries.

Egypt's experience illustrates dramatically the rate of expansion that occurs when private clinics are supplemented by public services. Although Egypt had permitted private clinics to conduct family planning services since 1953, they were not officially recognized until 1962 when Nasser perceived their value. The Ministry of Public Health thereafter began to assist them; by 1966, 1,991 centers were in operation. That total rose in 1970 to 3,030 units served by 3,200 medical doctors, 5,600 midwives, and 1,900 social workers, though still only 800,000 acceptors were being reached out of a target group of 5 million.[24] This rapid expansion, replicated in scale in many other countries, helps explain the somewhat dismaying decline in unit effectiveness as programs expanded. The very size of the current program in Egypt reduced the scope and commitment of the average medical and paramedical clinician. It also meant assigning a rather austere level of physical resources for family planning activities on a per capita basis.

Elsewhere in this volume David Korten has described the administrative variations that have emerged as countries have confronted the declining marginal utility of expanding a family planning program by using a standard public health base. These variations imply two different strategies—"separatist" and "communal"—for overcoming the professional and bureaucratic shortcomings displayed as the traditional base expands. The first strategy calls for creating independent family planning units staffed by a new career bureaucracy (possibly paramedical, possibly interministerial generalists) that is committed solely to family planning. The second relies on decentralized community services to provide both the means of contraception and the social support required to gain and retain large numbers of new acceptors. Both of these approaches are described in detail by Korten.[25]

Administrative experience in family planning is not well enough documented to permit policymakers to learn the advantages and weaknesses of alternative delivery systems. Some informative experiments can now be consulted, however. In the Philippines, the Commission on Population experimented with different incentive systems to see whether "piecework" pay on a per acceptor basis provided better motivation to lay workers attached to family planning clinics than either flat salaries, or salaries with a "performance" bonus.[26] The risk of overreporting (informally estimated as high as 40 percent) is, of course, enhanced by piecework methods of payment. Fairly reliable information is also available as to the relative effectiveness of different contraceptive technologies (though experimentation is necessary before relying on any single technology because country preferences and practices differ). But there exist almost no comparative studies of the effectiveness of different organizational arrangements as such.[27] Even intermediate indicators of effectiveness have not been systematically linked to program variations as yet. In spite of the fact that more than 500 studies have been conducted in the past five years to discover the range of public knowledge, attitudes, and practices (KAP) regarding family planning, there are no accepted linkages between these findings and actual behavior. The extent to which either is influenced by population policies is not yet documented.

It is clear that the most important remaining area for policy research is in the relation between different styles of policy intervention and family-level motivations and behavior. Countries that have reached the plateau of acceptance and can demonstrate high levels of public knowledge about family planning are just beginning to experiment with incentive policies that lie "beyond family planning." As they do so, doubts about the patterns of behavior associated with traditional family planning programs are producing new coalitions seeking to develop policies to affect family-level population decisions.

Transitional Phases: Termination and Change

Even routine aspects of population policy undergo change, both random and purposive. New technologies appear; public expectations fluctuate; standards of performance rise or decline; other service organizations make their entrances and exits; and the ebb and flow of politics change preferences and styles in all forms of public intervention. The history of implementation in population policies is certainly not a record of steadily increasing efficiency. Even a standard family planning prorgram working toward designated targets is not approaching a fixed objective.

Policy transitions can occur in seemingly contrary directions without changing a name, legal prescription, organization, or even a budget. The trends identified in the previous sections were on a rising curve of involvement, implying a sequence moving "upward" from pronatalist policies to those of neutrality and then to antinatalism as governments responded to a recognition of the costs of exponential population increase. These early phases call for constant bureaucratic acceleration, moving from moderate support for private clinics to the beginning and enlargement of new public services. But programmatic expansion is hardly ever exponential for long. In family planning, public response levels off; more strenuous recruiting efforts follow; the program strives to maintain its momentum; communication programs and saturation campaigns get under way; there is a brief intensification of program activity involving different specialists and organizations. Family planning becomes broader but less professional as media and information technicians introduce new activities that are unfamiliar to the medical leaders and perhaps somewhat distrusted by them. The more broadly a family planning program extends its reach, the more diluted its technical content becomes and the greater the number of administrative resources it requires.

Singapore's experience in policy transitions illustrates the scope of such changes. In the 1960s it was offering incentives to immigration (in order to provide labor for the rapidly expanding industrial sector), but soon it was expressing concern over the resulting rise in demand for public services. The first quick-action policy of stimulating population was followed by a slow-action but aggressive antinatalist campaign. Parents who rejected family planning in Singapore were discouraged from applying for government housing; income tax deductions became available only for the first three children; maternal leave was provided for only two, not three, confinements; and government clinics and hospitals charged steeply rising obstetrical fees after the first childbirth, while sterilizations and abortions were subsidized.[28] All of these activities went far beyond family planning as official policies, and they required mutually reinforcing efforts among agencies administering welfare, housing, and tax functions as well as those in medicine and public health. Population policy was no longer a strictly medical service.

Even the purely medical aspects of family planning are subject to change, and not always along a rising curve of commitment. The sheer cost of program activities in the Philippines was said to account for declining support in 1957.[29] Tunisia changed course in 1968 by cutting down on the IUD campaign on the ground that the original program had moved too fast to anticipate and prepare for the side effects that followed.[30] After some initial success, Sri Lanka at one point decided to reduce publicity on behalf of family planning, cancelled the use of monetary incentives for family planning workers, refused to accept AID funding for population programs, and withheld the distribution of booklets on family planning even though they had been prepared by its own family planning bureau. In this case the explanation was the government's concern over ethnic-based attacks by the Sinhalese and other groups who objected that their population "would gradually disappear" if family planning succeeded.[31]

Nowhere have transitions in population policy been more dramatic than in eastern Europe, where a series of stops and starts provides data that approximate a social laboratory. The basic pattern of the transitions first appeared in the Soviet Union in the 1920s, when free abortion was introduced not as a family planning instrument but to reduce illegal abortions and assert a human right of choice. The abortion rate at once rose rapidly, and officials decided to impose a small fee for the service. Continued concern led to gradually increasing restrictions until in 1935 abortion was forbidden altogether in the case of first pregnancies. In 1936 the state sought to discourage the practice by offering family allowances scaled to family size. As legal abortions became more difficult, the illegal abortions increased and restrictions on access to abortion were again removed in 1955.[32]

This sequence of events was repeated in the 1950s and 1960s in the socialist countries of eastern Europe. Hungary, Czechoslovakia, Bulgaria, and Rumania abruptly reduced birth rates in the 1950s by making abortion facilities available—the Gross Rate of Reproduction declining 0.5 in both Hungary and Rumania between 1955 and 1962.[33] In Rumania abortions were made available without any advance application or medical approval, producing extraordinary numbers of legal abortions.[34] In Hungary the number of abortions per thousand exceeded the number of births.[35] Again, political concern led to major policy reversals, starting with the introduction of pronatalist incentives such as lengthened paid maternity leaves, sharply progressive family allowances, cash payments for births, preferential access to new housing for large families, and even taxes on childless couples. Soon the abortion privilege itself was under attack, leading to administrative restrictions on access to the service in Czechoslovakia in 1962 and Bulgaria in 1967. In Rumania abortion was made almost impossible in 1966. The results closely paralleled Soviet experience: in Czechoslovakia there were great increases in recourse to illegal abortions and a consequent rise in maternal mortality followed in 1966 by a return to liberalization after considerable public controversy. Family incentives also appeared to produce a slight increase in birth rates in Hungary after 1967.[36]

Other discernible patterns emerge from these transitions that suggest the apparent irreversibility of certain specific changes and sequences. No country that forbids the sale of contraceptives, for example, permits their advertising, though some forbid advertising and permit sales. No country that permits abortion forbids the sale of contraceptives, though the reverse combination is frequent. Efforts to make abortions illegal, once they have been legitimized, result in increased recourse to illegal abortion and thus increased deaths, and do not recapture the low levels that prevailed before abortion was legitimized in the first plcace. Family allowances, tax exemptions, and other pronatalist policies, once introduced, also tend to survive (perhaps because their beneficiaries constitute an easily identified and mobilized constituency), though their significance and effectiveness appear everywhere to be in a state of decline. In recent times, at least, the antinatalist momentum has not been easily reversed by deliberate policy. For the moment, the major policy changes appear to be unidirectional, though exceptions can be found. There are changes in administrative procedures and organizational preferences, but these reflect resource constraints more than reverses of doctrine.

LEARNING FROM EXPERIENCE: POLICY AS DATA

Most policy decisions are made on the basis of incomplete learning from the immediate national experience. The administration of family planning programs tends to follow general doctrines and procedures somewhat casually drawn from other sectors or from international guidelines. This inadequate use of experience is compounded when politics forces decision makers to zig-zag from one extreme reaction to another in the hope of avoiding excesses of the past. While such policy fluctuations can be viewed as a form of cybernetic learning, they are an inefficient method of translating experience into an improved performance.

But carefully structured policy evaluations can run the opposite risk: that of excessive precision, based on fragmentary findings that usually make experience look worse than it is. It is this problem that provides the greatest current challenge to policy scientists.

Learning from on-going programs is a task in longitudinal analysis equal in importance to the more conventional procedures of examining structures comparatively in the hope of discovering evidence of social causation. Structuring longitudinal social theory around population behavior is not a matter of developing simple correlations between immediate inputs and delayed outputs; there is no "end state" or "product" in the social process of population change. The task of comparing longitudinal data requires the use of some kind of social process model that will permit decision makers to link policy elements and responses to each other.

The use of "policy links" is an attempt to learn from experience in motion; it reveals classes of events that confirm or invalidate working hypotheses. Unexpected outcomes are often more valuable as experimental data than are confirmations of predictions, since they force the observer to restructure his theories. But both confirmations and surprise occur best in the context of structured observation, which permits assumptions to be tested and revised. One way of conceiving of the analysis is to hypothesize that the link between population policy and social response can be subdivided into basic elements (see Figure 2). Longitudinal policy analysis requires consideration of all of these elements. Incomplete, link-by-link analysis is an informative first stage, although if it is taken in isolation, the conclusions may be misleading. Thus the links described below should be interpreted as elements in a total configuration that is still conjectural.

Figure 2
Hypothesized Links between Population Policy and Social Change

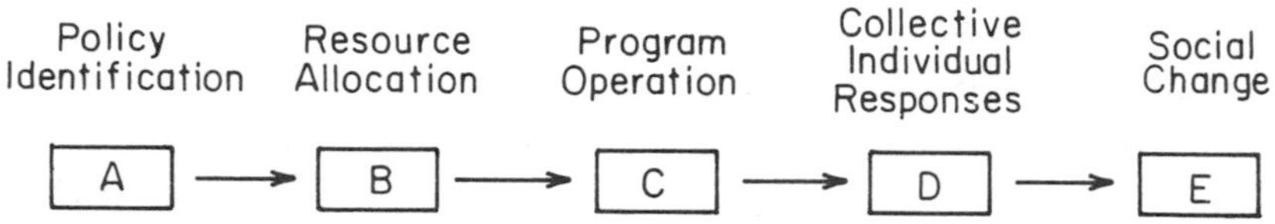

Policy Identification	Resource Allocation	Program Operation	Collective Individual Responses	Social Change
A	B	C	D	E

The Allocation Link

The simplest form of appraisal is management evaluation, a procedure that permits analysts to determine the appropriateness of actions taken to link policy identification with resource allocation. These actions can be judged in terms of the presumed adequacy of the planned administrative-technical system to achieve the announced targets. The criterion of adequacy as applied to family planning was at first essentially judgmental, based on extrapolation of management experience from other programs and becoming more certain as experience corrected previous judgments. An early study by Lapham and Mauldin sought to evaluate programs by listing the hypothetical prerequisites to success, such as whether the "leader of the country" speaks "publicly and favorably about family planning once or twice a year," whether the ministry of health carries out a "vigorous effort," whether the administrative structure is "adequate to provide family planning services" to those desiring them, whether there are "adequate family planning training facilities" available for health personnel, and whether the mass media "frequently provide family planning information."[37] Other questions addressed the availability of abortion and sterilization services, the use of nonmedical field workers as motivators, the existence of training facilities for health personnel, the provision of family planning information to maternity workers, the use of national funding to support family planning, the keeping of adequate records, and a "serious and continuing" evaluation effort.

Most of these variables proved to be difficult to quantify for comparative purposes, but Lapham and Mauldin proceded to classify family planning efforts in twenty countries into four categories of relative effectiveness according to these criteria. When they compared these ratings with acceptor data, two indicators stood out as highly correlated with acceptor rates: ready availability of contraception and vigorous efforts to provide family planning services. Useful advice can be offered on the basis of such findings, but as social theory the evidence is inconclusive since other factors may have been more important in achieving the desired outcome. The countries with the best family planning services on this scale—Korea, Singapore, Taiwan, Hong Kong—also enjoyed the most favorable economic, social, and health conditions. Changes in the birth rate in these countries are correlated with both sets of factors. Thus the Lapham-Mauldin correlation did not demonstrate how effective the family planning inputs would have been in the absence of the other factors. Since fertility declines have occurred without the benefit of family planning services, other methods will be required to show how such inputs can be combined to reinforce other favorable factors.

A more subtle problem in establishing the resource-allocating link is that of evaluating the appropriateness of resources allocated. When an evaluation report stated that Korea achieved 81 percent of its "fertility target" by "overfulfilling" part of it (distribution of condoms) and underfulfilling another part (IUD insertions), it underestimated the significance of the differential effectiveness of the two methods. It is hard to avoid the conclusion that such use of acceptor targets as goals in measuring progress is more of a political ploy than a serious administrative appraisal.

The Operations Link

Testing the adequacy of program inputs requires a second form of appraisal, linking resource allocation (B) with program operation

(C), which focuses attention on the provision of services intended by the policy. Such a study was recently undertaken by the American University in Cairo (AUC), which began in 1971 to examine ten clinics intensively to see how their quality could be upgraded. Its preliminary conclusions offered specific managerial advice on the rendering of services, a set of recommendations that can be made without reference to their ultimate effort on social responses (D). The major finding was that the Family Planning Association should develop standardized procedures for dealing with client problems and train staff in their use so as to reduce the "capricious character of staff/client interaction." The study also identified instances of overstaffing, excessive salaries, and costly procedures in the clinics. In an effort to increase the rigor and utility of these evaluations, AUC proposed in 1975 to test four different family planning systems over an eighteenth-month period to select those most cost-effective in terms of acceptor data. Four major program variants were to be examined: free services versus nominal fee charges, each with and without reinforcement follow-up by staff monitors.[38]

Another approach to measuring the effectiveness of family planning clinics at the operating level is to compare clients' waiting time for different services under alternative staffing and management arrangements. At moderate costs in evaluation, major savings in client time can be effected by changing procedures and sequences. Proposed changes can be tested by means of simple, hand-processed simulation techniques in order to avoid disruption of the clinics themselves while optimal arrangements are developed.[39] Since time lost in waiting is a principal cause of discontinuance of family planning service, even modest improvements on the score can eventually affect social responses (the C-D link). Operating effectiveness (link B-C) is also tested by knowledge, attitude, and practice (KAP) surveys, which can provide a basis for comparing communication campaigns and contraceptive delivery systems. The design and execution of these studies make it possible to derive such comparisons even though they have rarely been used to make management decisions.[40] It would appear, however, that KAP studies have traditionally been used for promotion—that is, to persuade the apathetic and disarm the opposition—rather than for evaluation.[41] Surveys have nevertheless affirmed the feasibility of asking questions and securing answers on family planning and contraceptive knowledge and practice. They have also shown that although everywhere there are increases in knowledge, they occur at somewhat different rates depending on the communication techniques used. But only a few studies have been designed to show whether administrative and organizational styles for implementing family planning programs make any difference in obtaining such results.[42]

The Taichung experiment in Taiwan demonstrated the relative effectiveness of different delivery systems in reaching clients. In one system only wives were approached; in another more costly program the clients were married couples. The communications means, too, were tested, comparing group meetings with home visits and other means of promoting the program.[43] Follow-up studies then compared the effectiveness of different marketing techniques that were used to supplement clinical operations, such as posters and meetings, along with supplemental use of mailings and personal visits to husbands. The conclusion was that the value of the added, more costly functions was marginal.[44] Such findings, limited as they are, assisted in program design and resource allocation and thus served important management needs, even though their focus was on only the first links in the chain of events that family planning seeks to influence.

The Social Response Link

Evaluations of the effectiveness of family planning often seek to establish the link to social response by relying on output indicators such as the numbers of IUDs inserted and sterilization obtained. Using such indicators, Jason Finkle has concluded that Pakistan was much more successful in its family planning programs than India during the period 1964-69 despite India's head start and supposedly more favorable setting (India possessed the larger infrastructure of health facilities and theoretically better cultural prospects). Pakistan's superior performance was attributed to its greater political commitment to development and specifically to family planning, a by-product of its more authoritarian political style under Ayub. Where India was subjecting its program decisions to political maneuvers and bureaucratic preferments, Pakistan was governed by technocratic objectives and performance norms. Finkle argues that this political style permitted it to introduce several cost-effective innovations that would have been otherwise impossible. Thus paramedical personnel replaced physicians (an economy that the medical profession could veto in India), and streamlined administrative procedures and organization permitted more effective use of the budgeted resources than that prevailing in India.[45] The validity of his judgment can now be tested against subsequent events. In the years that followed, Ayub's successors faced political objections that focused on family planning and compelled a retrenchment in the program itself, while India resorted to a tutelary political style similar to that of the displaced Ayub. Extremes in the injection of technocratic criteria in India produced a popular backlash that is said to have been a primary force in unseating the government of Indira Ghandi in 1977. Excessive reliance on procedures and experimental uses of performance incentives might reverse the original judgment on the relative effectiveness of family planning in India and Pakistan, but it would confirm the wisdom of a more politicized style of policymaking.

Establishing the social response link using acceptor rates as the dependent variables has proven extremely difficult. The greatest success stories are those of Taiwan, Singapore, Hong Kong, Korea, Malaysia, Sri Lanka, Trinidad, and Tobago—all countries where economic growth or other evidence of improving the quality of life has been marked.[46] Some interpretations have suggested that family planning is not effective unless economic development has occurred. If so, forces other than family planning efficiency are more immediately linked to acceptor rates. The Taichung program in Taiwan has provided evidence, however, that family planning does succeed in reaching low-income, traditional groups that have not yet benefitted from much economic development.[47] In Taiwan, at least, family planning has had its greatest effects in the less modern areas of the country.[48] Whether this experience can be generalized to less favorable environments is, of course, uncertain.

The Social Change Link

Other forms of administrative experimentation in family planning extend the analysis to long-term social change effects. An ambitious example is a current effort by the International Center for Health Research (formerly Cholera Research Laboratory) in Dacca, Bangladesh. Midwives will distribute contraceptives in one half of Matlab Thana (total population 260,000), but not in the other half; the two sections are separated by a river. The objective is to see whether intensive forms of family planning delivery provide superior access to supplies in a poor Moslem community, and whether there is any difference in fertility behavior after three to five years of the service. The laboratory already has a file of vital statistics that it has kept for the Thana since 1966 and therefore possesses adequate baseline data from which to examine future trends.

The usual means of establishing the D-E link is by analysis of the demographic consequences of "acceptance." These consequences challenge any temptation to complacency about the effectiveness of contraceptive acceptance as equivalent to "birth control." Contraceptives have not entirely eliminated unwanted births even under the most favorable circumstances. In areas where longtitudinal records of desired family size have been compared with actual births, the measurable decline in the numbers of unwanted children born seems to parallel the rise in contraceptive use.[49] But in the United States, contraceptives are reported as failing 12 to 39 percent of the time, depending on the method used. And none is perfect.[50] More than a third of American couples using contraceptives to prevent pregnancy reported that they had conceived children within five years. The number of unwanted pregnancies in the United States has been described as reaching an "epidemic proportion."[51] The incidence of so many unwanted births partly explains the continued extensive research in contraceptive technology.

The widespread desire for fewer births is itself an important manifestation of social change. An active public commitment to family planning responds to, and affects, an altered social perception of the value of children. When children are no longer considered a universal blessing, society begins to provide protection against unwanted births; the proposition that parents have a civil right to decide whether and when to have children means that the desirability ("value") of each unborn child is rationally calculable. Such calculations can be made in economic or social terms, and at family or national levels. The most elaborate calculations are those that attempt to quantify the economic gains that accrue to society for each birth averted through the use of contraception. This form of macro-level benefit/cost assessment has often served to justify public support of family planning programs and to provide an objective measure of the D-E link.[52]

The details of the calculus are conceptually simple. Each averted birth is assumed to be that of an average or marginal worker. His consumption over a lifetime of low productivity would therefore be greater than his output and a burden on the society, reducing the national capacity to save and thus slowing the rate of economic growth. In computing the social gains of each birth averted, the net benefits are discounted (on the assumption that the production and the consumption of the hypothetical "nonperson" would have taken place over time and are not therefore immediately available for investment). Further refinements take age-specific survival rates into account to calculate likely childhood consumption costs and adult productivity. On the basis of such calculations promoters of family planning have argued that each birth averted can save amounts ranging from $150 to $1000; the costs of the birth control facility, calculated in terms of the number of contraceptive users, the statistical effectiveness of the method involved, and the per acceptor unit costs of the family planning program are estimated to be as little as $18 to $24. The theoretical weaknesses of the argument are well recognized,[53] but the concept recurs frequently in the attempts to provide justification for the rising costs of family planning programs.

The concepts used in defining these links and the tools available for measuring their strength are useful not because of their immediate applicability, but because they make it possible to structure more systematically the observation of policy experience.

CONCLUSION

Fertility decline is rare in the recent history of mankind, and its social consequences are still obscure and hard to document. There is still no test of Adam Smith's mercantilist expectation that a "no growth" society in economic terms would necessarily be stagnant and melancholy in its cultural or social dimensions. But indefinite population increase is surely a more melancholy prospect.

What evidence there is reinforces the appeal of the "no growth" demographic model. There is a strong relationship between low fertility and equality of income distribution, along with a continuing growth of opportunity for individual self-expression in countries with limited population growth. "Higher fertility tends to increase the concentration of income," according to one formulation of the data.[54] Several reasons are offered for this relationship: the lowered educational opportunity in large families diminishes lifetime earning capacity; the opportunity for capital formation is reduced in large (usually poor) families; in high-fertility societies dependency rates are higher because there are more children and therefore savings are lower; female participation in the work force is reduced when large families are the norm; productivity and earning power are greater in societies with higher average ages (i.e., low birth rates); wage levels are higher in a labor-scarce society; malnutrition and infant mortality rates are lower among smaller families; and land is more equitably distributed in societies characterized by low birth rates.[55]

These somewhat involuted arguments suggest an array of policy interventions that have been defined as population policies. Indeed, there is a noteworthy inclination among politicians and planners to use anticipated population effects to justify policies that are considered desirable for other reasons. Among the suggested policy choices are more comprehensive development planning, extended educational opportunities, protection of human dignity and women's rights, improved nutrition levels, public day-care centers, and even controls on the use of nuclear energy. It is possible that the relationships now perceived among these events may turn out to be spurious as a guide to policy. But the present evidence, aggregated cross-nationally, has shown supportive correlations between improvements in the condition of the poor, for example, and lowered fertility rates.[56] The problem is that the evidence is not strong enough or detailed enough yet to provide a basis for choice among the alternatives just described, or to permit decision makers to assign priorities among them. Nor are the reasons for such correlations well understood. Without knowing the social processes at work, planners cannot calculate how much investment in these sectors will be necessary, or over how long a period, to produce changes in either fertility or mobility. Thus the attempt to link development policies with population policies may be better politics than social science, though it certainly deserves encouragement on moral grounds.

The ultimate test of such consequences will require longtitudinal studies in which links of social response can be predicted and tested. Studies of this type can be performed retrospectively, as Lubin has done in her analysis of the regional differences in the impact of family allowances on fertility in the Soviet Union, as Clark has done in his study of immigration policies in Australia, and as Iqbal has done in his description of the population effects of land reform in Pakistan elsewhere in this volume. At the moment such studies usually have to rely on data gathered haphazardly or generated for other purposes. But once their value is recognized, more deliberate data-gathering efforts will begin. The optimal approach to data of this order would be a carefully designed analysis of policy experience based on assessments and predictions that can be tested as events unfold. This preferred strategy would use policies as experiments, setting forth as accurately as possible the expected consequences of each program function or activity and recording events as they confirm predictions or deviate from them. The kind of knowledge generated by such studies is likely to be both site-relevant and operational, and to create information linking policies with population that extends far beyond the associations derived from cross-sectional data.

The increased emphasis on population as a factor in the development of national plans creates a favorable environment for the treatment of policies as social experiments. Plans can be viewed as structured predictions of the consequences of proposed interventions. Gathering evidence to confirm or challenge such predictions is one of the most promising means of applying the policy science to the planning process.

In most settings plans are used primarily to encourage and measure progress; ordinarily no official has the responsibility for analyzing the significance of unexpected deviations. A most promising source of new information about policies is therefore lost. In the absence of such structured predictions and a policy analysis unit to study events in light of them, the best sources of data for population decision makers remains retrospective predictions and comparative policy analysis of the type presented in these pages. Better knowledge will depend on the cooperative participation of program planners and managers in observing the policy experiments of the future.

NOTES

The author gratefully acknowledges the critical comments he received from his colleagues Joel Migdal, David Korten, and Donald Warwick and for the careful work of his research assistant, Eugenio Ocampo.

1. *Policy Sciences*, special issue on Comparative Policy Analysis (December 1975), Craig Liske, William Loehr, and John McCamant (eds.), *Comparative Public Policy: Issues, Theories, and Methods* (New York: Wiley for Sage Publications, 1975); Hugh Heclo, *Modern Social Policies in Britain and Sweden: From Relief to Income Maintenance* (New Haven: Yale University Press, 1974); Arnold Heidenheimer et al., *Comparative Public Policy: The Politics of Social Choice in Europe and America* (New York: St. Martins Press, 1975).

2. Luke Lee, "Law and Family Planning," *Studies in Family Planning*, 2 (April 1971). Ward F.Y. Elliott, "Federal Law and Population Control," *Federal Environmental Law*, edited by Erica L. Dolgin and Thomas G.P. Guilbert (St. Paul: West Publishing Co., 1974); *Population Reports Series E*, no. 1 (July 1974); and no. 2 (November 1974); D. Maxwell Stamper, "Population Policy in Development Planning," *Reports on Population/Family Planning*, 13 (May 1963); Jan Stepan and Edmund H. Kellogg, *Comparative Study of World Law on Contraceptives: Revised and Updated* (Washington: Interdisciplinary Communications Program, Smithsonian Institution, Occasional Monograph Series no. 1, 1974).

3. Christopher Tietze and Marjorie Cooper Murstein, "Induced Abortion: 1975 Factbook," *Reports on Population/Family Planning* (December 14, 1975); Ronald Friedman and Bernard Berelson, "The Record of Family Planning Programs," *Studies in Family Planning* 7 (January 1976).

4. Dorothy Nortman, "Population and Family Planning Programs: A Factbook," *Reports on Population/Family Planning*, no. 2 (7th Edition: October 1975).

5. Walter D. Watson and Robert J. Latham (eds.), "Family Planning

Programs: World Review 1974," *Studies in Family Planning*, 6 (August 1975).

6. T.E. Smith (ed.), *Politics of Family Planning in the Third World* (London: Allen & Unwin, 1973); Bernard Berelson, *Population Policy in Developed Countries* (New York: McGraw-Hill, 1974), ch. 3.

7. One school of policy scientists has standardized these policy functions as follows: *intelligence* (that is, the gathering of information about population conditions and trends); *promotion* (the process of developing coalitions for and against policies); *prescriptions* (the authoritative announcement of policy decisions); *invocation* (the mobilization of resources for program action); *application* (establishing the actual routines of program implementation); *termination*; and *appraisal*. See Harold D. Lasswell's essay in Warren Ilchman et al., *Policy Sciences and Population* (Lexington: D.C. Heath, Lexington Books, 1975). See also Lasswell's *A Preview of The Policy Sciences* (New York: Elsevier, 1971). On the major lines of controversy over the appraisal function, see C. Chandrasekaran and Albert I. Hermalin, *Measuring the Effect of Family Planning Programs on Fertility*, Dolhain (Belgium 4830) for International Union for the Scientific Study of Population (Paris, OECD, n.d. 1975).

8. Loren Fessler, *American University Field Studies*, no. 20 (May 1973); and *Asia*, no. 17 (April 1971).

9. A. Chandra Sekhar and G.R. Nair, "The Administrative Implications of Rapid Population Growth in India," Eastern Regional Organization for Public Administration, 6th general assembly and conference on *Administration Implications of Rapid Population Growth in Asia* (Manila: EROPA 1971), vol. 3, p. 197.

10. John Owusu, "Information Systems, Policy Measures, and Data Needs for Fertility Planning in Ghana," unpublished paper prepared in 1975.

11. Muhammad Sattar, "On Two Determinants of Population Policy in Bangladesh," unpublished paper prepared in 1975.

12. John Owusu, cited.

13. Victor D. duBois, "Population Problems, Perception, and Policy in Rwanda," *American University Field Staff Reports Service: Central and Southern Africa Series*, vol. 17, no. 2 (March 1973), pp. 6-11.

14. Shadi A. Karam, "Projections of Industrial Work Force in Lebanon," unpublished paper prepared in 1975.

15. John S. Aird, *Population Policy and Demographic Prospects in the People's Republic of China* (Washington: HEW/NIH, 1972), p. 226; Leo A. Orleans, "China's Population Figures: Can the Contradictions be Resolved?" *Studies in Family Planning*, 7 (February 1976).

16. John Owusu, cited.

17. Chile, Colombia, Costa Rica, Mauritius, Philippines, Singapore, Sri Lanka, Malaysia, and Uganda.

18. Bangladesh, Indonesia, Japan, Mexico, and Uganda.

19. People's Republic of China, and (double-counting) Japan and Mexico.

20. J. Mayconne Stycos, "Love the World's People: Demographic Chic at the UN," *Family Planning Perspectives*, 6 (Summer 1974). On the differences between European and Third World demographic preconditions to population decline associated with development, see Michael S. Teitelbaum, "Relevance of Demographic Transition Theory for Developing Countries," *Science*,

vol. 188 (May 1975), pp. 420-425.

21. In the United States, the reproductive potential of the black races is nearly three times that of the white, and projections to the year 2000 continue to show greater childbearing potential. Donald J. Bogue, "The Demographic Potential of the United States," in J.R. Udry and E.E. Huyck (eds.), *The Demographic Evaluation of Domestic Family Planning Programs* (Cambridge, Mass.: Ballinger, 1975), p. 12.

22. The 16 countries for which continuous and comparable data for the period 1971–75 are available are: Costa Rica, Dominican Republic, Ghana, Hong Kong, Indonesia, Iran, Korea, Malaysia, Mauritius, Nepal, Philippines, Singapore, Taiwan, Thailand, Tunisia, and Turkey.

23. The annual total per-capita expenditures represent both government and nongovernment expenditures. Nongovernment expenditures are mostly by international organizations, foreign governments, and private agencies.

24. John Waterbury, "Egypt," *American University Field Staff Reports Service*, vol. 17 (December 1971) and vol. 17 (February 1972).

25. See also David R. Seidman, "Alternative Modes of Delivering Family Planning Services," *Studies in Family Planning*, no. 52 (April 1970).

26. James F. Phillips, Aurora Silayan-go, and Aurora Pal-Montano, "An Experiment with Payment, Quota, and Clinic Affiliation Schemes for Lay Motivators in the Philippines," *Studies in Family Planning*, 6 (September 1975).

27. An exception is Jason Finkle, "Politics, Development Strategy, and Family Planning Programs in India and Pakistan," *Journal of Comparative Administration*, vol. 3 (1971).

28. Willard A. Hanna, "Singapore: Success Syndrome," *American University Field Staff Reports Service*, vol. 21 (January 1973).

29. Albert Ravenholt, "So Many Makes for Malnutrition," *American University Field Staff Reports Service*, vol. 22, no. 5 (1974).

30. W.G. Povey and G.F. Brown, "Tunisia's Experience in Family Planning," *Demography*, 5 (1968).

31. S.V. Kodikara, "Ceylon," in T.E. Smith (ed.), *Politics of Family Planning in the Third World*, cited, pp. 310-313.

32. Robert J. McIntyre. "Effects of Liberalized Abortion Laws in East Europe," R. Clinton and R. Godwin, *Research in the Politics of Population*, 1972.

33. McIntyre, p. 186.

34. McIntyre, p. 205.

35. Nathan Keyfitz, "How Birth Control Affects Births," *Social Biology*, 18 (1972).

36. Maria Zsophia Langyel, "Evaluation of Present and Future Effects of Hungarian Pro-Natalist Policies 1975," unpublished paper prepared in 1975, p. 2.

37. *Studies in Family Planning*, 3 (March 1972).

38. AID project summary, *Family Planning Sutration Project: Egypt*, 1-75; Leila el-Hamansy and Saad-Gadalla, "Grant Request presented to Population Division, AID," March 1975.

39. Alan Keller and others, "The Impact of Organization of Family Planning Clinics on Waiting Time," *Studies in Family Planning*, 6 (May 1975).

40. John Cleland, "A Critique of KAP Studies," *Studies in Family Plan-*

ning, 4 (February 1973), p. 42.

41. Cleland, p. 43; see also Dudley Kirk, "The Effectiveness of Family Planning in Less Developed Countries: Evidence from Survey Data," (Palo Alto: Stanford Research Institute, 1971).

42. John B. Wyon and John E. Gordon, "A Long-Term Prospective-Type Field Study of Population Dynamics in the Punjab, India," in Clyde V. Kiser (ed.), *Research in Family Planning* (Princeton: Princeton University Press, 1962) proposed the first systematic study. The results appear in Wyon and Gordon, *The Khanna Study: Population Problems in the Rural Punjab* (Cambridge: Harvard University Press, 1971). M.C. Chang, George P. Cernada, and T.H. Sun reported a small-scale study comparing a management technique in "A Field Worker Incentive Experimental Study," *Studies in Family Planning*, 3 (1972). Another such study is the recent experiment in incentives to lay motivators in the Philippines, reported in *Studies in Family Planning* (September 1975).

43. Ronald Freedman and J. Takeshita, *Family Planning in Taiwan* (Princeton: Princeton Unviersity Press, 1969), p. 355.

44. George Cernada and T.H. Sun, "Knowledge Into Action: Use of Research in Taiwan's Family Planning Program," (Honolulu: East-West Center, paper no. 10, July 1974).

45. Jason Finkle, "The Political Environment of Population Control in India and Pakistan," in R.L. Clinton, W.J. Flash, and R.K. Godwin (eds.), *Political Science in Population Studies* (Lexington: D.C. Heath, 1972).

46. Ronald Freedman and Bernard Berelson, "The Record of Family Planning Programs," *Studies in Family Planning*, 7 (January 1976); Elihu Bergman, "The Evaluation of Population Policy: Some Missing Links," (Cambridge, Mass.: Harvard Center for Population Studies, 1973); Philip M. Hauser, "Family Planning and Population Program," *Demography*, 4 (1967).

47. Freedman and Takeshita, cited, pp. 354 and 358-362.

48. Albert I. Hermalin, "Taiwan: Appraising the Effect of a Family Planning Program Through an Areal Analysis," *Taiwan Population Studies Working Paper*, no. 14 (Ann Arbor, Mich.: University of Michigan Press, 1971); T.P. Schultz, "Explanation of Birth Rate Changes Over Space and Time: A Study of Taiwan," *Journal of Political Economy*, 81 (1973).

49. Freedman and Takeshita, cited.

50. Norman B. Ryder, "Contraceptive Failure in the United States," *Family Planning Perspectives* (Summer 1973), p. 133.

51. Commission on Population Growth and the American Future, Population and the American Future (Washington: Government Printing Office, 1972), p. 97; Fred S. Jaffe, "Commentary," *Family Planning Perspectives*, 5 (Summer 1973), p. 144; N.B. Ryder and C.F. Westoff, "Wanted and Unwanted Fertility in the United States: 1965 and 1970," in Westhoff and R. Parke, Jr. (eds.), *Demographic and Social Aspects of Population Growth* (Washington: Government Printing Office, 1972).

52. Stephen Enke, "The Economics of Government Payments to Limit Population," *Economic Development and Cultural Change* (July 1960), vol. 8, no. 4, pp. 339-348.

53. Harvey Leibenstein, "Pitfalls in Benefit Cost Analysis of Birth Prevention," *Population Studies*, 23 (July 1969). The methodological pitfalls in the statistical techniques used to evaluate family planning are carefully

appraised in Chandrasekaran and Hermalin, cited (1975).

54. Robert Repetto, "Interaction of Fertility and Size Distribution of Income," (Cambridge, Mass.: Harvard Center for Population Studies, 1974), p. 1.

55. Most of these relationships were identified in a static cross-national regression analysis in the Repetto study. When data were confined to forty-one LDCs only, the regression coefficient of income distribution and fertility fell below a statistically significant relationship. But when developing countries that were in or near the "demographic transition" were arranged into groups (according to improved income distribution, and unchanged and worsened income distribution on a gini index), birth rates again correlated with the improved equity status. Other socioeconomic correlates of reduced fertility are reviewed in William P. McGreevy et al., *The Policy Relevance of Recent Social Research on Fertility* (Washington: Smithsonian Institution, Interdisciplinary Communications Program, Occasional Monograph Series, no. 2, 1974).

56. Ruth Simmons et al., "Organizing Government Intervention in Family Planning," *World Politics*, 27 (July 1975); William Rich, *Smaller Families Through Social and Economic Progress* (Washington: Overseas Development Council, monograph no. 7, 1973).

2

THE STRATEGY OF FAMILY PLANNING PROMOTION IN EL SALVADOR

John C. Ickis

Though "family planning" was a taboo subject in El Salvador through the 1950s, it had been embraced as an official government program by 1968 with ambitious plans for the nationwide expansion of clinic services. In a country bound by centuries of Catholic tradition and pronatalist values, this represented a rather startling and perhaps revealing policy shift. In this paper I shall examine the strategic process through which this policy emerged and raise questions about some puzzling occurrences which accompanied this process. Finally, I shall offer some explanatory interpretations and explore those conceptual frameworks underlying them which appear to have utility in the analysis of strategies for promoting social action programs.

DESCRIPTION

The Setting

El Salvador is the smallest of the Central American republics with an area of some 21,000 square kilometers and a landscape which rises dramatically from Pacific coastal lowlands to low, rugged mountains and towering volcanoes. Within its boundaries are over 3.5 million inhabitants, making it by far the most densely populated country within Central America.

The birth rate of El Salvador was among the highest in the world in 1960 at 49.5 per thousand, though this figure had dropped to 42.1 per thousand by 1968. Though socioeconomic changes provided the impetus for this trend, some of the decline was undoubtedly due to the increasing availability of contraceptives through private initiatives and government acquiescence.

Initial Impulses

Though the main focus of our attention will be directed toward the period from 1962 to 1968, there were several initial impulses which surfaced the issue of family planning and which resulted in the coalescence of a visible group that would undertake the task of promotion. The first of these impulses was the formation in the 1940s of "Amigos de la Tierra" by conservation-minded industrialists, agronomists, and demographers. The "Amigos" members, among whom were some of the most influential and progressive of Salvadorean elite society, were concerned with the relationship of man and the land. In 1948 one of their number, Mario Pacheco, spoke to conservationists at a conference in Denver, Colorado, about the problems for the man/land relationship presented by a rapidly increasing population. This was one of the first public statements of concern about population problems by a Salvadorean.

The second impulse toward family planning was the appearance and gradual dissemination of two significant publications on contraception. The first, a paper written in 1943 by Dr. Gregorio Avila Agacio entitled "The Contraceptive Problem in El Salvador," urged the abolishment of a law prohibiting the importation of contraceptives as a protective measure for materal health. The second, prize-winning book by Dr. Cesar Emilio Lopez entitled *Social Obstetrics*, argued that many women in fact have more children than they really want. In neither of these publications, however, was there any expression of concern about population growth in El Salvador. Even so, their authors had approached the issues of contraception and family planning—certainly a necessary component of any population program—much more directly than the "Amigos" members had.

The third impulse, in 1958, was the organization of a series of seminars at the National University on "Major Problems of Public

Health in El Salvador" by Dr. Juan Allwood, founder and head of the newly formed Department of Preventive Medicine and Public Health at the university's School of Medicine. During a panel discussion on the demographic problem one of the participants, newspaper editor Napoleon Altamirano, became involved in a heated debate with Dr. Allwood which, rather than resolving their different points of view, crystallized Altamirano's opposition to family planning and moved him to lead the fight against it in his newspaper *El Diario de Hoy*.

In 1960, when the seminars at the School of Medicine had run their course, one of Dr. Allwood's associates on the faculty, Dr. Bustamante, organized a television debate on the topic of abortion. The abortion problem in El Salvador was critical: each year there were an estimated 50,000 abortions as compared to 145,000 live births.[1] Bustamante was a vocal spokesman for family planning as a means of alleviating the problem. The general result of his efforts was to strengthen the arguments of family planning proponents by relating them to a widely recognized national problem.

During the early 1960s the family planning movement received an added injection of strength from an almost continuous stream of visitors from the north. Among them were David Burleson, active in the family planning field in the United States, who arrived in November 1961 as visiting professor of social anthropology at the School of Medicine, and Mrs. John Garst, professor emeritus of gynecology at Stanford University, who arrived in April 1962 and was asked by Burleson to make an address at the medical school.

Formation and Legalization of the ADS

The group addressed by Mrs. Garst in April 1962 included fifteen or twenty individuals who were becoming increasingly visible as proponents of family planning. These included many "Amigos de la Tierra" members as well as faculty at the School of Medicine. After her address, the meeting quickly turned into an organizing session and before it broke up the "Asociacion Demografica Salvadorena" (ADS) was formed with the immediate objective of creating a consciousness among decision makers in the government of the social and economic problems arising from a rapidly growing population. The longer-range objective was to convince the government to offer family planning services through the ministry of health, which had clinical facilities located throughout the country.

The ADS would not be a legally recognized institution, however, until its statutes had been approved by the minister of the interior, a

position at that time occupied by Colonel Fidel Sanchez Hernandez.
With ever-mounting attacks on family planning in *El Diario de Hoy*,
legalization would be no small matter particularly if it were publicized and became an issue of national debate. To foreclose this
possibility, Allwood placed a call to his personal friend Sanchez
Hernandez and less than one month after the statutes were drafted in
final form, in early 1963, they were approved.

The leadership of the ADS was exercised by a twelve-man board of
directors among which were some prominent members of the small
Salvadorean business elite. Other members included well-known
physicians and gynecologists, such as Drs. Roberto Pacheco and Bustamante, who had become closely identified with family planning.
They formed a close interpersonal network, not only among themselves, but also with other Salvadoreans in high social and political
circles—including those who held opposing views on family planning.

Introduction of Clinic Services

In September 1963 Burleson approached Bustamante (now vice-
president of the ADS board) and two other leading Salvadorean
gynecologists—Drs. Quan and Orellana—about the possibility of the
ADS performing intrauterine device (IUD) insertions in San Salvador's public maternity hospital, La Maternidad, as part of a study
to be financed by a private U.S. foundation, the Pathfinder Fund. He
was cautioned that there would be opposition to any form of family
planning in La Maternidad, but the doctors did agree to use their
private consultation rooms for the Pathfinder project. Soon the volume of women requesting IUDs became so great that some fifteen
other doctors were recruited to participate in the study. It was not,
however, carried out under the auspices of the ADS.

As a first step toward using the ADS itself to offer family planning
clinical services, the president of the ADS board, Roberto Pacheco,
proposed a study of the knowledge and attitudes toward contraceptive use by women who visited public health clinics. But the minister
of health, Ernesto Lima, advised Pacheco in early 1964 that he did not
want such studies conducted in public facilities.

The next attempt toward moving the ADS into clinic services
occurred in late 1964 when it medical advisor, Oscar Beneke, suggested that the ADS might now seek to sponsor an IUD insertion
program in the spare consultation rooms at La Maternidad during
the evening hours when these rooms were vacant. The director of La
Maternidad, Dr. Roldan, promised to consider the idea but when he
discussed it with the minister he received a flat rejection.

The ADS continued without providing clinical services until February 1965 when Juan Allwood, now an active ADS board member, offered the facilities of the School of Medicine's Department of Preventive Medicine and Public Health for use as family planning clinics. The doctors who offered these first ADS clinical services did so on a voluntary basis, and only about half of those who had participated in the Pathfinder IUD study chose to become involved.

Shortly after Allwood extended this vital assistance to the ADS, he was named minister of health. In this new position, he experienced strong pressure from the archbishop and the Catholic hierarchy to close down the ADS. Allwood resisted these pressures, but when the ADS made yet another request to open a clinic in La Maternidad, he turned it down.

Unable to expand clinical services from the university's School of Medicine to the Ministry of Health's La Maternidad, ADS leaders approached the Agency for Intenational Development (AID) to request funds for the establishment of independent clinics. A formal budget request was made to AID in November 1965, and in December Guillermo Borja Nathan, head of the National Planning Council and an ADS member and family planning supporter, delivered the required government approval of the request. In March 1966 a contract was signed by the ADS and AID for $30,000 to finance the installation of family planning clinics. In the same month the IPPF donated $15,000 for the establishment of three family planning clinics, one in the major population center of the eastern region, San Miguel, and two in the capital city of San Salvador.

By November 1966 there were sixteen ADS clinics located throughout the country. Many of these were in free-standing rented facilities, but some were actually located within health centers operated by the ministry. This had been done quietly with the acquiescence of some regional and local health officials but without government acknowledgement of protest.

Emergence of Opposition

The most serious opposition to the expansion of clinical services by the ADS came not from the politically conservative Altamirano and *El Diario de Hoy* but from two doctors, Bracamonte and Barba, described as left-wing or communist. Both had written vehement articles against family planning in late 1965, condemning in particular the use of university facilities for this purpose.

Bracamonte had uncovered an obscure law that required all private associations to obtain permission of the *Consejo Superior de*

Salud to operate clinics. The *consejo* was a consultative body which advised the Salvadorean government on all matters concerning health. It contained ten members, three from each of three professions (medical, dental, and pharmaceutical) and one government representative. Specific actions taken by the *consejo* were generally based on the recommendation of a five-man "vigilante committee" representing the profession involved.

In December 1966 Bracamonte asked the *consejo* to close the ADS clinics since they were being operated without its permission. He charged that they were being run in an improper manner and were part of a massive effort to control the Salvadorean population. Most, including the *consejo* members, had forgotten about the law, but they agreed to have the medical vigilante committee investigate the allegations.

Barba, an associate of Bracamonte and a strong opponent of family planning, was a member of this vigilante committee, and ADS board members feared a negative recommendation. But elections for a new committee by members of the Salvadorean professional association of doctors and surgeons were to be held in February 1967. The board members sought to delay action on the clinics until after the election, and at the same time they began an aggressive campaign for their own candidates. During the month of January they obtained the signatures of a number of medical association members in favor of these candidates, and at the February election convention seventy of the eighty doctors present voted for the ADS slate.

The newly elected vigilante committee not only recommended that ADS clinics not be closed but expressed the hope that other similar clinics be opened throughout the country. Their report concluded that:

> There has been no massive program of population control, but rather it was individual cases that were being treated, and it was completely voluntary. We found that doctors in La Maternidad are asked by patients for information. And we found that clinics were not endangering the health of patients.

Contracts with the Government

The first official interest shown by the government of El Salvador in a family planning program came in the form of a request to the Pan American Health Organization (PAHO) by the then minister of health, Interiano, for advice on how to initiate such a program. Sylvia Platha of PAHO visited El Salvador in early 1967 and recommended that the ministry prepare its personnel so that once a program was formally established it could be put into effect immediately.

Meanwhile the ADS had begun to organize a national training program for medical and paramedical personnel under the direction of a well-known Salvadorean gynecologist, Angel Quan. Ministry of Health personnel were readily accepted into the program and large numbers of them received training during the months of March, April, and May of 1967.

One of the graduates of the ADS training program was the director of the Chalatenango clinic, located in a village in the northwestern region of the country. Upon returning to his clinic in August 1967 he became increasingly aware that many of the women that he saw during maternal-child health (MCH) consultations were anxious to obtain family planning services. Upon his request the regional director granted him permission to dedicate two of the four "MCH hours" per day to family planning. The minister, who had not been consulted beforehand, reportedly said, "I don't want to know anything about it."

In late 1967, a series of conversations took place between the population officer of AID, Vernon Scott, and Ministry of Health officials regarding the establishment of a national family planning program. Scott was particularly anxious to see the AID-funded ADS clinics, which now numbered over thirty nationwide, gradually transferred to the government where the dependence on external assistance could be reduced. Finally in early 1968 a tripartite agreement was drawn up among AID, the ADS, and the Salvadorean government for just such a transfer. It would take place gradually by regions, as Scott had envisioned: during 1968, all ADS clinics in the paracentral region would be transferred to the ministry; clinics in the oriental, occidental, and central regions would be transferred in 1969 and 1970; and clinics in the San Salvador metropolitan region would be transferred during 1971 and 1972.

ADS members reacted to the first news of this agreement with a sense of finally having accomplished a major objective: after over five years the organization had finally obtained government sponsorship for a national program of family planning clinic services.

SOME QUESTIONS

This slice of history as it has been presented seems, at first glance, to be fairly straightforward. People interested in family planning banded together to form an organization with a particular objective in mind and after some "politicking" on the part of the ADS membership and some "softening" on the part of government officials the objective was attained.

But on second glance we are struck by several occurrences which are not so readily explainable. For example, how is it that what began as a conservationist movement in the forties becomes a platform for antiabortion rhetoric in the sixties? What does the man-land relationship have to do with combatting clandestine abortions through contraception? How can it be that both groups—the conservationists and the doctors—became so cohesive?

A second cluster of questions revolves around the early inactivity of the ADS. It was founded by these two groups of zealots in early 1962 and yet it did not really do anything as an organization until Allwood offered clinical facilities at the School of Medicine nearly three years later. Why?

But Allwood, as a Japanese commentator once said of MacArthur, was "not a simple man." Though a decisive promoter of family planning in the early years, he reversed himself as minister of health and denied the ADS access to La Maternidad. Again, Why?

Despite the slow start of the ADS, it was amazingly successful once it had begun to establish independent clinics in early 1966. How is it that the ADS was virtually able to blanket the country with thirty-plus clinics in the face of multiple centers of opposition? Napoleon Altamirano and *El Diario de Hoy*, Bracamonte and Barba, and the church were all intent upon sinking the ADS yet it expanded very rapidly in a very short time. The opposition was powerful; why was it not more effective? In broader terms we can ask what kinds of strategies were adopted in a hostile environment in order to minimize the opposition to family planning?

Coalition-Building: Fusing Conservation and Abortion Prevention

Businessmen and agriculturalists concerned about soil erosion and the relationship of man and the land were joined during the 1950s by a loose coalition of gynecologists and obstetricians from the School of Medicine who were interested in maternal health. In family planning both groups found a means to their desired objective. No one raised the possibility that those objectives were quite different and might be inconsistent. Ideally, the conservationist interested in population control would want to identify young women with few children as

users of family planning services thus maximizing the number of
births avoided, while the maternal health advocate would seek out
older women with many children whose well-being would be most
endangered by an additional pregnancy.

The objectives and ideal strategies of those opposing abortion were
even more divergent from those of the conservationists. If family
planning was seen as an alternative to abortion it would be most
efficient if directed only toward those women whose desire for no
more children was so strong that they would risk death from the
complications of a clandestine operation rather than give birth. Thus
despite the obvious humanitarian benefits, it would not result in a
net reduction of births. Of course it is not possible to segregate target
population with such precision and, possibly recognizing this, the
various coalition members pragmatically chose to cooperate in implementing commonly shared means toward distinct ends.

Like most explanations this one is incomplete. It offers a theoretical rationale for the way in which coalitions were able to avoid
conflict by attending to different goals at different times, but it
ignores that these coalitions are composed of individuals, each of
whom has a unique network of interpersonal relationships. In El
Salvador where the number of actors on the national scene is quite
limited and the family ties are intricate and interwoven even by
Central American standards, the interpersonal factor assumes especially large proportions.

One example will suffice to illustrate this. Mario Pacheco was
unquestionably one of the foremost "conservationists" and his 1948
paper, "The Population of El Salvador," still stands as a significant
historical document. His brother Roberto was a well-known public
health official and esteemed among the doctors concerned about the
abortion problem. Both embraced family planning, encouraging
friends and associates to join them in forming the ADS.

To seek further levels of explanation requires some guesswork. It is
perfectly plausible, for example, that members of the conservationist
coalition, recognizing the strength of church opposition to any form of
population control (which, after all, was essential to the conservationists' ultimate objective), embraced the antiabortion cause as a
means of "legitimizing" family planning or at least of presenting it to
the Catholic hierarchy as the better of two evils.

Context: Explaining Inactivity

The structure and composition of the ADS coalitions assured that
family planning would develop in a medical context. All public chan-

nels, however, were initially blocked by government reticence. Having repeatedly tried and failed to introduce family planning services in La Maternidad, where most of the ADS doctors worked part time, they proceeded to the next most immediate medical alternative: services through their private consultation rooms. This approach was encouraged by the Pathfinder Fund through its distribution of IUDs. Once placed in this context there was no need to bring the ADS structure to bear on service delivery, and the organization floundered.

"Posibilismo" and the Salvadorean Political Process

Another cluster of questions concerned the actions of Allwood before and after becoming minister of health. To many ardent ADS members recalling the events years later these actions were "unexplainable." They acknowledged that he must have been under some pressure from the Catholic hierarchy to reject the ADS request for a clinic in La Maternidad, but he had always resisted such pressures on previous occasions. He had risked his career to bring a family planning clinic to the university above the outraged cries of Bracamonte and Barba. Why did he now appear to be so faint-hearted?

In an insightful analysis of events during the Cuban missile crisis, Allison quotes the aphorism, "Where you stand depends upon where you sit."[2] From his chair in the council of ministers, the family planning issue might have shown a very different face to Allwood than it had from his chair on the Faculty of Medicine. To understand why, we must seek some information about recent Salvadorean political history.

Allwood was offered the ministry by Col. Julio Adalberto Rivera, who had ruled the country since January 1961 when a countercoup against pro-Castro officers (who in turn had overthrown the civilian government in October 1960) had brought him to power. The new U.S. president, John F. Kennedy, reacted angrily to these events and had temporarily suspended assistance programs. Rivera, anxious to prove that he was interested in free elections and social reforms, resigned from the ruling military junta in January 1962 to organize a new "Party of National Conciliation" (*Partido de Conciliacion Nacional*, or PCN) and to campaign for the presidency. Elections were held in April but a number of opposition groups denounced it as fraudulent and refused to enter candidates. As a result Rivera found himself to be the sole contender and was elected for a five-year term.

Over the following three years he launched a sweeping reform program that was guided by what might be called *posibilismo*—accomplishing whatever possible to improve the life of the poor without seriously risking his own position by disturbing the structure of Salvadorean society. His program included agrarian reform through distribution of state-owned lands, enactment of minimum wage laws and legislation providing worker benefits, and the facilitating of subsidized benefits to small farmers. Most significantly, he scrupulously enforced an income tax law which called for a levy of as high as 76.5 percent on incomes over $78,000. This was not done in brutal confrontation but rather in collaboration with progressive elements of the elite structure: one of the proponents of the tax law was Don Francisco De Sola, a highly influential businessman and a founder of the ADS.

Though both social and economic progress was made under Rivera, strong opposition to his rule persisted and in the 1964 legislative elections, twenty seats were lost to the Christian Democratic party (*Partido Democrata-Cristiano*, or PDC) and the Party of Renovating Action (*Partido de Accion Renovadora*, or PAR). Both were to the left of PCN although by 1965 some conservative elements of both the PCN and PAR had allied to form the Salvadorean Popular party (*Partido Popular Salvadoreno*, or PPS), which had a rightist or nationalist orientation and was supported by some wealthy interests and large corporations.

New legislative elections were approaching in early 1966 and Rivera realized that further loss of PCN power could place the upcoming 1967 presidential elections in serious jeopardy. Although he could not succeed himself by law, he would personally choose a successor who would continue his reform policies. The most likely successor, by all accounts, was Fidel Sanchez Hernandez.

Up to the time of Allwood's appointment, family planning had not emerged as a visible political issue and President Rivera was particularly anxious to keep it that way. Most elements of the PDC opposed it on principle (although some individual PDCers, like Mario Pacheco, did not); the more doctrinaire leftist elements of the PAR saw family planning as part of a foreign-based conspiracy; and finally, most members of the PPS opposed it on both moral and nationalistic grounds. Any hint of government support for family planning clinics would draw a barrage of charges and accusations from all these quarters, which was precisely what President Rivera least needed at this moment.

If Allwood did not understand all this when he became minister, the president surely wasted no time in explaining it to him. Allwood's support of family planning was a matter of public record; he would be closely watched by the opposition. But many of Allwood's associates in the ADS did not understand, and some of those who did— particularly among the "conservationists"—may have wondered why he accepted the position at all under those circumstances.

The most obvious answer is that Allwood was, above all, dedicated to improving the quality of public health in El Salvador and from his new position he could draw upon the vast resources of the ministry in pursuing this aim. Family planning was important, but it had to be placed in perspective—and the perspective of his ADS colleagues was simply too narrow. They were not thinking about the control of intestinal diseases and malnutrition or about inoculation and antimalarial campaigns but he, as minister of health, had to design effective programs to deal with these critical problems. Why risk all this to make an unwise stand on a single issue?

Even if Allwood remained more concerned about family planning than all other public health issues, his actions could still be explained by the idea of *posibilismo*. Recognizing the magnitude of the current political stakes, he may have been looking ahead to the election of his friend, Fidel Sanchez Hernandez, in 1967. Sanchez Hernandez had been a key figure in the legalization of the ADS and could be counted upon, as president, to support family planning. But a PDC or a PAR victory at the polls would mean a severe setback to the family planning movement as well as to Rivera's program of reforms. Once it is seen what hung in the balance in 1965, Allwood's "faint-heartedness" should not surprise us.

THE CRITICAL SUCCESS FACTORS

Despite Allwood's caution, the more zealous members of the ADS did in fact push ahead with a clinic service delivery program in early 1966 as a means of convincing the government that demand for family planning services was strong among the lower-income groups in Salvadorean society. The fact that this effort proceeded with so little restraint in such a politically charged atmosphere may be attributed to the policies adhered to by ADS leadership and to certain favorable external factors.

Policies

Incorporation of diverse elements in a broad-based coalition. As we have noted earlier, a pragmatic agreement on short-term, operational goals served to suppress conflict among differing ultimate objectives. Interpersonal relationships helped to smooth this process. Identification with any single social class, profession, or political affiliation was carefully avoided, and this diversity was an important source of strength. There were no exclusionary doctrines; the ADS could be all things to all people.

Avoidance of controversy. The ADS leadership had learned the lessons of the School of Medicine seminars: don't push people into extreme positions; don't prematurely create vociferous opposition. Once Napoleon Altamirano had been "created" as an opponent, ADS leadership pursued a policy of silence and never answered his editorials. Some younger ADS members were annoyed by this policy and felt that wider public controversy would actually benefit the family planning movement. In this respect they misunderstood both the ADS strategy and the nature of the change process in El Salvador.

Accommodation of potential opposition. Neither the church nor the political left were looked upon by ADS leadership as the "enemy," and neither were placed in a position where they would feel obligated to take a stand on family planning. Catholic attitudes were respected and the rhythm method was offered as an alternative. The secretary to the archbishop, Padre Ramon Vega, accepted an ADS invitation to attend an international conference on family planning in Puerto Rico in May 1965, and thereafter he was an important channel of communication and understanding between the ADS leadership and the church hierarchy. Similarly several ADS members provided links with the democratic left and helped to communicate the ADS concern with social and health benefits arising from a voluntary family planning program.

Cultivation of government contacts. ADS leadership was particularly sensitive to the action channels of Salvadorean government and to the individuals who were strategically placed in positions along them. Fidel Sanchez Hernandez, as minister of the interior, was critical to the legalization process and Guillermo Borja Nathan, as executive secretary of the National Planning Council, played a vital role in obtaining resources for clinic expansion. When Bracamonte tried to dismantle its clinic infrastructure through a long-forgotten channel, ADS leadership moved quickly to place allies in position. Given this strategy we can begin to understand the surprise and disappointment of the ADS leadership when Allwood, suddenly placed on a direct action channel in the Ministry of Health, failed to act.

Creation of constituencies in the Ministry of Health. ADS leadership understood that the decision by a minister to provide family planning services when it came would not in itself be sufficient to ensure implementation at the clinical level. Opposition to family planning was strong among some medical and nursing personnel, while many others knew very little about it or were simply indifferent. The ADS training program, launched in early 1967, was intended to break down this indifference and to create a commitment to family planning among individuals situated in health centers in diverse regions of the country. The success of this policy was demonstrated in August 1967 when a recent participant in the program, the director of the Chalatenango clinic, took the initiative in offering family planning services on government time.

Each of these policies comprises an element of the ADS strategy from 1962 to 1968. The elements, in themselves, are internally consistent and mutually supportive. But how well do they respond to factors in the external environment? It is to this question that we shall now turn.

External Factors

Grass-roots demand for the service. At the center of the ADS strategy was the assumption that there was a demand for family planning services at the grassroots level among low-income rural families and marginal urban dwellers, so that once the services were made available they would be used without the need for noisy promotional campaigns which might wake the church hierarchy or other potential opponents. This assumption of grassroots demand was supported by the experience of ADS members who had worked in public health centers, but there was little solid evidence that demand was widespread—hence the importance of Roberto Pacheco's proposed "knowledge and attitudes" study (which could not be carried out because of ministry opposition). Though further evidence was provided by the Pathfinder study, it was not until free-standing clinics were established in 1966 that the assumption of grassroots demand was confirmed.

International agency support. It was a political fact of life in the 1960s, and probably still is, that no Salvadorean head of state could long exist without U.S. support. This is not to imply that the United States would have intervened directly; rather, that the individuals and interests which benefitted from friendly United States-Salvadorean relations were powerful enough to change the situation by themselves. Imagine the surprise of Col. Rivera upon overthrowing pro-Castro officers in January 1961—an act worthy of a medal from the Eisenhower administration—only to find himself regarded as a military dictator by Kennedy. His reformist zeal during the early 1960s might well have been influenced by his desire to prove himself a friend of Kennedy's "Alliance for Progress." Though family planning was politically too problematical for him to touch, he was not about to force a confrontation with the U.S. Embassy by closing private AID-funded clinics.

The "intentional ambivalence of government." Manheim observed that there was often a wide breach between the stated positions of the Rivera and Sanchez Hernandez governments and their positions in practice. He concluded that "this pattern becomes a way of easing into change . . . a way of making sure that something is accepted before it is announced."[3] The policy of the Sanchez Hernandez government, which took office in mid-1967, was to work quietly in supporting family planning through the unpublicized use of its facilities by the ADS until the program was accepted as a *fait accompli*. Korten points out that the role of the private demographic association as "stalking horse" for a cautious government is not at all uncommon in Central America.[4]

The nature of the opposition. It has already been noted that the ADS leadership did not consider the Catholic church to be a monolithic enemy and they intentionally pursued policies that would minimize its opposition to clinical programs. Far more relentless as an opponent, ever since his 1958 confrontation with Allwood, was Napoleon Altamirano. His arguments, which frequently appeared on the pages of *El Diario de Hoy*, centered on the value of human resources to El Salvador and on the physical and moral danger that might arise from the use of contraceptives. However, Altamirano worked only through his editorials and never tried to organize opposition to family planning. His firmest potential allies were on the political left, and the possibilities of an alliance with them were remote. "Before anything else, Altamirano is an anticommunist," said one of his personal acquaintances.

THE ADS STRATEGY REVIEWED

The Strategy as a Plan

"Strategy," is most commonly found in military usage where it refers to the broad array of actions or tactics used to achieve a specified objective, or in relation to the business firm where its meaning has been broadened to include the definition of objectives as well as means. In the latter spirit, Andrews defined strategy as "the pattern of major objectives, purposes, or goals, and essential policies and plans for achieving those goals, stated in such a way as to define what business the company is in or is to be in and the kind of company it is or is to be."[5] According to Andrews, strategy is more likely to be successful when its internal elements are consistent and when it achieves a balance or "matching" of corporate resources, environmental opportunities, and the personal values of the organization members. Although this definition was not formulated with Central American demographic associations in mind, it may serve as a helpful yardstick in reviewing the "critical success factors" described above.

The pragmatic, operational objective of ADS leadership was to convince the government of El Salvador to implement a broad program of family planning services through its public health centers. To do this it chose to quietly establish its own network of clinics and to create, in Selznick's terms, "grassroots constituencies" for these services which could be absorbed into the government program at some future date with minimal political risk.[6]

Younger ADS members, eager to "take on" Altamirano in print, failed to recognize the importance of "avoidance of controversy" as an element of this strategy. ADS leadership certainly realized that the impact of an editorial battle on their target population, the grassroots, would have been minimal since most could not read even if they did have access to daily newspapers. However the effect upon the middle classes who were able to obtain contraceptives from private physicians and thus had no interest in ADS clinical services almost certainly would have been negative. The last thing the middle-class housewife wanted to see were daily editorials that screamed the sinfulness of what she was doing.

A public debate also would have endangered the usefulness of government contacts that had been cultivated on key action channels. Suppose, for example, that a furor over family planning had erupted immediately before Allwood called the minister of the interior in 1963 or before the ADS had sent its loan agreement with AID to the National Planning Council for approval. These action channels were particularly useful because they had the advantage of low visibility; the position of minister of health was not useful as a channel for precisely the opposite reason.

Finally, a strategy of confrontation would not have been consistent with the preferred styles of interaction among members of the ADS leadership and representatives of the various sectors of Salvadorean society. This style was characterized by highly personalized exchanges and the relative absence of conflict. As one ADS board member put it, "It's a small country." Interactions among Salvadorean elites were frequent and they were careful not to alienate one another over particular issues.

In his discussion of corporate strategy, Andrews underlines the importance of making strategy explicit both as a means of critical review and as a vehicle for communicating key goals and policies to organization members. If ADS leadership had subjected itself to the discipline of writing, as Andrews advocates, one paragraph describing their strategy, it might have looked something like this:

> The ADS is a private, voluntary association with a broad base of membership which seeks to promote the delivery of government family planning services to low-income segments of the Salvadorean population through public health centers by demonstrating the existing demand for these services through the establishment, with international assistance, of its own clinic infrastructure. To facilitate this, it cultivates government contacts in those areas critical to its clinic operations, it avoids controversy that might endanger those operations, and it accommodates potential opposition to clinic service delivery. Finally, it seeks to create constituencies among medical personnel in public health clinics through its training programs so that implementation of a government program will be swift.

As we have seen, this strategy was highly successful in yielding a government decision to launch a family planning program at an earlier date than even the ADS leadership thought possible.[7] Its elements were consistent, reinforcing, and well in tune with the surrounding environment as well as with predominant ADS values.

The Strategy as an Outcome or Resultant

The only problem with the above description of ADS strategy, as pointed out by one former board member, is that "it just didn't happen that way." When the faculty of medicine people and the "Amigos" members met in 1962, their discussions turned more to the wording of statutes than to elements of strategy. Unlike the private corporation there was no chief executive officer; "ADS leadership" was instead a coalition that included at least two major subcoalitions, the "conservationists," and the doctors. How could such a coalition be capable of formulating and articulating a strategy with the power and coherence of that described above?

Some would argue that this strategy is in fact merely the outcome of organizational processes or the resultant of bargaining among individuals. Cyert and March have developed a behavioral theory of the firm which seeks to explain the actions of an organization through its attempts to avoid uncertainty by negotiating with the environment, to search for alternative solutions in the neighborhood of the problem symptoms, and to discontinue the search once an acceptable-level solution has been found.[8] The Cyert and March organization "learns" to the extent that it develops programs and repertoires for responding to certain stimuli.

Much of what we have described as the ADS strategy may be explained through the concepts and language of Cyert and March. Efforts of the ADS to incorporate diverse elements into its midst, avoid controversy, accommodate potential opposition, cultivate government contacts, and create constituencies within the Ministry of Health may be seen not as elements of a conscious plan but rather as instances of reactive negotiation with the environment to reduce the uncertainty of its own organizational survival. Its decisions to doggedly pursue the installation of a clinic in La Maternidad or to offer a medical training program may be understood as having been based upon acceptable-level goals and arrived upon through localized search procedures. When seen from this frame of reference, the ADS had no "strategy" in the Andrews sense; it simply behaved in a predictable manner.

But the explanatory power of these concepts is not without its limits. They are less helpful in understanding why, for example, Allwood reversed himself in 1965 or how the ADS was able to meet the Bracamonte-Barba challenge in 1967. Our analysis of these occurrences relied much more upon notions of pluralistic politics in which action is neither the product of a conscious plan nor the output of organizational processes, but rather it is the resultant of the interacting personal strategies of individuals in key positions. As we observed, some of these individuals occupied positions on action channels which enabled them to provide essential assistance to the ADS when its survival was threatened.[9]

The Strategy as a Process

In the promotion of family planning, strategy must occur in an institutional environment where the "laws" of politics and bureaucracy hold sway. It must be partial and adaptive; indeed, there may be no single actor or coalition able to conceive of strategy in holistic terms. Even in these circumstances, however, we are inclined to regard strategy as something more than the product of adaptive response, and the success of the ADS from 1962 to 1968 reinforces this view. Successful strategy, in this context, must involve a process of creatively working through political and interorganizational networks whose structure and values will, in turn, influence the plans and policies for goal achievement. Andrews notes the reiterative nature of strategy formulation and implementation and Bower actually models this interactive process for the phenomenon of resource allocation,[10] but less is known about it outside the corporate context. If we are to work toward the more effective promotion of social action programs like family planning, it will be necessary to expand our knowledge of the strategic process in situations of high organizational and political interdependence through analysis that bears upon particular cases.

POSTSCRIPT: THE DECLINE OF STRATEGY

Beyond the process of promotion, these concepts of strategy lose much of their explanatory power. Promotion is directed toward the acceptance of an idea, and once this objective has been attained the question of institutional responsibility for translating the idea into action must be addressed. It is at this point that the guardians of institutional domains square off in a contest where the stakes may be no less than organizational survival.

Scarcely two years after the ADS had promoted government sponsorship of family planning clinics in 1968, some of its members began to voice concern about the course of events. The Ministry of Health had introduced many new clinics in rural areas during this period, but its very aggressiveness provoked strong reactions from the church and renewed attacks from *El Diario de Hoy*. Medical students, informed that they might have to administer family planning clinics during the one year of required social service in the field, threatened to go on strike. The atmosphere had begun to grow ugly, and this was especially distasteful to the older ADS members who had been the architects of a strategy which placed so much emphasis upon the avoidance of conflict.

Younger ADS members were even more upset at the transfer of clinics to the Ministry of Health, but for a very different reason. This younger group included aggressive businessmen who watched in dismay as the number of ADS clinics declined from year to year. Convinced that a private association of dedicated individuals could provide more specialized attention and better services than the ministry, they demanded that the ADS reassert leadership in family planning by opening new clinics and showing the government "how to get the job done."

By late 1971 the ADS membership was sharply divided on this issue, with older members emphasizing the need for the ADS to seek a supportive role in a national family planning effort which would include not only the ministry but also the Salvadorean Social Security Institute. "The ADS is not a ministry," explained founder Francisco De Sola, "but rather a body for training and research. Its major thrust should be in the area of opinion formation." And while this view eventually prevailed, conflicting perceptions of one another continued to hamper cooperation between the ADS and the Ministry of Health.

These delicate relationships were further complicated in 1973 by developments in CONAPLAN, the national planning arm of the presidency. In June of that year the Population and Human Resources Unit was created within CONAPLAN's Social Planning Department and charged with the task of incorporating population considerations in El Salvador's third five-year development plan. By October a group of CONAPLAN technicians, with the encouragement of international agency representatives, had drafted a document which would lay the bases for a national population policy.

As the draft underwent successive revisions in early 1974, it became clear that a policy in itself would not necessarily strengthen the position of the family planning advocates within the ADS. Indeed, in the final document family planning was mentioned only as one of seven programs through which the modification of population dynamics might be achieved, and this in turn was only one of eight policy objectives.[11] This approach was in keeping with the spirit of the recently celebrated World Population Conference in Bucharest, which urged that governments attempt to deal with population problems in their broad developmental context rather than to focus exclusively, or even primarily, upon programs designed to lower birth rates.

As of late 1976, the ADS continued as one of eight members of a technical committee on population charged with making recommendations on the implementation of the Integral Population Policy to an interministerial commission.[12] Jurisdictional disputes were frequent and the current ADS director, a nephew of *El Diario de Hoy* editor Napoleon Viera Altamirano, felt that the autonomy and flexibility of his organization were being restrained by the new structure. "The central question is whether the ADS is going to be an active or a passive organization," he told the other representative on the technical committee, "because if it is going to be passive, then in another year or so there will no longer be any reason for it to exist."

This gloomy remark captures the frustration of the strategist caught up in the multiinstitutional dimensions of the implementation process. He and his fellow players are no longer the promoters of new ideas but rather are the protectors of the claims staked out by their respective institutions. The transition from the promotion to the implementation process has been accompanied by a fundamental change of purpose, from one of goal attainment to one of survival.

NOTES

Prepared for the Seminar in Population Policy, Population Center, Harvard University, this paper is based upon information in *El Salvador Country Report: A Management Oriented Description of its Family Planning Program*, by John C. Ickis, and was made possible by a grant from the Ford Foundation to the Instituto Centroamericano de Administracion de Empresas (INCAE) of Managua, Nicaragua, for research on the administration of family planning programs.

1. Recently this figure has been questioned and it is possible that the actual number of clandestine abortions was less than half this amount.

2. Graham T. Allison, *Essence of Decision: Explaining the Cuban Missile Crisis* (Boston: Little, Brown & Co., 1971).

3. Michael A. Manheim, "The Politics of the Birth Control Movement in El Salvador" (Cambridge, Mass.: Harvard University, unpublished thesis, 1968).

4. David C. Korten, *Defining Institutional Roles in the National Family Planning Program* (Managua, Nicaragua: INCAE, 1973).

5. Kenneth R. Andrews, *The Concept of Corporate Strategy* (Homewood, Ill.: Dow Jones-Irwin, 1971).

6. Philip Selznick, *TVA and the Grass Roots* (Berkeley: University of California Press, 1949).

7. But the strategy as stated here did not include a consideration of purposes or policies beyond the attainment of this objective. The question of how the ADS leadership faced the issue of what it should do once it had been successful is beyond the scope of this paper. For an excellent discussion of this issue, see Korten.

8. Richard M. Cyert and James March, *A Behavioral Theory of the Firm*

(Englewood Cliffs, New Jersey: Prentice Hall, 1963).

9. On the conceptual framework, see Charles E. Lindbloom, *The Policy-Making Process* (Englewood Cliffs, New Jersey: Prentice-Hall, 1968); and Richard E. Neustadt, *Presidential Power* (New York: John Wiley and Sons, 1960). Also, see Allison on the use of several "conceptual lenses" to develop a more comprehensive view of events. Also helpful here are the descriptive model of Cyert and March and the prescriptive model of Andrews.

10. Joseph L. Bower, *Managing the Resource Allocation Process* (Homewood, Ill.: Richard D. Irwin, 1970).

11. Other population objectives were set in the areas of skills training; nutrition; health; employment; population distribution; women's participation; and demographic research.

12. The other seven members were: the head of the Population and Human Resources Unit, CONAPLAN; the chief of Maternal-Child Health, Ministry of Health; the head of Adult Education, Ministry of Education; the assistant director of the Bureau of Statistics and the Census, Ministry of Economy; a representative from the Office of Sectoral Planning, Ministry of Agriculture; the director of the National Manpower Department, Ministry of Labor; and the director of the National Council on Minors.

3

STRATEGY, LEADERSHIP, AND CONTEXT IN FAMILY PLANNING: A THREE-COUNTRY COMPARISON

David C. Korten and Frances F. Korten

In 1960 there were only three countries in the world with population policies and only one actually offering family planning services.[1] By 1975, 93 percent of the population of the developing world was living in nations which had either an official policy to reduce population growth rates or provided support for family planning activities, or both.[2] As E.N. Rogers has suggested, "Probably no other idea in man's history has spread so rapidly from nation to nation."[3]

That such basic changes in social policy perspectives and values can take place on a global scale with such rapidity is of major interest and relevance to future, potentially global, social changes currently appearing on the horizon.

The present paper examines how three basically conservative Catholic countries came to accept family planning programs as an implicit instrument of national social policy. We will draw on the case of El Salvador in the preceding chapter, adding data on Costa Rica and Nicaragua to provide the basis for a three-country comparison of the evolution of policy toward family planning. This comparison reveals both the common external forces impinging upon the three countries and each country's unique response. We shall see that while the countries had much in common, the style of leadership, the channels of influence, and the programs which eventually resulted differed substantially from country to country, reflecting the differences in socioeconomic and political context. From the consequences in these three countries we will attempt to draw insights into the patterns and possibilities relevant to future efforts at social change.

SOCIOECONOMIC AND POLITICAL CHARACTERISTICS OF THE THREE COUNTRIES

Visitors to Central America are often impressed by the extent to which the small, contiguous nations of the isthmus differ from one another. While all Spanish-speaking and Catholic, each has distinct socioeconomic and political characteristics which are important to understanding the differences in the ways each country's government came to support family planning.

Socioeconomic Characteristics

Comparative data on selected socioeconomic indicators for the three countries under study are presented in Table 1. These figures show Costa Rica to be clearly the wealthiest and most modernized of the three, with a per capita income more than twice that of El Salvador. It has the highest life expectancy, the highest percentage of its population covered by social security, the best water supply system, and the most highly developed health infrastructure. In recent years it also achieved the largest increases in food production.

Costa Rica is known among Central American countries for the predominance of its middle class, whereas both El Salvador and Nicaragua usually are characterized as highly stratified, with enormous contrasts between rich and poor. However, statistics on income distribution do not reflect these widely held perceptions. Rather, the data in Table 1 show remarkable consistency among the three countries in the distribution of income. It appears that the source of the perception of Costa Rica's strong middle class comes less from the actual distribution of income than from other factors such as (1) its higher income at all levels, (2) its more fully developed social services

Table 1
Selected Social and Economic Indicators

	Costa Rica	El Salvador	Nicaragua
Population (in millions) 1974 est.[*]	1.9	4.0	2.1
Density: 1974 population/sq. km.[*]	3€	183	16
% urban of total population 1975 est.[*]	40	40	48
Estimated rate per 1,000 population 1973[*]			
Births	29.5	40.3	46–50
Deaths	5.4	8.3	14–17
Life expectancy at birth: 1970–75 est.[*]			
Male	66.5	56.0	51.2
Female	69.9	59.7	54.6
% of population 15 and over literate 1970[**]	89	58	60
% of population ages 5–14 years in elementary school 1970[**]	67.4	54.0	47.3
% of population 15–19 years in secondary school 1970[**]	40.6	24.0	20.7
% of population 20–29 years in university 1970[**]	5.0	1.7	2.2
Population in thousands[*]			
Per physician	1.4	4	2.1
Per nurse	1.4	1.4	00.7
Per midwife			
Per hospital bed	0.2	0.7	0.4
YEAR	(1973)	(1973)	(1969)
Per capita gross domestic product[*]			
Per capita in US $ (1972)	634	307	496
% derived from agriculture (1972)	20	26	26
Per capita food production[*]			
Index (1961–65=100)			
1972–74 average	133	100	112

Table 1
(cont'd.)

	Costa Rica	El Salvador	Nicaragua
Per capita energy consumed: 1972[*]			
(kilograms of coal equivalent)	478	199	408
Economically active population by type of activity, % 1970[**]			
Primary	43.2	60.3	56.5
Secondary	19.9	16.9	15.8
Tertiary	36.9	21.8	27.7
Economically active population covered by social security 1970[**]	38.0%	17.5%	12.7%
Calories per person per day (units), 1966[**]	2,610	1,840	2,350
Protein per person per day (grams), 1966[**]	57.9	44.2	59.0
Population with potable water source, 1970[**]	100%	70%	
Urban	100%	70%	95%
Rural	56%	27%	10%
Urban Population with sewage services, 1970[**]	23.9%	73.7%	43.6%
Income distribution (% of total income received by each strata)[**]			

Strata	% of population			
Low	50%	18	16	15
Middle	30%	26	24	25
High	15%	27	33	32
Very High	5%	29	27	28

[*]Dorothy Nortman and Ellen Hofstatter, "Population and Family Planning Programs: A Factbook," *Reports on Population/Family Planning*, No. 2 (seventh edition, October 1975).

[**]UNICEF, SIECA and ODECA, *Las Sociedades Centroamericanas Actuales* (Guatemala: 1972).

which provide middle-class living standards to a larger proportion of its population, and (3) its long-standing democratic traditions which give visibility and power to the middle class.

Between El Salvador and Nicaragua, Nicaragua is the wealthier on a per capita basis, is more urbanized, and has a slightly more modern economy. It also leads El Salvador on nutritional indicators and has more hospital beds and medical personnel on a per capita basis. Yet in spite of Nicaragua's edge in health inputs and in basic wealth, El Salvador enjoys higher indicators of achievement in health and education as well as in family planning. Its life expectancy is higher, its death rate substantially lower, and its birth rate somewhat lower.

Table 1 also reflects the rather striking demographic contrasts among the three countries. El Savador, by far the smallest with a land area less than 20 percent that of Nicaragua, has a population of four million, nearly twice that of either of the other two countries. As a result the population density of El Salvador at 183 persons per square kilometer is nearly five times that of Costa Rica and more than eleven times that of Nicaragua.

These figures tend to understate the demographic pressures felt by all three countries due to the unevenness of population distribution. For example, Costa Rica's overall density of thirty-eight persons per square kilometer disguises the reality that approximately 50 percent of its population is clustered in its relatively small central plateau. The 1971 census for Nicaragua reveals that its Atlantic region, which accounts for over half its land area, had a density of only 1.6 persons per square kilometer, reflecting the fact that much of it is rendered undesirable for habitation by excessive rainfall (approximately 150 inches per year), jungles, swamps, pests, and infertile soil. By contrast the more desirable Pacific region in which the capital city of Managua is located had a density of 47.7 persons per square kilometer. Within this region much of the rural population is crowded on the poor lands not already taken for large commercial farming operations.

In 1960 Costa Rica had a population growth rate of 3.8 percent, one of the highest in the world. Since that year birth rates have fallen steadily from 47.5 per thousand to 29.5 per thousand in 1973, with indications that the decline is continuing. (Preliminary U.S. census estimates placed the rate for 1975 at 24 per thousand.) The absolute number of annual births reached a peak of 62,909 in 1965 and then began a decline to 53,455 births recorded in 1973. These rapid declines make Costa Rica something of a demographic phenomenon among contemporary developing nations.

El Salvador's demographic trends have been much less spectacular than Costa Rica's. Nevertheless its birth rates have been dropping steadily from 49 per thousand in 1963 to an estimated 40.3 in 1973.

Nicaragua, with an estimated birth rate of 46 to 50 per thousand in 1973, has experienced little if any decline.

Political Context

The three countries offer interesting political contrasts, from the social equality and democratic traditions of Costa Rica to the dynastic one-man rule of Nicaragua. The influence of these differences on the patterns of family planning policy development is striking, as will become evident in our later analysis.

Costa Rica. The Spaniards who populated the central plateau region of Costa Rica were an industrious group who worked the rich soil with their own hands, a pattern which was to continue until the rise of the coffee barons in the nineteenth and early twentieth centuries. This new wealthy class, which benefited from a Costa Rican version of laissez-faire government, gradually came to dominate the government as well as the economy until a revolution brought José Figueres and his National Liberationist party (PLN) to power in 1948. Believing that a legitimate function of the state was to provide for the welfare of its citizens, the founders of the PLN embarked upon a series of social reforms intended to break down the class structures and achieve a redistribution of wealth. However, not all Costa Ricans share the PLN ideology and Costa Rican elections are hotly contested, with regular changes of government. Basically Costa Rica is a pluralistic democracy with equalitarian traditions, an influential middle class, and a commitment to progressive social policies which for Central America is quite strong.

El Salvador. Periodic instability with a continuing succession of military presidents gaining power by constitutional and extraconstitutional means continues to characterize El Salvador. An elected president was overthrown in a coup in 1960. In the subsequent election in 1962, the winner from the newly formed National Conciliation party (PCN) was unopposed. Though individual presidents have honored the constitutional provision against an individual retaining office beyond one term, the PCN has remained in power since that election. There is a very active left-of-center opposition which staged an unsuccessful coup in 1972. In addition a militant leftist element pressures the government with guerilla activity. El

Salvador may be characterized as a somewhat unstable democracy with strong influence from a generally conservative, traditional oligarchy which has supported a succession of military governments and social reforms to justify and defend itself in the face of active leftist elements. The military governments have in turn sought to maintain the balance between the conservative oligarchy and the leftist interests required to remain in power.

Nicaragua. From the 1820s to the 1930s Nicaraguan history was largely a record of power struggles between the leaders of its liberal and conservative parties, punctuated by periods of U.S. intervention.[4] Then after a U.S.-supervised election in 1928 and a long struggle in which a guerrilla hero named Sandino fought the U.S. Marines to a stand-off, the United States withdrew from Nicaragua, leaving General Anastasio Somoza Garcia as head of the National Guard. Sandino was assassinated by the National Guard in 1934, and three years later Somoza became president. D.B. Heath observes that "in a tradition that some refer to as 'dynastic,' the Somoza family has monopolized the presidency and much of the national economy for forty years."[5] While Nicaragua is nominally a constitutional democracy, there remains no effective challenge to Somoza's rule, and any potentially serious opposition has been quickly suppressed.[6] Relations between the U.S. government and the Somoza family have been very close. Basically Nicaragua is an oligarchy in which a firmly entrenched ruler has a greater stake in a vigorous economy than in serious social reforms.

This, in summary form, is the context within which family planning was introduced in three Central American countries.

THE DEVELOPMENT OF FAMILY PLANNING IN COSTA RICA

Initial Impulses

The family planning movement in Costa Rica received its initial impulse from activities begun by two individuals in the early 1960s. One was Dr. Arturo Cabezas Lopez who directed a Protestant-sponsored clinic located in the capital city of San José and who helped lead a volunteer mobile medical program which provided services to the rural poor. Cabezas introduced family planning services as a major activity in both programs. He quickly became well known in Costa Rica and abroad for his aggressive and successful promotion of vasectomy operations carried out in remote villages.

The second key individual was Alberto Gonzalez whose involvement in family planning services delivery began in the early 1960s while he was a student enrolled at the Inter-American Institute for Agricultural Sciences in Turrialba, Costa Rica. At that time contraceptives were unavailable in Turrialba. Since Gonzalez frequently made the two-hour trip to San José, some women in the area began asking him to buy contraceptive pills for them in the city. Finding the number of requests increasing, he sought out a wholesaler who agreed to sell to him in bulk at one-fourth the retail price, a saving that Gonzalez passed on to the women.

As demand continued to grow, young Gonzalez became interested in making oral contraceptives more readily available to women who wanted them. He suggested that the women he was supplying organize themselves into informal groups or cells of eight women. The woman who organized and led a cell would receive her pills free in return for acting as the distributor. The others would receive their pills for half the retail price. The proceeds would be used to finance the system and to provide the free pills to the cell leaders.

The idea caught on quickly. Not only did the participants obtain their contraceptive supplies at attractive prices, but the regular meeting which the cells held to distribute the pills had the effect of getting women together to talk about their experiences with family planning and helped reinforce their motivation. Within a short time, there were about thirty different groups involving 250 women. Gonzalez could no longer keep track of all the newly forming groups and effectively manage the system in his spare time.

As a result he decided to try a more stable distribution system based on local women whose jobs placed them in close contact with the public such as nurses, school teachers, and hairdressers. They sold pills for four *colones* per cycle, compared to the normal pharmacy retail price of fourteen *colones*.

At the same time as these initial impulses by a medical practitioner and a budding young entrepreneur were being felt, a number of international organizations involved with demographic concerns began demonstrating interest in Costa Rica. A stream of visitors from foreign family planning groups began to appear in Costa Rica. Beginning in 1964, external groups became involved in supporting a number of studies of family planning practices and attitudes in Costa Rica.

An Action Coalition

Gonzalez had been financing his program in part through a small profit margin on pill sales and in part through donations received from a group of interested friends in Turrialba. Looking for further sources of support during a period when his program was in financial difficulty, Gonzalez approached Cabezas in 1965 to seek assistance from him and the group of supporters he had developed. Soon Gonzalez began organizing meetings among these people which led in March 1966 to the formation of the Costa Rican Demographic Association (ADC). The association was committed to developing an awareness of population problems in Costa Rica and to encouraging public support for family planning programs. A board of directors was elected with Cabezas as its president. Alberto Gonzalez was named by the board as the first executive director.

Cabezas and Gonzalez became committed to extending family planning services to the widest possible population, working from a conviction based on personal experience with rural peoples that excessive numbers of children were major contributors to the conditions of malnutrition, ill health, and poverty in which these people lived.

With initial funds from the U.S. Agency for International Development (AID) and the International Planned Parenthood Federation (IPPF), the ADC assumed sponsorship of the family planning services in the clinic which Cabezas headed and established six family planning clinics in hospitals and Ministry of Health centers. Gonzalez now worked through the ADC to expand to the San José area the distribution system for oral contraceptives which he had initiated in Turrialba.

Opposition

The use of government facilities implied at least tolerance by the government. There were strong pockets of unorganized opposition to the use of birth control methods, but little organized opposition. To avoid any visible stimulus which might serve to coalesce an opposition, no mass communications programs were launched to announce the clinic services.

The church avoided taking a stand. Perhaps the major single source of resistance was the Medical College, a professional association of physicians whose elected directors were the maximum authority on medical practice in Costa Rica. On one occasion the college, a private association not to be confused with the Faculty of Medicine at the university, denied the use of its auditorium for a conference on family planning.

The College of Pharmacists, a Costa Rican professional association to which all practicing pharmacists were required to belong, gave the program its only real setback. In 1964 the college had decreed that oral contraceptives could be sold only through pharmacies and other authorized establishments and only on receipt of a medical prescription. According to Thein and Reynolds, although the public justification of the decree was to protect the health of the public, the major purpose was to halt the door-to-door sales of contraceptive pills by one local distributor whose activities were cutting heavily into pharmacy profits.[7] Citing their 1964 decree, the college charged that the ADC was distributing a prescription product without proper medical control and insisted that this practice must stop. (It was common knowledge, however, that many pharmacists themselves sold oral contraceptives and other drugs freely without prescription.)

The Coupon Distribution System

After a period of difficult negotiation, Gonzalez and the College of Pharmacists agreed in June 1967 to a compromise whereby the college granted the ADC a special classification as a drug distributor authorized to import contraceptives and to distribute them through pharmacies. The ADC in turn agreed to employ a full-time pharmacist to supervise the distribution. Thus ended Gonzalez's successful and pioneering community-based distribution program. Instead the ADC enrolled a number of pharmacies in the program as distributors. It then arranged with private doctors, as well as the ADC's own clinics, to distribute coupons to women who came to them for contraceptive assistance. These coupons could then be redeemed at cooperating pharmacies for the purchase of ADC-supplied pills at well below the regular retail price.

Even with this change, the distribution program continued to grow rapidly and, according to Cabezas and Gonzalez, provided an important source of funds for crucial ADC activities. They were used, for example, to sponsor receptions and dinners to bring together influential Costa Rican opinion makers, including the president, other high government officials, radio and television people, newspapermen, professors, and clergy to discuss demographic themes. At the time the international donors were not willing to fund these activities.

The Creation of a National Program

The major objective of the ADC during the 1966-67 period was to convince influential politicians and public sector officials of the need for a government-sponsored program. Particularly helpful was a young economist in the Ministry of Public Health, Augusto Perera, an ally of the family planning movement who was sent with ADC funds to a course at Yale University on the demographic explosion and its implications. On his return, the Yale credentials lent credibility to his arguments that an office of population should be created in the ministry.

Once a beachhead of support was established in the ministry, ADC officials, accompanied by a group of Chilean doctors, approached the president of the Republic and the minister of public health with a formal request that the government participate in a family planning program. The president responded affirmatively and on April 7, 1967, an executive decree was published which created the Office of Population in the ministry. Its regular activities began in January 1968, under the direction of Perera, with the initial establishment of family planning clinics in nine health units. Collaboration between the ministry and the ADC was very close from the beginning, with the ministry agreeing to rely on the ADC coupon system for oral contraceptive distribution. Thus the ministry doctors gave out coupons which users could redeem at participating drug stores. Women who could not afford the small fee were given special coupons which could be redeemed without charge, the ADC giving the druggist a rebate to cover his costs and a small margin.

The third institution to become involved in family planning in Costa Rica was the Family Orientation Center (COF) created in January 1968 by an Episcopalian minister from Puerto Rico, Rev. José Carlo. Like Cabezas and Gonzales, Carlo was known for his strong personal dedication to the family planning movement and for his ability to generate enthusiasm and commitment among others. The COF provided a program of sex education based on short courses, counseling services, and a radio program.

A short time later the University of Costa Rica became the fourth institution to join the effort when it created a Center for Social and Population Studies to provide for medical training and social science research in family planning and population.

Recognizing a need for coordination, the leaders of these four institutions decided that it would be useful for them to meet on a regular basis for purposes of exchange of information on their respective activities. Thus the National Population Committee (CONAPO) was formed on November 30, 1968. It was an informal association without official status or paid staff, yet the CONAPO members proved to be an active and committed group. As a result CONAPO gradually came to be an important force in shaping the future directions of what had become a truly national program.

Shortly after the formation of CONAPO, Gonzalez became aware that a few of the doctors participating in the ADC programs were overcharging their clients. When he put pressure on them, they started a rumor campaign against him, implying irregularities in the use of ADC funds. At Gonzalez's request, the ADC board contracted an audit of the ADC accounts which completely exonerated Gonzalez. But he was discouraged by the ordeal and shortly afterwards announced his resignation. He redirected his entrepreneurial talents to setting himself up as a commodities trader and soon was engaged in dealings throughout Central America.[8] The new executive director of the ADC was Victor Morgan Alvarado, a successful businessman and former head of the Costa Rican civil service.[9] An effective administrator with considerable political skill, Morgan was to become a major factor in gradually elevating the role and prestige of CONAPO and in maintaining the interest and collaboration of its member institutions. He took an active interest in the affairs of the International Planned Parenthood Federation and was appointed its regional coordinator for Central America and Mexico. Through this position he gained an international visibility which was useful in attracting additional funding to Costa Rica. He also established a role for the ADC as informal secretariat to CONAPO. By the early 1970s funds were flowing through the ADC to CONAPO member organizations from a number of donors, including the Pan American Health Organization, the International Planned Parenthood Federation, the U.S. Agency for International Development, and later the United Nations Fund for Population Activities.

A Period of Continued Expansion

Family planning had become an open topic of discussion in Costa Rica by 1970. The Ministry of Public Health was operating eighty-eight clinics throughout the country, the ADC had begin mass communications campaigns, and the Family Orientation Center radio program "Dialogo" had attained respectability and popularity. The minister of public education, Victor Brenes, known to be a supporter of family planning and sex education, felt that the public acceptance of these topics was sufficient to create in March 1970 a "General Supervisory Office for Sex Education" to coordinate the ministry's sex education activities. After finishing his term as minister, Brenes assumed leadership of this office and became the fifth member of CONAPO.

In April 1970 the Costa Rican Institute of Social Security, which provided medical services to an estimated 50 percent of the population, opened its first family planning clinics and later named a representative to CONAPO.

The final addition to CONAPO, in February 1971, was the Family Integration Center, established by the Catholic-sponsored Christian Family Movement out of concern that the CONAPO organizations were not placing sufficient emphasis on the "natural" methods of birth control acceptable to the Catholic church.

The period from 1971 to 1973 was basically one of steady, systematic expansion of coverage within the governmental structures, building on new program initiatives of the government, while being careful not to test the limits of tolerance of the bureaucratic or political system by pushing major innovations.

THE DEVELOPMENT OF FAMILY PLANNING IN NICARAGUA

Initial Impulses

Although the governmental family planning program in Nicaragua apparently blossomed suddenly in 1968 and grew quickly thereafter, it actually was born out of both external and internal processes set in motion earlier.

In March 1965 the U.S. Agency for International Development (AID) sent an airgram to all of its missions outlining basic AID policy in population and asking each mission to assign one officer to become familiar with population dynamics and related programs.[10] In Nicaragua, Louis Gardella, the mission's public health advisor, was given the additional title of population officer.

Gardella had friendly relationships with a number of Nicaraguan doctors whom he knew to have an interest in family planning, including Noel Sandino and Gardella's neighbor, Emilio Bandes. Gardella talked with Sandino and Bandes about how to stimulate interest in family planning, and they decided to hold a series of meetings at Gardella's house inviting outside speakers whenever possible. Sandino and Bandes were instrumental in drawing a number of other doctors into the group. This group included Dr. Castillo Quant, who in 1967 as vice-minister of health was instrumental in organizing the family planning program within the ministry, and Dr. Rodrigo Portocarrero, who in 1969 organized the family planning program within the Nicaraguan Social Security Institute. In 1971 Bandes himself became the executive director of the local International Planned Parenthood Federation chapter, the Nicaraguan Demographic Association.

In 1966 AID sponsored fifteen Nicaraguans to attend a Latin-America-wide conference of IPPF in Honduras. This experience served to intensify interest in the meetings at Gardella's home. However, this group of Nicaraguan activists was stymied by staunch governmental opposition. President René Schick, who had been approached by both IPPF and AID about family planning, was irrevocably opposed to it saying he would never have such a program in Nicaragua. The minister of health at that time was also firmly against it. Thus while interest in the problem was growing in Nicaragua and while AID's increasing support for family planning activities throughout Latin America made it clear that potential resources were available, government action was impossible.

The year 1967 proved to be a turning point. At their April 1967 meeting at Punta del Este, the Latin American heads of state formally recognized the population problem—opening the way for programs which dealt with it. At the same time, Nicaragua was moving toward a new regime as elections neared following the death of René Schick. The official candidate whose victory seemed assured was Anastasio Somoza Debayle. He and his health and welfare advocate wife, Hope, appeared open-minded on family planning.

Prior to the elections, a group of doctors including Sandino, Bandes, Quant, and Portocarrero (Hope de Somoza's cousin) met with Hope and obtained her agreement that Nicaragua should have a family planning program. Following the elections, the U.S. ambassador to Nicaragua and the local AID director, both strongly profamily planning, went directly to Somoza and proposed the establishment of a family planning program. Quant and Portocarrero continued to contact Hope periodically to maintain her support for the plan. As soon as Somoza appointed his minister of health, Quant and Sandino met with him to seek his support for a family planning program. He indicated that he would accept such a program in the ministry if approved by the National Health Committee, headed by Hope de Somoza.

At the next meeting of the committee, Portocarrero proposed the establishment of a family planning program. Hope approved a program for the ministry, but would not approve one for social security for fear that insured workers might feel they were being pressured to enroll. Gardella and Quant were ready with a plan for a ministry program. On September 27, 1967, only one week after the minister of health gave his formal approval based on the committee decision, and only three months after Somoza's election, a formal agreement was signed between AID and the Nicaraguan government to implement a family planning program.

Initial Controversy

The program aroused a strong negative reaction from the church, with the archbishop for Nicaragua announcing that he would excommunicate anyone who participated in the family planning program. This brought a counterreaction from a number of influential priests and lay persons who stressed that the program was necessary to reduce the number of abortions and the high rate of illegitimacy. The archbishop backed off, the family planning people made a point of quietly seeking the support of Catholic leaders in each community where they opened a clinic, and the controversy quickly died. The country's opposition newspaper, *La Prensa*, used its editorial columns to emphasize that the use of contraceptives was against the edict of the pope and for several years refused to print news stories about the program, but it did not attack the government program directly. The basic strategy of the leaders of the family planning effort was to maintain public silence in the face of the early attacks and simply let things run their course.

Development of Institutions and Programs

Ministry of Public Health. The ministry's family planning program, entitled the "Family Welfare Program,," was considered part of its maternal and child health effort. However with its independent funding from AID, it was organized as a separate unit within the Ministry of Health, and its coordinator reported directly to the Minister of health through Quant, the vice minister. A social worker with strong commitment to family planning was appointed as the first coordinator. However personality conflicts and the feelings of some ministry personnel that the program should be headed by a physician led to the appointment a year later of Dr. Francisco Gutierrez as director of the program.

The first six months were devoted mainly to ordering necessary equipment and supplies and to sending medical personnel from the ministry's health centers to the El Salvadorean Demographic Association for short training courses in family planning. Also, educational activities were begun in areas surrounding the clinics where the family planning services would first be introduced.

In March 1968 the first ministry clinic was opened in Managua, followed in May by the opening of three clinics in the northern provinces and one in Granada. The program grew quickly thereafter, adding family planning services in additional clinics as the personnel became trained.

There was considerable resistance among the ministry's clinic personnel to the program at the outset. This was due in part to an ignorance of what family planning was and in part to the fact that it added one more duty to the already numerous duties they were expected to perform during the morning hours of the clinic. It soon became evident that a combination of staff resistance and a heavy existing demand for MCH care, especially in the Managua clinics, placed considerable pressure on clinic personnel to neglect family planning in favor of what they saw as more immediate needs. Thus it was decided to provide special afternoon hours exclusively for family planning services. AID agreed to pay the salaries of these clinic personnel during the special hours. This helped in overcoming the resistance of clinic personnel. The extra pay was appreciated, especially by those working in rural areas where other sources of supplemental income were scarce.

Resistance was also encountered among some of the ministry's central office personnel, partly due to the fact that many did not believe in family planning—feeling that it would corrupt the women of the country, that it was an expression of U.S. imperialism, or that Nicaragua needed more population, not less. Another source of resentment was the fact that the administratively separate program provided its central office personnel with higher salaries than other ministry personnel, due to the fact that they were employed for seven and a half hours each day (contrasted to the normal six-hour ministry schedule).

Time and education were principal factors in overcoming resistance. The training in El Salvador appeared to be influential in changing opinions about family planning among the clinic personnel who attended. At these courses the personnel learned that family planning was being offered in a neighboring country. They talked with fellow Latins who saw family planning as acceptable and needed, and they obtained the medical knowledge needed to carry out their new duties.

As the program became established, the ministry's family planning office began offering a family planning course for all nurses and auxiliaries who worked for the ministry, regardless of whether they did family planning work. According to the head nursing supervisor for the family planning program, this served to improve the general climate for family planning work at the clinics. Also, according to one public health doctor, once doctors began working in the family planning program their attitudes generally became more positive.

Within the central office of the Ministry of Health, there were no specific efforts aimed at reducing resistance, although the educational efforts mentioned above most likely had some effect. According to an AID public health advisor, Hope de Somoza's positive attitudes on family planning had a favorable influence on ministry personnel. However there continued to be some resentment of the separate status and periodically the possibility was raised of returning to an integrated program with no special hours or extra pay.

In mid-1972 Castillo Quant resigned as vice-minister of Health, at which time family planning services were offered in sixty of the 118 Ministry of Health clinics. This marked the end of the expansion of the ministry program, with only a few clinics being added to the family planning program in the next three years.

Social security. While Hope's decision initially prevented the social security from offering family planning services, by 1969 Portocarrero, then director of medical services for the Nicaraguan Social Security Institute (INSS), obtained approval to start a family planning program within the institute. On May 29, 1969, an agreement was signed between AID and INSS to provide services within five of social security's nine health facilities.

Although the social security's "Family Orientation Program" was officially considered part of its maternal-child health section, it, like the family planning program in the Ministry of Health, was actually administratively separate, with a special staff which reported directly to Portocarrero. The social security program from the beginning had separate family planning hours with clinic personnel paid by AID. The Social Security Institute's contribution to this program consisted primarily of providing the clinic space and some basic equipment and supplies.

Once the agreement was signed the first six months of the program were devoted to educational activities. Social security personnel were sent for training to the Salvadorean Demographic Association and educational activities were carried out within the clinic to prepare the women for the new service. Hope de Somoza had requested that careful educational programs be carried out before clinic services began so that users would understand the concept of planning a family and know that the program was strictly voluntary. When in February 1970 Portocarrero resigned as director of medical services, family planning was being offered in five clinics. By 1971 it was expanded to seven clinics, and after the December 1972 earthquake which destroyed most of Managua, the services were expanded to ten clinics.

Moravian Mission. The Moravian Mission was a Protestant religious group which had been active in providing health services in the isolated, inaccessible, and politically ignored Atlantic region of Nicaragua since 1935. In 1965, the same year that the Nicaraguan doctors started meeting in Gardella's home in Managua, they began quietly offering family planning services. These services were limited to consultations conducted within the mission's hospital in Puerto Cabezas, supported by the Pathfinder Fund and the International Planned Parenthood Federation.

In May 1969 the Moravian effort became a part of the official national program when a three-party agreement was signed between the Ministry of Health, the Moravian Mission, and AID under which AID would fund family planning services in the Moravian hospitals. Later AID funded outreach services to some of the remote villages.

Nicaraguan Demographic Association. The last institution of the national program to develop in Nicaragua was the private Demographic Association. In 1970 Castillo Quant, in his capacity as vice-minister of public health, invited fifteen persons interested in family planning to travel at AID expense to the Dominican Republic to visit their demographic association. The group returned from that visit interested in starting a local chapter of the International Planned Parenthood Federation. Nicaragua at that time was one of the two Latin American countries still lacking chapters of the International Planned Parenthood Federation (IPPF), the other being Bolivia. On July 3, 1970, at the home of Emilio Bandes, a Nicaragua affiliate was officially founded. A board of directors was set up and Bandes was elected executive director. Funds were obtained from IPPF to support the executive director, his secretary, and a small educational program.

The early educational efforts consisted of seminars, conferences, and short courses aimed at increasing awareness of the consequences of rapid population growth and at developing understanding of the spiritual, moral, and material benefits of family planning. The association often made use on a volunteer basis of staff members from the Ministry of Health and the Ministry of Education in conducting its courses.

While Bandes had from the beginning sought funds for a clinic program, the donors, observing that the government was already offering services, were unsympathetic until the emergency situation which followed the December 1972 earthquake. Then the Pathfinder Fund authorized funding for five clinics to be located in the Managua area on land donated by the government to provide family planning, prenatal, and pediatric services. These clinics were to be transferred to the government within two years. Postearthquake funding was also received from IPPF to open a "model" clinic for the purposes of training family planning personnel from the ministry in medical techniques and human relations.

In March 1973 the Demographic Association initiated an intensive radio campaign based primarily on spot announcements aimed at encouraging use of the government's clinics.

National Program Coordination

So long as Louis Gardella, the local AID population officer, remained in Nicaragua, the meetings at his house provided an effective mechanism for coordinating the efforts of those involved in promoting family planning in Nicaragua. When he was reassigned to Honduras in 1969, these meetings stopped. Thereafter coordination came primarily from initiatives taken by Gardella's AID replacement on whom the ministry, social security, and Moravian programs were all dependent for their funding.

This resulted in some integration of functions. The ministry supplied the other programs with contraceptives through its warehouse. It also ran the cytology laboratory to which specimen slides were sent from both the ministry and the social security programs. It organized training programs for personnel from the other programs and coordinated scholarships for study abroad in family planning. Until 1973 it also assumed responsibility for promoting family planning through mass communication and community educational efforts.

Formation of the Demographic Association in 1970 introduced the need for some rethinking of previous institutional roles. Thus in December 1971 a meeting was held between the heads of the ministry, social security, and association programs, the AID population officer, and the regional representative of the International Planned

Parenthood Federation. This meeting produced an understanding that the ministry and the Social Security Institute would provide the basic clinical services in family planning as well as the person-to-person motivational efforts; the ministry would provide, compile, and report statistics on the work accomplished; and the newly formed association would carry out mass communication campaigns, research related to demography and attitudes toward family planning, and training of personnel to work in family planning through a model clinic which it was to establish.

No further meetings were held on either a formal or informal basis. By the time the association opened its model clinic in 1973 for the purpose of training ministry personnel, the ministry had its own training program well established and planned to continue it. The delineation of roles further broke down when the association opened five additional clinics in Managua in 1973, even though their intent was to pass them on to the government eventually.

COMPARATIVE ANALYSIS

The preceding descriptions of the development of family planning programs in Costa Rica and Nicaragua, plus Ickis's case on the Salvadorean program, reveal several major patterns. Four major aspects of the policy process were similar in all three countries.

1. In each country political leaders maintained low personal profiles on family planning, even when they supported the concept.
2. In each country the program came about through a step-by-step expansion of family planning activities, with each increment small enough to avoid confrontation.
3. In each country family planning leaders justified the program in terms of maternal and child health rather than population objectives.
4. The governments of all three countries adopted official family planning programs at nearly the same time.

In spite of these major similarities, there were also significant differences in the ways each country's program developed: (1) the origins and patterns of efforts to establish a government policy in family planning were quite different; (2) the nature and style of the leadership during the promotion stage differed significantly; (3) the private family planning associations played substantially different roles in the three countries.

Similarities

The similarities suggest that a number of forces were at work that were external to, or at least independent of, the marked contextual differences among the three countries. These are worth exploring in search of insights into how a potentially controversial policy was able to gain official support in a relatively short time.

Stance of political leaders. A remarkable aspect of the development of family planning in these three conservative, Catholic countries is that each was able to reach a de facto policy in support of family planning without any major political leader publicly taking a stand on the issue. Rather than publicly either supporting or opposing the concept of family planning, the political leaders in each country responded in a low-key and cautious manner. Family planning as a political issue in Latin America in the 1960s appears to have had about the same status as did abortion in the United States in the mid-1970s. There was more to be lost than gained politically from taking a public stand.

This was most evident in El Salvador in Allwood's sudden shift from a leader in the family planning movement to a hands-off posture as soon as he became minister of health. We may presume that he saw the political losses to be suffered by incurring the bitter attacks of the family planning opposition as greater than any potential benefits accruing from the good will of the family planning advocates. Even President Somoza of Nicaragua, with his relative political security, preferred to put his wife between himself and the issue.

How was it possible for these controversial programs to be established without open political support? One reason is that many political figures probably were either privately supportive or indifferent toward the issue. A consistent characteristic in the three countries is that while mainstream political leaders did not publicly support family planning, neither did they publicly oppose it. Thus there was no base of opposition within the political mainstream which would necessitate open political support to move the policy forward. A survey taken of the members of the legislative body in El Salvador revealed that in fact most members were privately supportive of family planning.[11]

A second reason was that foreign funding of the programs avoided the need to raise budgetary issues, allowing an approach of government acquiescence rather than government support, at least until the program became well-established and publicly accepted. A third important reason was the nonconfronting, incremental approach used by the family planning advocates.

Nonconfronting incrementalism. In each of the three countries family planning activities were established through a series of small increments with advocates seeking to avoid controversy at every step. While the strategy followed turned out to be the same in each country and consistent over time, there is no indication that the leaders in any of the programs were working according to a predetermined long-term plan. Rather they proceeded one step at a time, testing and negotiating, using a localized search pattern to identify those actions doable at the moment which carried minimum risk. No one step was of sufficient significance or visibility to coalesce opposition; yet each step ultimately prepared the way for the next.

The pattern was clearest in Costa Rica and El Salvador where by the time the government was called upon to make a decision, the basic demand for and acceptance of contraceptive services was well established. It was also clear that the service could be delivered, even within government clinics, without producing a political holocaust. Each step was measured. First, private services were provided outside government clinics, then private services were offered within government facilities, and finally, government services were available in government facilities. In El Salvador this was done first in more remote and less visible clinics and in a manner that allowed the central government, if challenged, to deny knowledge of and responsibility for the occurrence. When a public government decision was eventually needed, it was little more than a confirmation and acceptance of responsibility for what already existed. Certainly there was no fanfare in announcing new national priorities or a groundbreaking new social program. The government services were well established before the risk was accepted of introducing mass communication campaigns to draw public attention to them.

Nicaragua was something of an exception to this pattern. Prior to the government decision, there was no testing of acceptance for family planning services outside the Moravian Mission activities in the politically inconsequential and isolated Atlantic coastal region. Yet the successful experience in El Salvador, Costa Rica, and Honduras, the three immediate neighbors of Nicaragua, basically established the concept. Once the decision to offer family planning services was made, an incremental approach was followed even in Nicaragua. The Social Security Institute was initially excluded until the service was tested in the less socially visible Ministry of Health programs. Initial time was spent sending personnel for training and carrying out low-profile, person-to-person public relations work in the communities where the service was to be offered. Services were expanded to additional clinics one at a time and were available only during regular clinic hours. There initially were no separate clinics or special hours. During the program's first two years there was no use of the mass media. Nearly all added costs were borne by AID.

In all three countries every effort was made to avoid open public confrontation with the opposition. The one exception was the early experience in El Salvador with the debates which crystallized the opposition of an influential newspaper editor. This was widely recognized as a tactical error by family planning advocates throughout Central America. Subsequently the leaders in El Salvador, Costa Rica, and Nicaragua all adhered to the general policy of never answering public attacks directly.

Maternal and child health objectives. In each of the three countries, the government chose to justify the family planning program in terms of health rather than demographic objectives. Service delivery was executed through the existing health structures, which in each country were comprised of a combination of hospitals and clinics distributed throughout the country. Only Alberto Gonzalez's program of distributing oral contraceptives through locally based women did not make use of the health system, and eventually was shut down for precisely that reason.

This use of the health system was important in insulating the program from attack. It was much more difficult to oppose a policy intended to improve the health of mothers and children than a policy intended to reduce fertility. Furthermore, the advocacy by a number of prominent physicians made opposition even more difficult, as the word of a physician is generally not questioned in matters relating to health.

Concurrent decisions. Within the space of nine months—between mid-1967 and early 1968—the governments of all three countries had adopted an official family planning program.

How was this convergence of action possible when program support had been evolving in such different ways? Our look at the history of each program revealed in each case an exciting local drama with the outcome at each stage in apparent doubt. Or was it? Were there broader forces at work of which the local dramas were only a supporting element?

As it turned out the introduction of modern contraceptive services was a global social innovation. The concern about population pressures and the attention to family planning as one feasible action was rising around the world. By the mid-1960s the climate of opinion in the United States was such that the U.S. government was able to provide major support to family planning efforts around the world.

The U.S. action in turn affected the momentum of the movement in other countries, if only for the substantial funding which it made available. Private assocations' efforts were stronger for the external funding which became available in the mid-1960s, much of it provided either directly or indirectly by AID. And the fact that AID was prepared to absorb the major share of the early costs of the government was no doubt a major factor in the ultimate governmental decisions to go ahead with the programs. Thus, the March 1965 AID directive to all missions to begin to promote family planning and other population-related programs was at least a necessary precondition for the speed with which the three governments took action and the coincidence of the timing.

The April 1967 meeting at Punta del Este of the Latin American heads of state, at which the population problem was formally recognized, also gave legitimacy to action on family planning, making action more likely following the meeting. In addition all three countries were affected by the same global milieu—most specifically through the inputs of visitors from abroad as well as foreign travel by local nationals for training and site visits.

Thus there were some similar external forces impinging on each country, but their responses were individualistic, reflecting the local context which these influences touched.

Differences

Several striking differences in the development of family planning in the three countries indicate the importance of local context in determining how world forces will translate into local realities. The characteristics of the regimes in each country seemed particularly important in coloring the patterns in each country.

Origins and patterns of activity in the promotion stage. Costa Rica was by far the most open and pluralistic of the three countries. The regime was openly competitive, stable, and broadly inclusive, but without radical extremes. It seems appropriate and consistent that this was the only one of the three countries where the first step in the policy process was action, in fact action at two independent points of origin. Apparently in Costa Rica when individuals saw a need, they felt free to respond to it. Furthermore, in the family planning case, they felt free to respond in quite innovative, nonconventional ways. "Intelligence" gathering was a function of the immediate action experience, and coalition building proceeded from the action rather than preceding it. Indeed it would appear that the intellectual rationale for the activity and the concern for building political support for a national program developed subsequent to the initial services delivery actions. There is no indication that when they started their respective action programs either Gonzalez or Cabezas were thinking in terms of laying the groundwork for a national, government-sponsored program. The coalition building was an open process based on receptions and dinners. These included persons outside of traditional elite social structures and involved building new lines of social communication between individuals and groups, as was generally more feasible in a more open and equalitarian society.

In El Salvador the class lines were more clearly delineated, competition more militant and potentially explosive, the assurance that a presidential term would be completed less certain. Generally it was a less open society, and those in visible positions were inclined to use considerable discretion in their public actions. The family planning movement in El Salvador developed as an upper-class effort, and action was preceded by a lengthy period of "intelligence" gathering and coalition building extending over several years. Coalition building was largely a private, personalized process involving established relationships. When action came it was taken within the most prestigious available setting, drawing on doctors who were well established and respected, with the visible emphasis given to less controversial methods within the conventional, medically protected delivery systems.

Nicaragua presents still other contrasts. Here we see the influence of the concentration of political power in one individual. The regime was neither competitive nor inclusive. When the reigning President Schick gave an unequivocal "no" to family planning, then advocates could only meet informally and hope for a new regime. Only in a small area of the remote eastern coast did a group of foreigners dare to engage in offering family planning services prior to a green light from the presidential family. But once it became clear that Anastasio Somoza would become the new president, all attention focused on obtaining his approval on the family planning issue.

A number of international forces made it likely that Somoza would at least tacitly give that approval. By the time of his election in 1967, the neighboring countries had active, though private, family planning programs. They demonstrated the fact that it was politically possible to carry out family planning activities. In addition, the U.S. government, a powerful ally of the Somoza government, had by this time taken a strong stand on family planning.

Once Somoza's tacit approval and the more open support of his wife were obtained, the family planning advocates were able to move directly into a governmental program. The preparatory steps of introducing family planning services under private auspices were not taken. Somoza's power was such that it was not necessary for this step. But it was necessary to proceed in a low-key manner, introducing the services slowly through the government programs. A counterreaction came and went, but the attacks were directed against the use of artificial means of contraception, not against the government's program. The opposition apparently was reluctant to test Somoza's power directly.

Somoza's handling of the situation demonstrated his substantial political skills. Putting his wife between himself and the issue and moving slowly on the introduction of the program, he took only minimal political risk. At the same time he gained points with the U.S. mission and could use the U.S.-funded program to provide patronage to a number of friendly doctors.

Leadership. Just as the differing political-cultural contexts in the three countries resulted in different approaches to influencing government policy, so did it result in significantly different types of leadership.

Most unique were the two early leaders in Costa Rica: Gonzalez, the entrepreneur, and Cabezas, the missionary doctor. These two men were perhaps as creative and activist as any who have appeared on the family planning scene anywhere in the world. Even before the ADC was founded, Gonzalez was operating what probably was the first community-based contraceptive pill distribution program in the world. Cabezas was openly conducting vasectomy camps while others in Latin America still feared that the machismo of the Latin male would lead him to violence at the suggestion of any form of fertility control. The programs these men boldly implemented in the mid-60s others in Latin America would be cautiously testing nearly ten years later.

Both men were doers, each responding to the perceived needs and desires of an immediate constituency, as well as to the drives of his own personality. They were not politicians and had little regard for the political consequences of their actions. Neither was a member of the upper strata of Costa Rican society. In fact, both were on the social periphery: Gonzalez was a Colombian national who began his involvement while a student in a trade school several hours distance from the capital city; Cabezas was a Baptist missionary in a predominantly Catholic country. Their status may well have facilitated their taking on roles as deviant actors in the introduction of a social innovation. Of the three countries, Costa Rica was the most likely to tolerate such deviance, at least until it threatened a strong vested interest, which Gonzalez's contraceptive distribution program eventually did, by cutting into pharmacy sales.

In El Salvador the early leadership came from members of the oligarchy and the pretenders to it. Each individual was constrained by his position at the same time as he made use of it, seeking to avoid any obtrusive actions which might undermine his standing within the oligarchy. Coalitions were carefully built, supporters were quietly maneuvered into key positions, and proper timing seemed to assure that decisions would not be taken until favorable outcomes were a foregone conclusion. Whether this came about by plan or by process, it appears to have taken place very much in accord with the values and conventions which have traditionally governed interactions at the upper levels of Salvadorean society.

In Nicaragua the key group was small and closed. Much of the leadership came from foreign aid official. The key Nicaraguan members were close to the political center through their positions, and/or their personal relationships with the Somoza family. The effort there had none of the trappings of a grassroots movement. The period of intelligence gathering and coalition building was low-key indeed. Each individual in the early group was in some way dependent on avoiding the displeasure of the president in a small and generally closed society, and none were about to take any overt action which might incur his displeasure.

When it came time to make a move, the pattern of personal relationships of the elite circles that we have seen used so effectively in El Salvador came into play. Perhaps none of the Nicaraguans involved was in a position to approach directly the powerful Anastasio Somoza Debayle, or perhaps, being aware of how he would want to play his political cards in the situation, they avoided putting him in a situation of having to take a position on the issue in the presence of any of his countrymen. In any event, they chose to work through his activist wife Hope, who also happened to be a cousin of Portocarrero.

It was the U.S. ambassador and the local AID mission director who could approach Somoza directly. Given the history of close relations between the Somoza family and the U.S. government, it would have been difficult for him to give them a flat refusal on a matter on which he had no particular strong personal feelings. As of the time the minister of health gave formal approval to the program, family planning had not to our knowledge been the subject of a single public meeting in Nicaragua.

The private family planning associations. In most countries throughout the world private family planning associations have been formed before the national governments have committed themselves to providing family planning services through their own facilities. Usually the primary objective of the associations is to move their governments to take on this commitment. But once they accomplish this, then what? The association very often experiences an identity crisis. It is a functioning organization with a growing membership, budget, and paid staff, but the government has just taken over most if not all of its previous functions. The experiences of Costa Rica, El Salvador, and Nicaragua in addressing this crisis point provide interesting contrasts. We can see the interaction between the local political structure in which each association operated and the association's internal leadership in determining the role the organization would play within the national setting.

In Costa Rica the association weathered the crisis with only a temporary loss of stride. It made a major role change, and then carried on, maintaining a central leadership role in the national program. In El Salvador the association continued to carry out a variety of activities, but failed for several years to find a meaningful new role. In Nicaragua, where the private family planning association was formed after the government had begun offering services, the crisis was more a matter of finding activities to justify its existence.

The history of the association in Costa Rica divides very clearly into two periods. The first was that of Cabezas and Gonzalez, an entrepreneurial period of creating a movement. The second was that of Morgan, a period of building a workable organization. The transition from one period to the next was precipitated by the attempt of the private doctors to discredit Gonzalez. This incident apparently helped to crystallize in Gonzalez's mind the fact that the family planning program in Costa Rica had moved into a new phase. It was no longer his type of game. He was an entrepreneur with a high need for achievement who became involved almost by accident in family planning, and got caught up in the excitement and challenge of generating ideas and putting them into action.

As to further radical innovation, the timing was wrong. The choice was to concentrate on the task of making the program function effectively within the health system model, or to get out. Working within a bureaucratic framework was not the sort of task with which a Gonzalez or a Cabezas could long be happy. The task needed a person who combined administrative and political skills, who had the patience to pull together diverse institutions and maintain the commitment of these institutions to a coherent national effort. Whether by chance or insight, Cabezas found this combination in Victor Morgan. Morgan led the Costa Rican association into a role within the national program which appears to be unique among the worldwide affiliates of the International Planned Parenthood Federation. Continuing the spirit of collaboration which had existed between the ministry and the association, Morgan carved out a role for the association as secretariat to CONAPO, the national family planning coordinating committee, with himself as chairman. Since all foreign funds were channeled through CONAPO, this allowed him to become de facto head of the national family planning program in Costa Rica. It also meant that Costa Rica had a mechanism for planning and coordinating the national program, and avoiding the development of destructive rivalries. In this it was unique among the three countries.

The evolution of the Demographic Association of El Salvador presents a series of almost mirror image contrasts to the Costa Rican association. During the period of program initiation when the Costa Ricans were maverick innovators, the Salvadoreans were cautious and conservative. Then, once the government program was established, the Costa Rican association became much more conservative and establishment-oriented, while the El Salvador association sought to maintain its clear autonomy from the government, to be the innovator, and to provide a competitive stimulus to the government efforts. But its efforts tended to be more talk than action. For the first few years after it had transferred its clinics to the government, it continued to operate its remaining two clinics and carry on its ongoing programs of training, education, mass communications, and research programs, mainly drawing on established momentum, but with little sign of new direction or creative innovation. Its autonomy from the government seemed to have little effect other than reducing its influence on government programs and policies.

At the end of the previous chapter, Ickis pointed out the difficulties experienced in El Salvador in building a new coalition around a common purpose or activity once the clinics were transferred. But why didn't this same problem arise in Costa Rica? The answer lies in the differences in the loci of leadership, which in turn seem to have been determined by the differences in the very natures of the two societies.

In Costa Rica, the founders of the association devoted themselves fully to the organization and gave it a tradition of strong leadership. They took the key positions of president and executive director. Even though they were not members of the elite, in the more open society of Costa Rica they were able to function as leaders, with the volunteers and board playing a largely supportive role.

By contrast, in El Salvador it was almost impossible for strong leadership to emerge in the association. The family planning movement had begun among the elite of the society. These people had many commitments other than to the Demographic Association, many of them with large businesses to run. None was able to take on the time-consuming and ill-paying (by their standards) job of executive director. Rather they became members of the association's board of directors. The job executive director and other paid positions in the association tended to be filled by members of the middle class, who in the elitist society of El Salvador could not compete for leadership with the prestigious board members. In fact, even as the organization evolved from being largely dependent on volunteer labor to being run by a paid staff, members continued to feel free to intervene in the operating matters at any staff level. Leadership was further diluted within the paid staff by the division of authority between the medical director and the executive director, both of whom reported directly to the board. This combination of circumstances created an almost impossible situation for anyone serving as executive director and largely accounted for the high turnover experienced in the position.

Following the transfer of its clinics to the government, the heterogeneous board seemed unable to develop consensus around a new strategy or purpose. Without the strong direction of a respected leader with a full-time commitment, the organization floundered.

The evolution of the Nicaraguan Demographic Association (ADN) provides yet another contrast. In other countries commitment to and involvement in the private association had been generated by the challenge of pioneering the introduction of family planning services and of gaining government acceptance of the idea that family planning should become an integral part of the government health service. But in Nicaragua that battle was won two years before the ADN was formed. It seems the association was formed almost to avoid having Nicaragua be the only country in Latin America without an IPPF affiliate. The association started out with the burden of justifying its very existence, in addition to trying to build a following and develop useful programs.

Because of its ambiguous role, it had trouble getting funding and struggled along on a skeleton staff, further hindering its efforts. There was some sense that since it was autonomous from the government, it should take on the more innovative activities which were too sensitive for a government program. However, given the nature of the Nicaraguan society, this was an unlikely role. Nicaragua was not a society of openly contending forces where small, private organizations were likely to have much effect on the government. Influence was more personalized in terms of contacts with the powerful Somoza family.

A different, less innovative role was eventually carved out for the association. In 1971 an agreement was reached, largely at the behest of AID, in which the Ministry of Health and the Social Security Institute were to carry out the clinical services, while the ADN would handle research, mass communications, and the training of program personnel. While this division of duties had a certain logical appeal, it did not match with the interests and talents of the executive director of the ADN. The tasks called for social science, administrative, and educational skills. Yet the executive director was a gynecologist, most at home with clinical tasks. Consequently movement was slow and hesitant in regard to the assigned tasks, with more than two years passing before its model clinic was ready to begin training government personnel.

All the while the association continued to look for funding to open clinics of its own contrary to the 1971 agreement. Its inquiries among foreign funders met a cold reception until the December 1972 Managua earthquake stimulated the necessary sense of crisis and sympathy, resulting in an assumption that additional service facilities were needed and could be best provided by the ADN. This move put the ADN directly in competition with the government programs. In fact, one of the ADN's new clinics was located next door to an already underutilized Ministry of Health clinic. As a result a feeling of hostility was generated between the ministry and the private association, undermining any effort at coordination and influence the ADN might have been able to exert.

The national family planning program in Nicaragua remained without clear role differentiation among its agencies, without a coordinating mechanism, and without the strong leadership needed to give it a sense of momentum. Each agency delivered services within the same medical framework with little imagination or innovation, viewing each other as rivals for the same limited pool of clients.

We might expect that these very different origins and evolutions of the programs in the three countries might result in differences in their effectiveness. We will now briefly examine their performance as of 1975, seven to eight years after the governments had begun supporting family planning activities.

FAMILY PLANNING PROGRAM PERFORMANCE

By 1975 the family planning programs of the three countries had achieved strikingly different levels of accomplishment. While the Salvadorean program was ahead in terms of absolute members of new acceptors and active users, the Costa Rican program served by far the highest proportion of women of reproductive age.

Was this difference simply due to a difference in the populace's desire for family planning? We would expect that the higher living standards in Costa Rica might indeed bring about higher demand. But the differences would also seem to relate to differences in the programs themselves which in turn relate to the way each program came into being and the structure under which it operated.

Examination of the data in Table 2 shows a direct relationship between the number of clinics per capita and the percentage of the females of reproductive age actively using the program. Costa Rica, which had one clinic for every 2,817 women of reproductive age, provided contraceptive services to 20 percent of them. El Salvador, with one clinic for every 4,225 women of reproductive age, served 12 percent of them. And Nicaragua, with only one clinic for every 6,250 women of reproductive age, was only able to serve 7 percent of these women. With greater numbers of clinics per capita, the services were likely to be located nearer to the people and this greater convenience could generate greater demand.[12]

Nicaragua's much smaller number of clinics was not simply due to a lack of health facilities. Nearly half of the ministry of health's 118 health clinics did not offer family planning services at the end of 1975. In contrast, by this time Costa Rica and El Salvador were offering family planning services in virtually all their health clinics.

Table 2
Family Planning Program Operating Data, 1975

	Costa Rica	El Salvador	Nicaragua
Females aged 15–44* (000)	400	900	500
New acceptors** (000)	30.9	72.0	20.7
Active users** (000)	78.8	106.4	35.6
Coverage of the female population			
of reproductive age			
Acceptors	7.7%	8%	4%
Users %	20%	12%	7%
Number of clinics offering family			
planning services**	142	213	80
Number of females of reproductive			
age per clinic	2,817	4,225	6,250
Average output per clinic			
Acceptors	218	338	259
Active users	555	499	445

*Dorothy Nortman and Ellen Hofstatter, "Population and Family Planning Programs: A Factbook" (1975).

**AID, *Family Planning Service Statistics: Annual Report 1975.*

What happened in Nicaragua? Why did the government program not continue to expand as it did in the other two countries? We believe this relates to the differences in the way the programs were generated in each country and to the sources of encouragement and support available. In Costa Rica a strong coordinating body developed, comprised of both governmental and nongovernmental people, which functioned both to spotlight family planning activities and to infuse enthusiasm into the government program. El Salvador also had a coordinating mechanism, though considerably weaker, serving similar functions. In addition, the growing acceptance of the need for population control in a crowded country provided a sense of importance to the Salvadorean program.[13]

However, in Nicaragua no mechanism existed for infusing enthusiasm or importance to the governmental programs. The lack of a coordinating board and the closed nature of the society made it crucial that commitment come from high levels within the governmental implementing organizations themselves. At the beginning this existed. Portocarrero and Castillo Quant were both strongly committed to family planning and their commitment resulted in the initiation and expansion of the program. Between May 1969 and Portocarrero's resignation as INSS director of medical services in February 1970, family planning services were established in five social security clinics. In the Ministry of Health, family planning services were established in sixty clinics before Castillo Quant's resignation as vice-minister in mid-1972. Thus, sixty-five clinics were started under the direction of the initial family planning advocates. By the end of 1975 the Social Security Institute and ministry together had opened only seven more clinics. Once the initial advocates left, the program lost its momentum. Since it had been formed at the initiative of only a few individuals, there remained no broader base of support and enthusiasm to fall back on once these leaders left positions of power.

CONCLUSIONS

As we review the evolution of family planning in the three countries, several lessons stand out regarding the establishment of a new and potentially controversial public policy.

A reversal in governmental attitude can come about in a relatively short time. In 1962 as the family planning movements stirred in Costa Rica and El Salvador, family planning was a taboo subject inciting strong negative reactions from many persons in powerful positions. Only five years later, the governments in both countries as well as in Nicaragua provided formal support to family planning programs. This is a remarkable achievement, demonstrating the speed with which social change can take place. The key to this rapid change is that the movement was riding with the current of global opinion. The increasing global interdependence, facilitated by pervasive instantaneous communication and jet air travel, worked primarily to speed change in the direction of a favorable response to action on family planning. A policy at odds with global opinion could probably not expect this kind of rapid change.

A controversial program can come into being without major political figures taking a strong stance. In each of the three countries we saw how the incremental approach allowed family planning programs to come into being without major political support. This was probably largely due to the fact that the programs threatened very few vested interests. The main conflict was with the upper echelons of the Catholic church, reflecting the continuing struggle so common to Latin American countries, of how much influence the church shall have on government policy. But due to external funding and the fact that the program provided a service, implementing family planning activities did not take anything away from anybody. It was an "add on," rather than a substitution, and so did not generate the kind of coalitions of opposition that would require strong political support to overcome.

Initial small-scale program activities can serve fears about the potential consequences of a supportive governmental policy. In both El Salvador and Costa Rica, family planning advocates did not wait for support on the policy level to begin initial activities. Rather, they began with action, and each action seemed to make the next easier until government support became a reality. The key here is probably the fact that the program in the abstract generated far more fears than the program in reality. There were fears of the reactions not only of the higher church authorities, but also of the people who would be asked to implement the program, and the catholic populace itself to whom the program was directed. In reality these latter fears were never realized. To the people served, the program was never controversial and they reacted either with enthusiasm or indifference. This fact in turn affected the attitudes of those providing the service, reinforcing positive attitudes as they saw they were meeting a real need.

Rapid change can be brought about through the use of traditional patterns of influence. In each country we saw a different approach to establish a policy, each approach appropriate for its own setting. The speed and effectiveness of the efforts were probably largely due to the consonance between the approach used and the basic regime structure. The efforts at change did not require any basic restructuring of power or change in the channels of influence.

The experience with the family planning movement has revealed patterns and possibilities regarding the social change process. Many other social changes lie on the horizon which may exhibit similar patterns of rapid global diffusion. Interventions to change women's roles, to integrate rural areas into the social and economic mainstream, to achieve greater equity in living standards, to bring about basic reforms in health systems might all be potential candidates for such change. All are likely to benefit from increasingly favorable world opinion, all are likely to receive external funding, yet all involve policies which are clearly domestic matters and under the direction of local initiative. From this perspective the process by which countries have arrived at a commitment to action in family planning assumes a special significance in providing insights into the patterns and possibilities regarding future social change.

NOTES

Most of the data on which this paper is based were developed by the authors and a number of associates under the auspices of the Family Planning Management Project of the Instituto Centroamericano de Administración de Empresas (INCAE) in Managua, Nicaragua. The original research was funded by a Ford Foundation grant to INCAE. Many of the data on Costa Rica were developed by John C. Ickis, who also contributed valuable suggestions to the manuscript. Deirdre Strachan, Carmen de Benard, and Valerie Ickis were also contributors to project documents from which this report draws freely. These documents, many of which elaborate on the case detail and go into much greater depth on management issues than does the present report, are listed among the notes. The opinions expressed are those of the present authors.

1. Bernard Berelson, "Family Planning Programs and Population Control" in Bernard Berelson (ed.), *Family Planning Programs: An International Study* (New York: Basic Books, 1969).

2. Dorothy Nortman and Ellen Hofstatter, "Population and Family Planning Programs: A Factbook," *Reports on Population/Family Planning*, no. 2 (seventh edition, October 1975).

3. Everett N. Rogers, *Communication Strategies for Family Planning* (New York: The Free Press, 1973) p. 6.

4. Arthur S. Banks (ed.), *Political Handbook of the World: 1975* (New York: McGraw-Hill, 1975).

5. Dwight B. Heath, "Current Trends in Central America," *Current History* 68, (January 1975) p. 32.

6. Eric Morganthaler, "The Boss: Somoza Combines Politics, Business, Military to Rule Nicaragua as Undisputed Strong Man," *Wall Street Journal* 182 (October 22, 1973) p. 22.

7. Tin Myiang Thein and Jack Reynolds, *Contraception in Costa Rica: The Role of the Private Sector, 1959-1969* (San Jose, Costa Rica, February 1972), p. 26.

8. When we first met Gonzalez in 1972, it was at a modest branch office facility his firm maintained in one of the markets of Managua, Nicaragua. He spoke with conviction of the difficulties the market women had in getting contraceptive assistance through the government clinics in Nicaragua and of how easy it would be, if the law permitted, to organize a community-based distribution system. But he was clearly tired of the battles and had no more involvement with any family planning work.

9. Shortly after he selected Victor Morgan as the new executive director of the ADC, Dr. Cabezas stepped down as president of the association to devote his full energies to his medical practice at the Clinica Biblica and the Goodwill Caravans, giving particular attention to family planning and continuing to experiment with forward-looking but controversial approaches to service delivery. But he no longer played a public role in the program.

10. Phyllis T. Piotrow, *World Population Crisis: The United States Response* (New York: Praeger, 1973), pp. 95 and 109.

11. Joel G. Verner, "Legislative Attitudes Toward Overpopulation: The Case of El Salvador," *The Journal of Developing Areas* 10 (October 1975) pp. 61-76.

12. Adding more clinics is, of course, only one of the many means to increase convenience to the client. However, since service delivery in the three countries was carried out in almost identical fashions, it is not surprising that the variable of clinics per capita might have a strong impact on performance.

13. On October 30, 1974, the Council of Ministers approved an Integral Population Policy for El Salvador, making the country the first in Central America with an articulated policy.

4

THE FERTILITY CONSEQUENCES OF LAND REFORM

Farrukh Iqbal

In recent years a consensus has emerged among social scientists dealing with population processes to the effect that socioeconomic variables that influence the demand for children are at least as crucial in inducing fertility change as variables such as family planning program inputs which seek to influence the supply considerations. It is not enough for families to be provided with the means to limit births—they must be provided with the motivation to do so. An important policy implication of this consensus for the developing countries is that economic development policies aimed primarily at some socioeconomic targets can have important demographic by-products. Hence the cost-benefit analysis used to select and rank such policies must include this demographic dimension. Some development policies may have a pronatal effect, while others may have an antinatal effect. If population policies are not coordinated with economic development policies, the effects of the two sets of policies might very well negate each other.

This paper is an attempt to clarify some of the conceptual and empirical relationships between one important and widely prescribed development policy, land reform, and one very important aspect to the population problem in most developing countries, fertility change. The connection between the two is found in the effects of land reform on income, employment, and equity in a given rural system and in the effects of changes in these three variables on rural fertility. An analysis of this sort departs from most of the literature on land reform which, to date, has dealt exclusively with its direct economic effects. By taking the step of relating land reform to rural fertility change, such an analysis adds a potentially crucial dimension to the debate on development through agricultural reorganization. Moreover, such a study could help to clarify some of the policy options that may be available to developing countries to achieve both an adequate pace of development and a socially desirable level of fertility.

After introducing the concept of land reform as it is to be used here, the paper will outline the course and content of the land reform initiated in Pakistan in March 1972 and the nature of the population question in that country. The major part of the paper is a critical theoretical analysis of the interaction between land reform and rural fertility and an examination of the existing empirical evidence relating farm size to the intervening variables of income, employment, and equity and these, in turn, to rural fertility. In particular we will refer the 1972 land reform of Pakistan in this framework.

LAND REFORM: CHARACTERISTICS

The term land reform is often taken to mean simply the confiscation of large land holdings and their redistribution. We shall use the term in a less restrictive sense as a catch-all term signifying intervention in the prevailing pattern of land ownership, control, and usage. Since this pattern varies widely among and within countries, the composition of land reform policies also varies. Broadly speaking, some or all of the following policies are involved: (1) redistribution, resulting in the case of most noncommunist countries in an increase in the number of small and medium farmers; (2) tenure legislation, which is usually characterised by the conferral of ownership rights on tenants and/or the regulation of rental rates and lease protection; (3) consolidation of individual holdings so as to reduce inefficiencies arising from fragmentation, an aspect which may or may not involve changes in the distribution of land; and (4) related measures such as the provision of credit facilities, marketing and transport arrangements, agricultural extension facilities, various fiscal policies with respect to the redistributed land, and continuing political commitment.

THE 1972 LAND REFORM IN PAKISTAN

Prior to the Ayub Khan land reform of 1959, land reform legislation in Pakistan proceeded in a piecemeal and spotty fashion. The political elite of the country was composed largely of landlord elements who were prone to drag their feet and effectively thwart legislation that sought to reduce their base of power in hand. For example, until 1950, in spite of repeated declarations affirming the necessity of new tenurial regulations, the only laws governing tenancy in the country continued to be the Punjab Tenancy Act of 1887.

In 1959 the new military ruler of the country, Ayub Khan, introduced the strongest measure until that time in an effort to weaken the political power of the landlord class, elevate that of the numerically greater medium farmer class, and cultivate a personal and direct base of support in the rural areas of the country. This measure set down a limit of 36,000 produce index units or 500 acres of irrigated and 1,000 acres of unirrigated land, whichever was greater. It also provided fresh regulations concerning the consolidation of holdings, the financial relationship of tenant to landlord, and security of tenure. A fast rate of rural population growth, a faster growth of rural expectations, and widespread circumvention of the announced reforms resulted in a minimal impact.[1] The cry for further agrarian reform rose again, gathered momentum in the political campaign of the Pakistan People's party in the late 1960s, and culminated in the imposition of a fresh land reform in the shape of Martial Law Regulation no. 115 under a new government headed by Prime Minister Sulfikar Ali Bhutto in March 1972.

The intelligence for this policy was derived from at least three sources: comparative data from the Japanese, Taiwanese, and Egyptian land reforms; the work and advice of foreign aid donors and experts working in Pakistan; and the experience gained under the 1959 measure of Ayub Khan.

The promotional aspects of the 1972 reform came with Bhutto's political ascendancy in the late 1960s. His campaign was largely built around agrarian appeals, and land reform was a major factor in his appeal to the masses. Other political parties also raised the cry for land reform in common opposition to the Ayub Khan regime. The proposals were not challenged in the campaign, however. Most voters did not expect the People's party to win very heavily in the elections of December 1970, and in any case the proposals were discussed so vaguely as to provoke skepticism about their real possibilities. Many landlords had, in fact, already divested themselves of much of their rural property and enough of them had joined the People's party that they expected to be able to bring internal pressure to bear to protect their interests if necessary.

The measure announced in March 1972 had the following main provisions: a ceiling of 15,000 "produce index units" was laid down with an additional 20 percent to be allowed to owners and users of tractors and tubewells; private land transfers made after December 20, 1971 were declared void; arbitrary ejection of tenants was prohibited, and landlords were made entirely responsible for the payment of land revenue, the water rate and other taxes, and any expenditure on seeds; orchards, and stud and livestock farms were to be confiscated without compensation whenever they were in excess of the 1959 ceiling.[2]

RELEVANT CHARACTERISTICS AND PROJECTIONS OF PAKISTAN'S POPULATION

The population table (Table 1) shows how the demographic characteristics of Pakistan have been changing over the past fifteen years and how they are likely to develop over the next decade under three different growth rate assumptions. Some of the salient points of Pakistan's "population problem" are the following:

By 1985 the total population could well be in the triple digits and the rural population in the neighborhood of 70 million people. The pressure on land, which is already quite severe, could become intolerable. The known resources of water already limit the size of potentially cultivable land to about fifty-five million acres. These figures imply that the land/man ratio could decline from approximately one acre per person currently to 0.75 acres by 1985.

The rural-urban mix is changing significantly as a consequence of economic and demographic pressure. Migration into the towns and cities continues unabated. The known water resources also suggest that a rural labor force of only 20 million can be supported comfortably on the land. This implies that over half of Pakistan's rural labor force will soon have to seek employment outside the farm sector or remain unemployed.

The number of "dependents"—children under fifteen and adults over sixty-five—has also been growing steadily. The dependency ratio (dependents per working age person) has already gone from one in 1961 to 1.05 in 1975 and could go to 1.09 by 1985. Since this group contributes little to national output, the implication is that the national economy is likely to come under increasing strain not only because of the sheer size of the population but also because of its composition.

Although per capita food grain availability has risen somewhat over the years, the rapidity of population growth over the next ten years and the faltering of the so-called Green Revolution leads to deep concern about the future food situation in Pakistan. Productivity on Pakistani grain farms will have to triple by the middle 1980s in order to maintain present levels of food grain availability without having to resort to imports; productivity rates of increase will have to be even higher than those achieved with miracle seeds and rapid exploitation of groundwater resources in the Green Revolution period of the late 1960s.

The foregoing should leave no doubt that the population problem faced by Pakistan is a serious one.[3] The outlook for improvements in the nutrition, housing, employment, education, savings, and productivity of the country hinges upon its population performance. Even the most optimistic assumption of population growth rate does not lead to a significantly brighter picture for at least the next decade. It would be much worse if some economic development strategies were to fail or produce undesirable demographic results, or if other strategies are not followed because their demographic payoff has not been considered and evaluated.

LAND REFORM, INCOME PER CAPITA, FERTILITY

Proponents of land reform have often had to contend with the charge that a decrease in agricultural productivity will be the inevitable consequence. The conventional interpretation of the Mexican land reform of the 1920s is that while certain social and political gains were achieved through them, a high economic cost was exacted in the form of lower productivity on the redistributed farms.[4] In a more recent analysis of Brazilian agricultural development prospects, Nicholls concludes that Brazil should opt for the higher productivity path available in industrialization and urbanization rather than the greater equity path available in land reform because the economic costs of the latter approach are likely to be prohibitive.[5]

Such arguments are based on one or more of the following contentions: (1) Land reform involves considerable unrest and upheaval and is likely to disrupt the economic infrastructure resulting in huge losses of output. (2) Land reform might introduce a lower quality management input in the form of untrained and uneducated small-

Table 1
Pakistan: Relevant Characteristics and Projections

ASSUMPTIONS

	Crude Birth Rate	Crude Death Rate	Crude Rate of Increase
I. constant fertility, constant mortality	52	20	3.2%
II. constant fertility, declining mortality	52	17	3.5%
III. declining fertility, declining mortality	44	17	2.9%

Population size (millions)	1961	1965	1970	1975	1980	1985
I	46.2	52.1	60.9	71.6	84.9	101.1
II	46.2	52.2	61.8	72.8	87.4	105.8
III	46.2	52.2	59.8	68.1	78.8	92.5

Working Age Population (15–64yrs)	1961	1965	1970	1975	1980	1985
I	22.8	25.5	30.2	35.5	42.3	50.1
II	22.8	25.5	30.2	35.5	42.4	50.6
III	22.8	25.5	30.2	35.5	42.4	49.3

Working Age
Males

I	11.9	13.2	15.5	18.2	21.6	25.6
II	11.9	13.2	15.5	18.2	21.7	25.8
III	11.9	13.2	15.5	18.2	21.7	25.2

Rural Population

I	39.7	44.5	51.1	59.4	67.3
II	39.8	44.6	52.0	60.2	70.5
III	39.8	44.6	48.6	56.4	61.8

Rates of Pop. Growth

I	3.0%	3.0%	3.2%	3.3%	3.4%	3.5%
II	3.0%	3.1%	3.4%	3.6%	3.7%	3.4%
III	3.0%	2.4%	2.5%	2.8%	3.1%	3.3%

Crude Rural Arable Land/Man Ratio: 1.35 in 1961;   0.99 in 1972;   0.75 in 1985
(acres per man)

Dependency Ration   : $\frac{91}{100}$ in 1961; $\frac{101}{100}$ in 1972; $\frac{109}{100}$ in 1985

Potential Cultivable Area   :   55 million acres
(by known water constraint)

holders thereby reducing productivity. (3) Land reform might foreclose the possibilities of introducing new technologies and inputs that could raise output substantially. Small farmers, lacking credit and sufficient land to effectively utilize modern technology, such as tractors, may create a technologically stagnant rural sector. In other words land reform might remove the innovative farmers at the agricultural technology frontier and reduce potential output.

These arguments, however, are convincingly challenged by empirical evidence from a growing number of countries that small farmers are more productive than large farmers and that land reforms have resulted in increases in productivity and total agricultural output.[6] The arguments for expecting a decline in productivity lose their force if we stipulate that the reform must include supportive measures such as sustained and improved credit arrangements and marketing and extension services. The argument from technological regressiveness is also diluted if we consider that yield-increasing biogenetic technology (improved seeds and fertilizers) can be as effectively used on small as on large farms.

In fact there are a number of persuasive reasons to believe that land reform should stimulate productivity and output: (1) The conferral of ownership rights on a tenant could provide economic motivation to work harder to increase production while security of tenure could encourage longer-term investments in new technology; it could also enable him to acquire managerial skills and credit-worthiness in his own right. (2) Agriculture of the developing countries, and particularly that of India and Pakistan, is dualistic in that a large number of small farms operated predominantly by family labor exist along with a small number of medium-to-large farms operated predominantly by hired labor. Since the opportunity cost of labor is lower for the family farm, more labor per unit of land is available, producing more output per unit of land. A redistribution of land from large farms to small family farms is therefore likely to raise average productivity and total output. (3) Agriculture in developing countries also tends to be characterized by imperfections in the market for land because large farmers with superior credit and other resources encounter an effectively lower land cost per acre. Thus large farmers will tend to use relatively more land per unit output than small farmers, again leading to lower productivity. These considerations produce a strong presumption in favor of rising productivity and agricultural incomes as a consequence of land reform of the sort outlined above.

The connection between income and fertility has been the focus of much recent theoretical and empirical work. The economic theory of fertility, as developed by Becker and others, conceives of the human family as a decision-making unit that maximizes a utility function in which children appear as economic factors along with other goods and services; i.e., children are considered as "commodities" that carry certain costs and convey certain benefits and the demand for which can be analyzed by a straightforward extension of consumer theory. Thus the household is supposed to allocate its resources of time and money among the various factors that enter its utility function in accordance with the principle of utility maximization, and such allocation change in accordance with factor changes depending upon availability thereby inducing an "income" effect, or with relative prices, thereby inducing a "substitution" effect.[7]

All other things remaining equal, a rise in income should increase the demand for children. In the rural context, an increase in land endowment should lead to an increase in fertility both because the farmer can now afford a larger family and also because the productive potential of farm children is now enhanced. All other things being equal, an increase in the supply of one factor, land, increases the marginal product of complementary factors, in this case labor, and given that the dual labor market hypothesis applies, this would imply a rise in the demand for family labor on small farms.

One may argue, however, that all other things do not remain equal. In particular, a rise in family income may be associated with an increased preference for higher-quality children and/or an increase in the opportunity cost of female time. This could happen if the rise in income was associated with increased educational attainment on the part of the parents, particularly the mother, and if this brought new and better employment opportunities within reach. In such cases it is possible that the substitution effect, operating through the raised relative price of time-intensive commodities such as children, might overcome the income effect and lead to a decline in the demand for children rather than an increase.

There are minimally three good reasons, however, to discount this possibility, at least in the short run, in the case with which we are concerned here. There is no reason to expect land reform to be associated with changes in the educational attainment of rural parents. It is likely to be a purely exogenous factor. Nor is it plausible to assume a quick change in preferences from larger numbers to better quality as far as children are concerned. The attitude towards natality has

Table 2
Children Born by Mothers of Different Ages (estimated by regression techniques)

Mothers born in	Farms by size in ha.										Value of p
	0–0.5	0.5–1	1–2	2–3	3–4	4–5	5–7	7–10	10–15	over 15	
	Average number of children born										
1855–1880	4.74	5.59	6.21	6.71	7.01	7.34	7.67	8.08	8.57	9.02	0.152
1881–1885	3.61	4.68	5.51	6.22	6.74	7.15	7.65	8.31	9.10	9.85	0.236
1886–1890	3.26	4.20	4.94	5.56	6.01	6.37	6.81	7.38	8.07	8.72	0.232
1891–1894	4.12	4.51	4.77	4.97	5.11	5.22	5.34	5.49	5.67	5.83	0.082
1895–1897	3.97	4.28	4.50	4.66	4.77	4.85	4.95	5.07	5.21	5.34	0.070
1898–1900	2.85	3.39	3.78	4.10	4.32	4.50	4.71	4.97	5.28	5.57	0.157
1901–1902	3.00	3.47	3.81	4.07	4.26	4.40	4.57	4.79	5.04	5.27	0.133
1903–1904	3.12	3.30	3.43	3.52	3.59	3.63	3.69	3.76	3.91	—	0.053
1905–1906	2.91	3.18	3.37	3.51	3.61	3.68	3.77	3.88	4.10	4.11	0.082
1907–1908	2.79	2.92	3.01	3.08	3.13	3.16	3.20	3.25	3.35	—	0.044
1909–1910	2.38	2.70	2.93	3.10	3.23	3.32	3.43	3.74	3.88	—	0.115
1911–1912	2.54	2.80	2.88	2.93	2.97	3.01	3.07	3.19	—	—	0.053
1913–1914	1.92	2.21	2.41	2.57	2.63	2.77	2.87	3.00	3.29	—	0.127
1915–1918	2.02	2.11	2.17	2.21	2.24	2.27	2.29	2.32	2.36	2.39	0.040
1919–1921	1.53	1.69	1.80	1.88	1.94	1.98	2.03	2.10	2.24	—	0.090
1922–1929	1.31	1.37	1.40	1.43	1.45	1.47	1.49	1.53	1.55	1.55	0.041

Note: p is the coefficient of land size obtained by estimating the equation: $y = cx^p$ where x refers to size of farm, y to mean number of children, and c is a constant.

Source: Stys (1957, p. 141).

proved one of the hardest to change in tradition-bound rural societies so far. Finally, as far as the cost of female time is concerned, even if the land reform presents new employment opportunities to the mother of the household, it is unlikely that family-farm employment will be much of a hindrance to child-rearing. For all these reasons one would expect the income effect to predominate and fertility to rise as a result of land reform. It is possible that the large farmers who lose substantial amounts of land might curtail their fertility but since the number of such farmers is likely to be very, very small in relation to those that receive land, the decline in fertility is unlikely to counter-balance or even seriously reduce the net increase in fertility.

Direct empirical evidence detailing the fertility effects of land reform is hard to come by. Ideally we would like to examine the results of a more or less controlled experiment which allowed us to measure farm fertility before and after a land reform. Needless to say, such evidence does not exist and the possibility of a controlled experiment of this sort seems quite remote. Some indirect evidence, however, is available and it tends to support the inferences derived above.

The classic study is that of Stys.[8] From an analysis of peasant fertility in rural southern Poland in 1948, Stys reports the following: (1) The larger the landholding, the larger the average number of children per woman. (2) This is true for both the mothers and the wives of the peasants studied. (3) This finding is upheld even when the families are differentiated according to the age of the mother. An ordinary least-squares regression revealed a positive coefficient for the farm-size variable for each of the sixteen age-groups considered by Stys. The regression results are reported in Table 2. Stys also cites similar observations made by other investigators in the cases of Russia, China, and Germany.

W.W. Hicks reporting on an economic analysis of the relationships between economic and demographic change in Mexico finds his results to be consistent with the hypothesis that "arable land is complementary with labor and fertility is likely to decline in response to a decrease in arable land per agricultural worker."[9] Using arable land per farm worker as a measure of land availability, and children ever born to women ages 40-44 as a measure of fertility, Hicks reports that in his study of rural sectors of thirty-one states of Mexico, the land availability variable is positive and statistically significant at the five percent level, in a regression that controlled for differences in female literacy, the crude death rate, and the relative size of the local non-mestizo population.

A study by Yasuba of fertility ratios in the rural areas of the United States over the period 1800-1860 finds population density to be the

Table 3
Number of Agricultural Families of Different Sizes, Classified by Size of Agricultural Holding

PERCENTAGE OF HOLDINGS WITH FAMILIES OF DIFFERENT SIZES

Size of Holding	Total Holdings	1-2 Members	3-4 Members	5-6 Members	7-8 Members	9-10 Members	10+ Members	Average Family Size
Under 1 acre	742216	10.6%	17.2%	52.4%	10.0%	4. %	5.1%	5.4
1 to 2.5 acres	855732	10.3	19.6	47.2	12.1	5.3	5.5	5.5
2.5 to 5 acres	805984	9.8	19.9	41.9	14.9	6.7	6.8	5.7
5 to 7.5 acres	580952	8.5	19.4	39.0	16.9	7.9	8.3	5.9
7.5 to 12.5 acres	758703	7.4	18.6	36.0	18.4	9.5	10.1	6.1
12.5 to 25 acres	728909	6.2	16.0	32.9	19.2	11.2	14.4	6.6
25 to 50 acres	285882	5.3	12.6	30.1	18.2	12.3	21.5	7.1
50 to 150 acres	87624	5.2	11.6	32.3	16.5	11	23.4	7.1
150 acres & over	13981	4.7	10.6	37.3	16.2	9.4	21.8	7.0
Total number of Farms	4859983	8.6	18.0	41	15.3	7.8	9.3	

Source: Government of Pakistan, Census of Agriculture 1960: A Summary of West Pakistan Data, Karachi, Pakistan 1964.

most important factor associated (inversely) with fertility differences and trends. Yasuba interprets population density as a measure of the availability of land or degree of land pressure and his explanation of his finding accords well with our own theoretical speculations: "(In) a community where the supply of land is limited, the value of children as earning assets is low and hence the demand for children may not be as great as when there is plenty of open land nearby."[10]

Finally, my own very preliminary examination of Pakistani data from the agricultural census of 1960 suggests that among rural farm-owning households the size of the family is positively associated with the size of farm that is operated by the head of household. Table 3 shows that as farm-size increases from one acre to 150 acres the average number of family members increases steadily from 5.4 to 7.1 per household. Note that this finding does not control for education, land quality, or any other factor that might be associated with rural fertility. It may not even have a reasonable proxy for fertility since the number of fecund women in the household is not reported. It is only a tabulation, not a regression, but it seems to be about as ambitious as we can get in the absence of data that would allow a multivariate analysis.

The upshot of the preceding is that land reform is likely to engender a rise in fertility in the short run. In the long run, it is possible that the improved state of agriculture brought about by the reform may foster changes in attitudes towards family-size and this may coincide with improvements in the general level of education, nutrition, health, and social welfare arrangements to bring down the fertility rate. What the time specifications might be in exact terms in a matter of complex and detailed empirical investigation. The evidence for this sort of short run-long run threshold effect is fairly substantial.[11] Indeed, ths so-called demographic transition of the now developed countries may in one sense be regarded as the manifestation of just such an effect, working not only through increased urbanization and declining mortality rates but also through the decreasing availability of land.

LAND REFORM EMPLOYMENT FERTILITY

The relationship between land reform and overall rural employment is fairly complex. On the one hand some people, particularly permanent and temporary hired hands, will inevitably be displaced when their employers lose land. On the other hand new employment opportunities will probably be created as some farmers increase their land holdings. Whether overall rural employment will rise or fall would seem to depend on at least the following factors: the differences in the marginal product of labor function between the small farmers who gain land and the larger farmers who lose land; the amount of surplus labor that is available in the small family farm sector; the scale of the land reform as measured perhaps in the average size of a redistributed plot; the ability of landless labor to shift out of cultivation into other rural activities; and the changes in farming practices that occur as a result of the land reform.

The dual labor market hypothesis leads us to believe that small farmers tend to use more labor per unit area because of the lower implicit costs of family labor. It is possible that all the new employment opportunities created by land reform may be taken up by female and child labor on the family farm. If, however, little surplus labor exists in the family farm sector, then increased land endowments will lead to a demand for hired labor and the extent of this demand will vary with the amount of extra land gained by the farmer. Furthermore, given the operation of an imperfect land market which raises the cost of land for the small farmer relative to the large farmer, we may even see the use of more hired labor per acre by small farmers than previously used by large farmers. Also, the greater the ability of landless laborers and smallholders on the margin to shift out of agriculture and the greater the number of additional rural activities created by the reorganization of the agrarian structure, the less the negative impact of land reform on overall rural employment is likely to be. If, for example, the land reform enables vigorous commercial farming to take place and if this type of farming creates considerable demand for auxiliary activities, the labor initially displaced from cultivation may find employment in other rural activities such as marketing, processing, and storage. If the land reform enables changes in cropping practices in the direction of multiple cropping, the outlook for landless laborers becomes much brighter.

The evidence to date argues rather favorably for land reform. In no case has land reform been observed to depress the absolute level of employment, although in many cases it has been found to have little or no beneficial effect. These would seem to be examples of inadequate or "paper" reforms more than anything else.[12] Country studies usually indicate that the MPL function for small farms lies above that of large farms.[13] And in many cases, land reform has enabled farmers to break out of primitive patterns of cultivation, adopt multiple cropping, and introduce labor-intensive biogenetic technology which increases the need for labor. Taiwan and Japan are cases in point.

In considering the relationship between employment and fertility behavior, it will be useful to distinguish between male, female, and child employment. Employment, of course, works on fertility primarily through the change in income that it brings about.[14] Thus an increase in total male employment, on or off the family farm, should raise incomes and thereby have a pronatal effect in the short run as discussed in the previous section.

The case of an overall increase in female employment is a lot more complicated. Increased female employment raises household income and could raise fertility through the income effect. The opportunity cost of children, however, may also rise because the females involved will now have less time to devote to children and because higher quality children may now be desired—the substitution effect may depress fertility. It is reasonable to ask to what extent a rural woman finds children a hindrance to her employment. Given the existence of extended family systems, older siblings, and the fact that children may be brought to the place of work (usually the family plot), one may doubt the existence of a strong substitution effect. If work and home roles are broadly compatible, then female employment should not be expected to lead to a decline in fertility; on the contrary, the unhampered working of the income effect should raise fertility. The empirical results available for rural sectors of developing countries are substantially in agreement with this expectation.

In a study of fertility differentials by type of occupation for women in Japan, Jaffe and Azumi find a higher fertility rate for women who work at home than for those whom do not contribute to family income, and lower fertility for those who have to leave their homes to work than for those who do not.[15] In a similar study for Turkish women, Stycos and Weller conclude that female employment does not affect fertility as long as the roles of mother and worker are compatible.[16] In a more direct test of the relationship between female employment and family size, utilizing data from Puerto Rico (for 3000 women, married and spouse present, between the ages of 35 to 44), McCabe and Rosenzweig report strong positive associations between female wages and fertility. Although their methodology is somewhat controversial, their results do tend to conform to those derived from more indirect tests and also accord with the theoretical notions discussed above.[17] In general, therefore, the following conclusion seems warranted: by itself, increasing the rate of female participation in the labor force is not likely to generate a reduction in the rural fertility rate. To the extent that land reform merely provides additional employment to females without engendering attitudinal changes or changes in sex-roles or changes in the place of employment of women, fertility may actually rise as a result of the income effect.

Although relatively few studies have been conducted to determine the relationship between child employment and fertility, the results achieved are consistent with what we might expect on theoretical grounds: child employment tends to raise fertility levels. Expanding employment opportunities for children tend to increase their asset value to parents, and, in the absence of measures designed to remove children from the labor force, such as compulsory schooling or minimum working age laws, tend to lead to higher fertility. In a study of the determinants of family size in the Philippines, Harman finds that child labor force participation is strongly related to larger family size.[18] DaVanzo finds a similarly strong positive relationship between economic activity of children and fertility in Chile.[19] Finally, a sophisticated two-stage, least-squares analysis by Rosenzweig and Evenson of the interrelationships of fertility, schooling and the economic contribution of children in rural India, finds confirmation of the hypothesis that "in districts where variables positively associated with the economic contribution of children have high values, fertility is also high—a 10 percent increase in the child wage rate is associated with a 5.5 percent rise in the age-adjusted child-women ratio."[20]

The fertility behavior of one particular group in rural society, the landless laborers and the marginal smallholders, deserves special attention. These are high-fertility groups and in many ways their fertility response to their economic situation appears perverse: greater poverty in their case has often been seen to lead to increased fertility, contrary to the predictions of the economic model stated here. Mamdani and others have argued, however, that this response is actually quite rational because children provide a superior source of income and security in the generally precarious economic environment in which such groups live.[21] As poverty increases, these marginal groups may increase fertility for at least two reasons: (1) a significant number of their children may migrate and hence more procreation becomes necessary to maintain a constant stock of working children; (2) declining economic position may paradoxically improve the relative investment value of children as compared to other assets for these people. It is also possible that the sheer desperateness of their situation may force them to take their chances with larger families. One might also mention that such groups may have high fertility rates merely because they are less efficient fertility controllers and have the least knowledge of and ability to buy contraceptives. This interpretation is rejected by Mamdani on the basis of his own investigations into the matter in a part of rural India. At any rate, whatever the reason for the fertility behavior of these groups it is important to consider the effects of land reform and similar policies which seek to influence the agrarian structure on these groups. If land reform does not significantly improve their position it is likely that their high fertility behavior will be maintained. If it actually worsens their position it is possible that they might respond by having more children.

LAND REFORM, INCOME DISTRIBUTION, FERTILITY

Since in most developing countries the ownership of land constitutes the major source of wealth and power, the primary motive behind land reform has often been a desire to achieve greater equity in the distribution of such wealth and power. It has usually been assumed that redistribution must automatically ensure greater equity. Theoretically speaking, however, this need not be the case: as we have shown above, a land reform that involves the distribution of land to farmers whose eventual demand for market labor is less than the sum of the labor displaced by the reform measure, leads to a worsening in the relative position of the least privileged and usually most numerous group in rural society. Such a worsening may or may not show up in comprehensive measures of income distribution such as the Gini coefficient because the decline in income of the lowest group may be offset by a decline in the income of the previously highest income group of large landlords.

In general the equity effect of land reform will vary with: the degree to which the ownership of land is important in the rural scheme of things; the scale of the reform in terms of the ceilings fixed, the tenancy regulations enacted, and the other protective measures introduced; and the overall employment and income effects on various rural groups. What this combination of conditioning factors will eventually produce in terms of equity is hard to predict from theory—there are no magic parameters whose invocation will produce optimal results in every case. The results are likely to vary with each specific case and this is amply borne out by empirical investigations conducted to date.

What is the relationship between equity and fertility? Unless we assume that the fertility response to income changes is the same at all income levels, a clearly unrealistic assumption, we must expect the distribution of income to exercise an independent influence on fertility at least at the macro level. But what should be the direction of the relationship? The answer to this question would seem to depend on two aspects of equity, one being the fact that it is likely to have an indirect, rather than direct, influence on fertility through its effects on perceptions, motivations, and the general level of welfare, and the other being the fact that this indirect influence is likely to be operative in the long run rather than the short run. A good theoretical explanation of the equity-fertility relationship has, unfortunately, yet to be developed. Some partial and tentative explanations are advanced below.

It seems reasonable, for example, to expect the substitution effect of income changes to be greater for lower income groups than for higher income groups, at least in the long run. If such be the case, a redistribution of income from the rich to the poor should in the long run be associated with a fall in fertility. There is some evidence to support this explanation. Ben-Porath reports that the negative effect on fertility of an increase of one year of education is greater at low than at higher levels of education.[22] If land redistribution encourages the beneficiaries to increase their education, then the result might well be a decline in fertility.

It is also possible that agricultural reorganization might broaden the tax base in the rural sector and lead to increased expenditure on social services that strengthen the operation of the factors responsible for the substitution effect. This is, of course, strictly hypothetical. There is no compelling reason to believe either that greater equity will lead to increased revenue generation in the rural sector or that a *quid pro quo* relationship must exist between revenues and expenditures in the sector.

Repetto ascribes the nonlinearity of the income-fertility relationship to the operation of a fertility adjustment factor that is different at different socioeconomic levels and reflects essentially the efficiency of fertility control.[23] This efficiency is determined by levels of health and nutrition, education, and exposure to contraceptive techniques. Since these levels vary significantly with income, poorer households being less efficient fertility controllers, increases in income at low levels produce large increases in efficiency of fertility control whereas increases (or decreases) in incomes at high levels have small effects on this efficiency. A similar sort of adjustment mechanism could be postulated for rural fertility responding to changing land endowments from different initial endowments.

Table 4
Some Dimensions of the Pakistani Land Reforms of 1972

Table 4a
Estimates of Tenants Benefitted by Redistribution

	A Cultivable Area Available for Redistribution (acres)	B Tenants Benefitted (at 6.5 acres per tenant)	C Column B as % of Total Agriculture Holdings [a]
If 100% cultivable	2,800,000	448,000	9.2%
If 72% cultivable	2,016,000	322,000	6.6%
If 50% cultivable	1,400,000	224,000	4.6%

[a]/Of a total of 4,859,983 holdings. See Table 3.

Finally, we may note the operation of the "Joneses effect" as motivation. This explanation argues that lower income groups or individuals emulate the consumption patterns of higher income groups or individuals. Hence, when they find themselves in a relatively higher income group as a result of redistribution they might respond by limiting their fertility for purely imitative reasons. Thus, in general it is probably safe to assert that a more equal distribution of income (or land in an agrarian society) is likely to be associated with lower fertility in the long run.

Casual empiricism, as well as some detailed econometric investigation, seem to support this assertion. Kocher, using an index of income distribution and fertility trends for thirteen selected countries, finds that the more unequal the income distribution, the less likely the prospects for a fertility decline irrespective of changes in income per capita.[24] Brazil and Mexico are cases in point. Repetto uncovers a similar result in a regression analysis covering sixty-eight countries. He finds the equity variable (measured by the Gini coefficient for income distribution) to have a significant positive relationship in each of two regressions, using two different measures of fertility as the dependent variable. (The absolute effect of a change in income distribution on fertility, however, is not found to be very large.) On the basis of this empirical evidence as well as the theoretical reasons discussed earlier, we may expect a decline in fertility to come about as a result of the "equity" effect of land reform as distinguished from the increase expected as a consequence of the "income" and the "employment" effects of this development policy.

ECONOMIC AND DEMOGRAPHIC IMPLICATIONS OF THE 1972 REFORM

There are four aspects that have to be considered in assessing the economic and demographic implications of the Pakistani land reform of 1972. First, we have to calculate what the total amount of resumable land (i.e., land that is in excess of the legal ceiling) is likely to be. Second, we have to establish who the likely beneficiaries of the reform are. Third, we have to calculate the total number of beneficiaries. Fourth, we have to estimate what the net gains are likely to be in terms of additional output and employment and improved equity.

The quantitative estimates of the economic impact of the land reform of 1972 are largely taken from a study by Herring and Chaudhry based on figures available around 1974.[25] According to their

Table 4b
Aggregate Output Gains from Land Redistribution

	Based on Authors' Estimate	Based on Official Figures
A. Resumable Land Area (acres)		
i) Cultivable Resumable Area (AX 0.5 acres)	2,800,000	850,000
ii) Self-cultivated Resumable Area (A(i) X 1/3 acres)	1,400,000	425,000
	467,000	142,000
B. Productivity Gain Per Acre (Rs.)	304.76	304,76
C. Total Production Increase (B X A(ii)) (Rs. million)	142.32	43.28
D. As Percentage of Agricultural Income of Rs. 20,155 million in 1972–73	0.71	0.21

calculation, a reasonable maximum estimate of the total resumable area would be in the region of 2.8 million acres (see Table 4a). This calculation is subject to two caveats: In the first place, because the legal ceiling is framed in terms of quality adjusted produce index units, the effective ceiling in terms of acres is likely to vary from region to region and the average ceiling could be in the region of 300 to 350 acres depending on whether or not a tubewell-tractor exemption is claimed. In the second place, the data available on land ownership in Pakistan are very sketchy, fairly dated, and insufficiently disaggregated.

As far as the beneficiaries are concerned, it is not clear from the provisions of the reform or the actions of the government who the final beneficiaries are likely to be. An appropriate order of priority for the allocation of the resumed land would be existing tenants, smallholders who are not tenants on the resumed land, and finally, landless laborers. The limited amount of resumable land makes it almost impossible that the last two groups will get much land from the reform. Thus the largest and by far the poorest rural groups stand to be ignored by the land reform because of its inadequate provisions. Of the tenants who do receive land, some are likely to be fairly large landholders in their own right and it is therefore quite possible that a considerable portion of the resumed land will find its way into the hands of the already well-off rural groups. This has disturbing implications for the equity aspect of the measure.

The next important question is to estimate how many people are likely to be net recipients of land. For this purpose we must make two sets of assumptions. We must assume a typical redistributed plot size and we must derive a value for the cultivability of the redistributed land. Under different assumptions for these two measures we achieve widely different results (see Table 4a). The most optimistic assumptions, an average redistributed plot size of 6.5 acres and 100 percent cultivability of redistributed land, indicates that only 9 percent of the total number of holdings are going to be affected. More realistic assumptions would put this figure at 5 percent. Indeed, the latest figures made available by the government show a total of 40,000 tenants or 2 percent of the total being beneficiaries so far of the reform.[26] When we consider that the rural population of Pakistan is likely to go up to 70 million people by 1985, 18 million of whom are going to be working-age farmers, it is obvious that the potential redistributive impact of this land reform is going to be very small indeed.

We have developed arguments in the previous sections to show that land reform can lead to an increase in productivity and thus in output

Table 4c
Employment Effects of Land Redistribution

		Based on Authors' Estimate	Based on Official Data
A.	Self-cultivated Resumable Area (acres)	467,000	142,000
B.	Increase in Labour Input (man-days per acre)	51.52	51.52
C.	Total Increase in Demand for Labour (man-days)	24,059,840	7,315,840
D.	Man-Years of Employment at 300 days per year	80,199	24,386

Table 4d
Income Redistribution Impact of Land Reforms

		Based on Authors' Estimate	Based on Official Data
A.	Total Redistribution in favor of new proprietors		Rs 190,022,000
B.	Total Redistributive Impact through changes		Rs 395,941,000
C.	Total Income Redistribution (A+B)		Rs 585,963,000
D.	Income Redistributed as % of National Agricultural Income		2.91%

Source of Tables 4a-d: R. Herring & M.G. Chaudhry (1974).

per capita: in the case of the Pakistani land reform it has been estimated that this increase will be of the order of Rs. 300 per acre (see Table 4b). The aggregate output gain which is the product of the total self-cultivated resumable land times the productivity gain per acre comes out to be approximately Rs. 142 million or 0.7 percent of total agricultural income. This figure should be taken with caution, however, since it is subject to a number of inaccuracies—all the redistributed land is taken to be of equal quality, 100 percent cultivable, and operated in like manner before and after transfer of ownership. Even so the bias is in favor of a large rather than small output gain and the relatively small percentage gain confirms our earlier suspicion that the 1972 reform will not achieve much in the way of benefits. The fertility impact of this aspect of the measure is, therefore, likely to be small and, in the short run, positive. There is no compelling reason to believe that the limited number of farmers who benefit by the reforms will undergo major motivational changes with respect to their fertility decisions.

The second link that we have developed between land reform and fertility works through the employment effect for males, females, and children. In the case of Pakistan, it has been estimated that the 1972 reforms are likely to generate a total increase of 24 million man days in the demand for labor on the most optimistic assumptions (see Table 4c). We do not, however, know to what extent this demand will be taken up by underemployed family labor and to what extent it will mean an increase in the use of hired hands. Most studies of the employment problem in Pakistan's rural sector, although partial in nature, indicate that a substantial amount of underemployment exists. Thus it is quite likely that there will be some increase in the on-farm employment of females and children and an insignificant increase in the demand for landless laborers and smallholders who offer themselves for temporary employment. If we connect this to the existing evidence on fertility-employment relations, we can derive the following generalization in the case of Pakistan: the rise in the employment of women and children is likely to lead to an increase in farm fertility, and the insignificant increase in the demand for landless labor is going to leave their fertility behaviour largely unaffected.

The third link we have constructed between land reform and rural fertility works through the income redistribution effect. Herring and Chaudhry estimate that the total amount of income redistributed should be of the order of Rs. 585,000. This, of course, affects only those who receive plots of land and thereby save up to Rs. 135 in rent per acre. For tenants who do not receive land, the redistributive effects

Figure 1
Fertility-Development Policy Relationship in the Case of Land Reform

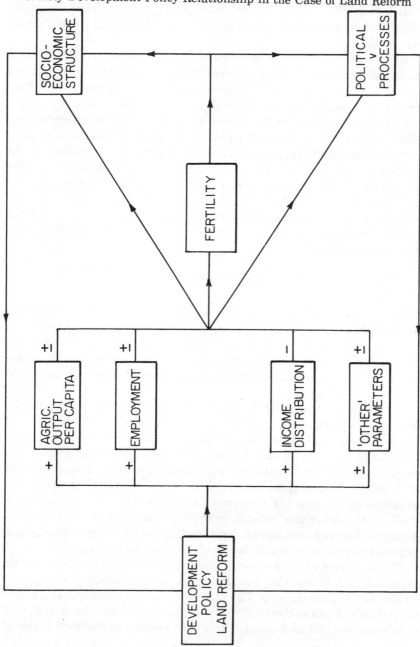

flow from the quantitative impact of the new tenurial regulations and amount to a meagre Rs. 22 per acre per year.[27] This estimate combined with the overall income and employment effects described above indicate that the overall equity effect is likely to be very small but positive.

In general we would expect the 1972 land reforms in Pakistan to have a pronatal effect. This will certainly be true in the short run and since the reforms are not deep enough nor pervasive enough to affect attitudes or generate expenditures whereby social overhead capital may be raised, the likelihood of a long-run antinatal effect is very slight. The equity effect, which is our only unambiguous antinatal factor, turns out to be very small and therefore quite ineffective. In fact, the high fertility rate maintained in rural Pakistan over the 1960s could be due in small part to the superficial land reforms passed in 1958 under Ayub Khan. (The major explanatory factor was probably the rise in rural incomes at all levels that accompanied the breakthrough in agricultural technology commonly referred to as the Green Revolution.)

CONCLUSION

Some complex policy issues are raised by the analysis undertaken in this paper. The major finding is that land reform is likely to have a pronatal effect in the short run and an antinatal effect in the long run. The strength and speed of these effects will, of course, depend on the scope of the reform and the characteristics of the socioeconomic groups affected by it.

One implication of this finding is that land reform should not be organized as a pure and unconditional transfer of income but should be carried out as a component of a package in which certain antinatal incentives are also included. This combination should enable the desirable economic effects to come about and should restrain the undesirable demographic effects of the short run provided, of course, that we are interested in reducing fertility in a given situation. It is difficult to define the most appropriate combination and level of counterbalancing incentives. As a result, decisions are often made haphazardly or in response to immediate political pressures.

This analysis of land reform, however, does suggest some of the ingredients that could go into the policy package involving this particular development policy. The fact that the long run antinatal effect of land reform works through variables such as education, health and nutrition, and reduced uncertainty with respect to the well-being of the parents in their old age, leads us to consider incentives built around these variables. Land reform could, for example, be tied to compulsory schooling for the children, male and especially female, of the family that is eligible to receive land. As another example, part of the revenue generated by transferred land could be taxed and held by the government specifically to finance an old-age insurance scheme for the recipients. Or part of the transferable land could be operated directly by the government and the intended beneficiaries could be given claims upon the revenue of this land which the government could satisfy through contributions to the education, medical care, and insurance of the families concerned. As a more stringent measure the government could make the transfer of land contingent upon the attainment of a prescribed fertility behavior over a given number of years on the part of the eligible family.

Our analysis has also indicated that it is important to identify the various socioeconomic groups that stand to be affected by the reform one way or the other. Different incentives, and different packages, may be needed for different target groups. If the threshold hypothesis is applicable then it follows that families near the threshold will need lesser incentives to cross it than families far from it. In particular, we have mentioned the "perverse" case of the landless and the marginal smallholders who seem to raise their fertility in response to increasing poverty. It is important that the land reform measure not bypass these high fertility groups or at least not worsen their position. In other words, the scale or scope of the reform is an important determinant of its fertility effects. A superficial land reform may produce only the short-run pronatal effects and none of the long-run antinatal effects as we have indicated is likely to be the case with the Pakistani land reform of 1972.

Finally it should be noted that the short-run pronatal effect should not automatically be considered an unfortunate result. Population growth is not necessarily an unqualified evil. And although many developing countries and certainly Pakistan could do much better if the fertility rate were to drop, there are worse ways of influencing population processes in a country. In the case of a serious land reform at least there are the promising prospects of increased productivity, greater food supplies, improved agrarian structure, and a long-run antinatal effect. The families that create more children are more likely to be able to feed and clothe them. This consequence, while not optimal, is better than having fertility rise as a consequence of desperate behavior by marginalized rural and urban groups who perceive their only chances of survival in ever greater numbers.

NOTES

1. For an account of the philosophy and politics underlying Ayub Khan's agrarian policies and the manner of their implementation, see S.J. Burki, "Interest-Group Involvement in West Pakistan's Rural Works Programme," *Public Policy*, 19 (1971) pp. 167-206.

2. Information regarding the provisions of the 1973 land reform in Pakistan has been taken from R. Herring and G. Chaudhry, "The 1972 Land Reforms in Pakistan and their Economic Implications: A Preliminary Analysis." *Pakistan Development Review*, (1974).

3. For a similar forecast constructed from slightly different assumptions, see S.J. Burki, "Pakistan: A Demographic Report," *Population Bulletin*, 29 (1973).

4. This interpretation of the Mexican land reforms has been challenged by recent studies of Mexican agricultural history. Folke Dovring, "Land Reform and Productivity in Mexico," *Land Economics*, 46 (1970), for example, lays the blame for productivity decline at the door of both bad data and the political manipulation of statistics.

5. This opinion is advanced in the context of a discussion of the Brazilian food supply and population growth in W.H. Nicholls "The Brazilian Food Supply: Problems and Prospects," *Economic Development and Cultural Change*, 19 (1971) pp. 378-90. It is undermined, however, by W.R. Cline, *Economic Consequences of a Land Reform in Brazil* (Amsterdam: North Holland, 1970) who finds that measures designed to promote equity in Brazil are compatible with growth of GNP.

6. For obvious reasons, the definition of small and large farmers differs from country to country. We will follow the conventional definitions in the case of Pakistan and identify small farmers as being those who own less than 6.5 acres of land. As far as empirical documentation of the relative superiority of small farmers and the benefits of land reforms is concerned, see P. Dorner (ed.), *Land Reform in Latin America: Issues and Cases* (Madison: University of Wisconsin Press, 1971); and World Bank, "Land Reform" Rural Development Series Paper, International Bank for Reconstruction and Development, Washington, D.C., 1974.

7. A model of this sort is presented in R. Willis, "A New Approach to the Economic Theory of Fertility Behavior," *Journal of Political Economy*, 81 (1973).

8. W. Stys, "The Influence of Economic Conditions on the Fertility of Peasant Women," *Population Studies*, 11 (1957/58) pp. 136-148.

9. W.W. Hicks, "Economic Development and Fertility Change in Mexico, 1950-70," *Demography*, 11 (1974) p. 416.

10. Y. Yasuba, *Birth Rates of the White Population in the United States, 1800-1860: An Economic Study* (Baltimore: Johns Hopkins University Press, 1962).

11. J. Simon, *The Effects of Income on Fertility*, monograph no. 19, Carolina Population Center, University of North Carolina, Chapel Hill (1974), is a good survey of the research on the income-fertility connection in both developed and less-developed countries.

12. Dorner.

13. See World Bank for a cross-national sample of labor-use patterns for

small and large farms as well as for individual cases such as that of Ferozepur, India and Colombia, Brazil and Argentina in Latin America.

14. It is also possible that employment may affect fertility through bringing about changes in occupational status. The empirical evidence on this point is inconclusive with some studies reporting a positive relationship between improved status and fertility, and others a negative one. The evidence is summarized in W. McGreevey, *The Policy Relevance of Recent Social Research on Fertility*, ICP occasional monograph no. 2, Smithsonian Institution, Washington, D.C. (1974) pp. 17-20.

15. A.J. Jaffe and K. Azumi, "The Birth Rate and Cottage Industries in Underdeveloped Countries," *Economic Development and Cultural Change*, 4 (1960) pp. 52-63.

16. J. Stycos and H. Weller, "Female Working Roles and Fertility," *Demography*, 4 (1967) pp. 210-217.

17. J. McCabe and M. Rozenzweig, "Female Employment Creation and Family Size," in R. Ridker (ed.), *Population Development*, (Baltimore: Johns Hopkins Press, 1976).

18. A.J. Harman, *Fertility and Economic Behavior of Families in the Philippines*, The Rand Corporation, Santa Monica, California (1970).

19. J. DaVanzo, *The Determination of Family Formation in Chile, 1960*, The Rand Corporation, Santa Monica, California (1972).

20. M. Rosenzweig and R. Evenson, "Fertility, Schooling and the Economic Contribution of Children in Rural India," (Forthcoming in *Econometrica*).

21. Mamdani, *The Myth of Population Control: Family, Caste, and Class in an Indian Village* (New York: Monthly Review Press, 1972).

22. Y. Ben-Porath, "Fertility in Israel: Point and Counter-Point," *Journal of Political Economy*, 81 (1973).

23. R. Repetto, "The Interaction of Fertility with the Size Distribution of Income," research paper no. 8, Center for Population Studies, Harvard University (1974).

24. J.E. Kocher, *Rural Development, Income Distribution, and Fertility Decline* (New York: The Population Council, 1973). Kocher also constructs plausible scenarios of how improving income distribution can release forces that eventually lead to lower fertility and how deteriorating income distribution can lead to the opposite.

25. Herring and Chaudhry

26. Ibid., p. 256.

27. Ibid., p. 269.

5

SEEKING ETHNIC EQUALITY: A CASE STUDY OF MIGRATION AND EMPLOYMENT POLICIES IN AN INDIAN STATE

Myron Weiner

The shift from colonial to independent status of many of the developing world's multiethnic societies often proved the most disruptive for the very groups that had been receptive to the educational and economic opportunities created by the imperial rulers.[1] Among the first to be both modernized and westernized, these ethnic groups tended to send their children to the new educational institutions created by the Europeans, where they acquired the skills, work habits, and languages that eased them into the newly created industries and made it possible for them to man the European-created administrative system. Many took the initiative themselves in creating new industries, establishing banks, opening new marketing networks, and in other ways playing a role in the creation of the institutions of a modern society.

Unfortunately for them, and even more unfortunately for their societies, these groups often belonged to an ethnic minority. In many instances they were migrants from other countries or from other parts of their own country. The rulers of the newly independent states, and the social classes which supported them, usually came from the majority ethnic communities, and they viewed the migrant minorities as interlopers who stood in the way of the full expression of the cultural and economic aspirations of the majority communities. Since the minorities were typically educators, businessmen, administrators, professionals, and middle-level clerks, they threatened the new middle classes emerging within the ethnic majorities. In Sri Lanka, the Sinhalese majority turned against educated Tamils; in Malaysia, the Malays, declaring themselves the "Bhumiputras" or "sons of the soil," legislated job preferences for themselves over the local Chinese population; in Nigeria, the Hausa and Fulani turned against the Ibos; and in Uganda, President Idi Amin expelled Pakistani and Indian settlers. In country after country migrant minorities were expelled, abused, or discriminated against—not because they had failed to contribute to the country's economic life, but rather because they had been successful; they were resented not because they were unemployed and imposed a burden on the country's social and welfare services, but because the dominant ethnic majority saw them as barriers to their own aspirations for jobs, status, and wealth.

The ethnic majorities that dominated the new governments pursued a variety of policies intended to increase their own share in the country's economy. When the ethnic minorities originated from outside the country, governments often expelled the migrants—or their locally born descendants. Several West Africa governments expelled migrants from neighboring countries. Uganda and Burma both expelled Indians and Pakistanis. Sri Lanka negotiated a treaty with India for the repatriation of part of the Tamil population. In both Indonesia and the Philippines, violent attacks against the Chinese led many Chinese to flee the country. Similarly, protectionist policies for the Malays in Malaysia have led some Chinese to move to neighboring Singapore.

When the ethnic minorities originated from areas within the same country, the process was a more complicated one. The Ibos, for example, are resented in Northern Nigeria, though they are after all Nigerians, entitled to the same rights as other Nigerians; similarly, Bengali white-collar workers in Assam, Gujarati merchants in Bombay, and Punjabi businessmen in Uttar Pradesh are all citizens of

India. State governments, so long as they operate within the framework of national law, are generally not able to adopt explicit policies intended to benefit the majority ethnic group, but there are a variety of indirect policies that can change the status of the ethnic majority in relation to the migrant communities.

This paper examines the policies adopted by one of the state governments in India to use migration and employment policies to achieve greater equality among ethnic groups by seeking to expand the employment opportunities for the local majority community, to reduce the opportunities for the migrants and descendants of migrants living within the state, and to reduce or halt the flow of migrants from other states. This case study has two objectives: (1) to show how a government attempts to regulate internal population movements for the achievement of social objectives; and (2) to examine and where possible measure the effects of these policies, including those that are unintended and indirect as well as those that are intended and direct.

We shall begin by describing the state of Assam, India, and the political problems which led government to adopt a set of policies; then turn to a description of the policies themselves; and finally we shall assess the consequences of these policies.

THE POLITICAL SETTING

The state of Assam is located in India's northeast. Except for a brief moment in world history during the Second World War when Japanese forces moved through northern Burma to Assam's border and Assam became a center for flying supplies to Chinese nationalist forces in southern China, Assam has been an obscure region in Southern Asia. Even to most Indians Assam is a relatively remote region of the subcontinent, linked to India by a small corridor between Bangladesh and Tibet. It has a population (in 1975) of about seventeen million, about the same as Algeria, but it remains one of India's smallest states. Its one major trade connection with the world is its tea, a plentiful crop whose rich color makes it an attractive addition to a variety of blends. When Chinese troops moved from Tibet to the gates of the Assamese town of Tezpur, Prime Minister Nehru in a memorable (but erroneous) statement bade farewell to Assam when it seemed inevitable that Chinese forces would occupy the entire region. To most Indians, few of whom had ever met any Assamese, Assam was nearly as remote as the border regions of

Ladakh which also fell under Chinese attack. Even India's national anthem, which mentions most of the regions of India, neglects Assam—a sore point, incidentally, to many Assamese.

Though obscure to the world and to most of India, Assam is very much a part of the consciousness of large numbers of people in the neighboring Indian state of West Bengal and the neighboring country of Bangladesh. To some 120 million Bengalis, Assam has been an historic frontier region, a place where the landless could seek land and the middle class could find urban employment.

From 1826, when the British dislodged the Burmese invaders who had conquered Assam a few years earlier, to 1874, when it was made a separate province, Assam was part of the presidency of Bengal. During this half-century the British created tea plantations in the hill areas and linked the region by steamship on the Brahmaputra river to the expanding port at Calcutta. Unable to persuade Assamese cultivators, most of whom owned their own land, that they should work as tea pickers in the plantations, the British "imported" a labor force from the tribal region of southern Bihar. This migration was soon followed by an influx of Bengali Muslim cultivators, by educated Bengali Hindus seeking positions in the administrative services and in the professions, and by a variety of other migrant traders, merchants, bankers, and industrialists. In time these migrations changed the ethnic composition of the entire region and resulted in the creation of a political system in which questions of ethnicity and migration became central.

Assam was separated from Bengal in 1874 to come under the administration of a chief commissioner; a decade later the area was given the status of a separate state responsible directly to the Viceroy. But its independent status did not last for long. The changes in the political geography of the new state were to play a critical role in the patterns of migration into the entire northeast, and in the kinds of political cleavages which characterized the area.

In 1905 the British partitioned the sprawling densely populated province of Bengal into a predominantly Bengali Muslim province in the east and a predominantly Bengali Hindu province in the west. Assam was incorporated into the eastern province. The partition of Bengal was deeply resented both by the Bengali Hindus and by the Assamese. In 1912 it was annulled and Assam was reestablished as a separate chief commissioners' province that included two Bengali districts—a predominantly Hindu district, Cachar, and a predominantly Muslim district, Sylhet. Assam also included the plains of the Brahmaputra valley, where the Assamese-speaking people were predominant, and the surrounding tribal areas—the Garo, Khasi, and Jaintia Hills; the Naga Hills; and the Mizo Hills.

In the latter part of the nineteenth century Bengali Muslim peasants moved into the plains of Assam. But it was not until after 1901 that the major influx took place. By 1911 there were 118,000 migrants, almost all Bengali Muslims, forming 20 percent of the district of Goalpara alone. The 1911 census commissioner, alarmed by the massive influx, wrote that the migration was "likely to alter permanently the whole future of Assam and to destroy more surely than did the Burmese invaders of 1820 the whole structure of Assamese culture and civilization."

Why the massive influx? Bengal was one of the most densely populated agricultural regions of the subcontinent. A gradual growth in population on this rice- and jute-producing delta, and a landlord system that contributed to tenancy and to the fragmentation of land holdings, resulted in the growth of the number of landless laborers and low income tenants.

In contrast nearby Assam had a relatively low population density, possibly because of the high mortality rate engendered by rampant malaria and the plague. One district officer, noting that in his district the indigenous population had decreased by 30 percent from 1891 to 1901, wrote that "not a single British district in the whole of the Indian Empire lost so large a proportion of its population as the unfortunate district of Nowgong."

As the public health situation improved in Assam, and the agrarian situation worsened in Bengal, the migration of landless Muslims accelerated. Assam had considerable virgin lands, some in the easily flooded lowlands along the Brahmaputra valley that are similar to the deltaic areas of East Bengal, and it had substantial forest tracts that were occupied, often illegally, by land-hungry peasant migrants.

Later on, political factors may have played a role in the migration. With the inclusion of Sylhet and Cachar districts in Assam in the reorganization of 1912, Assam had a large local Bengali Muslim population within its borders. As the Muslim population grew, Muslim political parties increased in political importance. A Muslim League government took power in 1937 and remained in office, except for a one-year interlude, until the close of the Second World War. During this period there was an increasing influx of Bengali Muslim migrants into the state, which aroused fears among both Assamese and Bengali Hindus that all of the province might be incorporated into the proposed Muslim state of Pakistan.

Bengali Hindus had been coming into the state ever since Assam had been incorporated into the presidency of Bengal. The British recruited their administrative staff from among the educated Bengali Hindus in the province. Bengali Hindus were among the first to join the administrative services. Later they entered the modern professions. By the beginning of the twentieth century, the doctors, lawyers, teachers, journalists, clerks, railway and post office officials, as well as officers of the state government in Assam, were Bengali Hindu migrants.

Bengali, along with English, became the language of the state government. Bengali became the medium of instruction in the primary and secondary schools, and Bengalis became the teachers of the Assamese. Soon the Assamese perceived themselves as having two sets of alien rules. Assamese nationalists fought back and by the 1880s managed to have Assamese adopted as the medium in the primary schools. As the number of educated Assamese increased in the twentieth century they turned against the Bengali Hindus, resentful of their domination of the administrative services, fearful of what they saw as a form of cultural imperialism on the part of many Bengalis, and angry at the efforts of Bengalis to treat them as culturally inferior provincial cousins.

In 1947, when independence was achieved, the political geography of Assam was again changed. The Muslim majority district of Sylhet was transferred to the new country of Pakistan. But even without Sylhet, Assam remained one of the most diverse cultural regions in the Indian subcontinent. It included three groups of native peoples: the Assamese-speaking Hindu population residing primarily in the Brahmaputra valley; the hill tribes (the Garo, Khasi, Naga, Mikir, and Mizo), and the indigenous plains' tribals known as the Bodo, or Kachari.

The migrant communities included: tribal laborers from Bihar and Orissa working in the British-owned tea gardens; Bengali Muslims, mainly from East Bengal, who settled primarily on land along the Brahmaputra valley; Bengali Hindus, originally from East Bengal and especially the Sylhet district, who settled in the towns throughout the Brahmaputra valley where they held middle-class jobs, and in the predominantly Bengali district of Cachar; the Marwaris, an entrepreneurial community from Rajasthan, who engaged in trade, commerce, and money lending; Nepalis who have settled in the low-lying hills around the valley tending cattle; Biharis who worked as seasonal migrants in construction projects and in the towns plying rickshaws; and a small but economically significant number of Punjabis working in the transport industry and in their own businesses.

The Assamese were the largest single ethnic group in the state, but they were not the largest ethnic group in the cities and towns. In 1961 (the last census for which language figures are available) 913,000 people lived in the urban areas of the Brahmaputra valley. Of this population, 38 percent were Bengali, 33 percent Assamese, and another 13 percent spoke Hindi. In their own urban centers the Assamese were outnumbered by the Bengalis, while the surrounding countryside was predominantly Assamese. The towns of Assam had become centers of alien life.

Why had this happened? One reason is that the jobs available in the urban areas of Assam were less attractive to the Assamese than they were to migrants from neighboring states. A predominantly agricultural people with relatively few landless laborers and tenant farmers, the Assamese had less economic incentive to seek low-paying urban jobs than the rural people of other states. According to the 1961 census only 3.8 percent of the rural labor force in Assam were agricultural laborers, as compared with 18.9 percent for India as a whole. Even a decade later when agricultural labor sharply increased in India to 30 percent, only 10 percent of the rural Assamese labor force were agricultural laborers. By contrast, 40.8 percent of the rural labor force in neighboring Bihar were agricultural laborers in 1971 (24.4 percent in 1961) and 33.8 percent in rural West Bengal (20.2 percent in 1961).

A second reason is that the skilled positions in urban Assam had been taken by educated workers from urban West Bengal and from other parts of India. A large proportion of the clerical positions, technical staffs, and managerial personnel consisted of migrants, or were native-born descendants of earlier waves of Bengali Hindu migrants.

As the Assamese middle class grew after independence, the major political problems for the Congress-controlled Assamese dominated government were how to expand the employment opportunities of the Assamese in general, and the Assamese middle classes in particular; how to halt (or at least slow) the flow of migrants into Assam's urban centers; and, though less explicit, how to diminish the role of the locally born Bengali Hindu population.

POLICIES

The government of Assam had to deal with three groups of employers whose actions affected the job opportunities for the Assamese, the locally born non-Assamese, and the migrants: (1) the state administration of Assam itself, including the large educational sector; (2) the central government, which not only maintains its own administrative staff within the state, but also runs a number of public sector enterprises, including railroads, an oil refinery, fertilizer plants, coal mines, and banks; and (3) the organized private sector.

Actually, only a small proportion of the entire labor force in the state falls within these three sectors. According to the 1971 census,[2] Assam had a total labor force of 4,240,000. Of these workers, a total of 722,000 (in 1974) were employed in the "organized" sector of the economy.[3] The remainder were in agriculture, household industry, self-employed, or engaged in services and industrial activities where less than ten workers were employed.

In the organized sector, 459,000 worked for private firms, and 263,000 were in the public sector. Most private sector workers, 404,000, were in tea plantations; the remainder were largely in veneer, plywood and match factories, in the repairing and servicing of motor vehicles, and in cotton spinning and weaving mills. In the public sector 31,000 were in central government services, 114,000 in the state or local government, and 43,000 in the central government railways. Another 75,000 persons were in public sector industries, including electric power, coal mining, oil refining, and banking.

The largest number of people working for state and local government were in education—about 70,000; the medical and health services employed another 11,000.

Only 55,000 workers in the state—8 percent of the labor force in the organized sector and a mere 1.3 percent of the total labor force in the entire state—were employed in the organized private sector. Nearly five times that number worked for the central government (including the public sector), and one and a half times that number were in educational services.

It is important to note, however, that while government policy was directed at affecting only a small portion of employment in the state, it was the organized sector that employed the bulk of the secondary school and college graduates, paid the highest wages, and provided ths greatest security of tenure, as compared with the unorganized sector of the economy. It was also the sector of the economy dominated by the non-Assamese, especially by Bengali Hindus, and Hindi-speakers. It was, in short, the "modern" sector into which the expanding Assamese middle class aspired to enter.

Three sets of policies were adopted by the state and central government to influence migration and employment: (1) education policies (2) employment policies, and (3) migration policies.

Education Policies

In an ethnically divided society, there are invariably struggles over the control of the school system. What is at stake are some of the most central values in a society: social mobility for the young, employment opportunities for graduates as teachers, and of course, control over an institution that shapes the fundamental, cultural symbols of the society. By the middle of the nineteenth century the Bengalis had established for themselves a central place in the educational system. Because Bengali was the medium of instruction, the teachers were Bengali. Local colleges were affiliated with Calcutta, and Assamese who sought higher education often went to Calcutta for advanced studies—again in Bengali.

The struggle by Assamese nationalists to gain control over the educational system began in the end of the nineteenth century when they established Assamese as the medium of instruction for Assamese children in the primary and secondary schools. After independence the primary and secondary school system was substantially expanded, and whenever possible the government created Assamese-medium schools even in areas in which Bengali Muslims or tea plantation migrant laborers were numerous. Under central government law, state governments were required to provide schools in the mother tongue of children if requested by parents. In Assam, however, Bengali Muslims and migrant tribals were generally provided with Assamese-language schools. Bengali Hindus continued to insist that their schools teach in Bengali. The Bengalis also opposed efforts to declare Assamese the exclusive official language of the state, a move they interpreted as a step by the Assamese to undermine the position of the Bengali-medium schools whose graduates might find themselves handicapped when they sought jobs in the state government.

Throughout the 1960s there were bitter clashes over the question of language medium in the schools and the status of Assamese as the official language of the state. Perhaps the most bitter and violent conflict took place in 1972 in a controversy over whether Bengali could be used for examinations at Gauhati University—a decision that had obvious implications for primary and secondary school language policies. The Academic Council of Gauhati University, whose jurisdiction extended to colleges in the predominantly Bengali Cachar district as well as throughout the Brahmaputra valley, ruled that Assamese would be the exclusive medium of instruction in the colleges and university, but that students could retain the option of answering examination questions in Bengali. Demonstrations by the student union, teachers at Gauhati University, and by the Assam Sahitya Sabha, the state's paramount literary association, led the council to reverse its decision on the question of a Bengali option. There was then an uproar in Cachar district where one of the colleges filed a petition in the Supreme Court arguing that the university's decision to restrict the medium of instruction to Assamese was a violation of a constitutional provision which assured protection for linguistic minorities. Large-scale arson and looting took place in several towns in the valley, and as the violence spread the central government called in the military to reestablish order. The chief minister announced that he would stand by the final decision of the Academic Council, and that he would not carry out a compromise proposal by the assembly to create a separate Bengali university for Cachar district. While the assembly's compromise was interpreted by Assamese militants as an unacceptable step toward a multilingual state, the new announcement of the chief minister was greeted by the Bengali Hindus as a step toward forced Assamization. One Bengali letter writer to a Calcutta newspaper expressed his fear that "the recurring disturbances are aimed not at usurping the Bengali language but at driving out the entire Bengali population from Assam."

The objectives of the policy itself thus became an issue. Some saw the Assamese guided by a cultural nationalism, concerned with assuring that their own language, and hence the Assamese themselves, would be in a politically and culturally dominant role. Others saw the policy directed at increasing the need for Assamese teachers in the colleges and secondary schools, since the use of Assamese as the medium of instruction in all subjects assured the Assamese they they would hold a dominant position in employment in all areas of education. And finally, some saw the policy as "driving out" Bengalis or at least discouraging potential Bengali migrants from entering the state. Most likely, among Assamese supporters of the chief minister there were individuals who held each of these views.

While data on the ethnic composition of school teachers and college faculty in Assam are not available—indeed, it is striking how little hard data there are on the relationship between ethnicity and education, employment or income in a state whose government is so explicitly concerned with improving the position of one ethnic community—it is generally agreed that there has been a substantial increase in the number and proportion of Assamese in the state's educational system at all levels.

Employment Policies

The pressure for a policy of giving preferences to local people both in public and private employment had been mounting for many years, but it became more acute in the 1960s at a time of growing educated unemployment. In 1959 the Employment Exchanges Compulsory Notification of Vacancies Act was passed by the national parliament requiring that all employers, both public and private, were required to inform local employment exchanges of newly available jobs. Employers were not, however, required to hire candidates submitted by the exchanges.

Two bodies pressed for a more active "hire-local" policy: the centrally appointed National Labor Commission, and the National Integration Council, which consists of state chief ministers and high officials of the central government.

The National Labor Commission recommended that both central and state governments actively pursue a policy of giving preferences to local people in their own employment and that they use their influence to urge private employers to do likewise.[4] The chairman of the National Labor Commission noted that the problem was less one of objectives than of implementation. He reported that the commission had received many complaints that instructions issued earlier by the central government to public sector undertakings to give preferences to local people were not properly observed. "In one public sector undertaking," he said, "not even a car driver was recruited locally." The tendency, he continued, "was that almost all the employees in a public sector undertaking were from the same region to which the top officials of the undertaking belonged."

The National Integration Council similarly recommended that the public sector give preferences to local people in order to "remove the discontent in the States arising from the inadequate share of the local people in employment opportunities in the public and private sectors."[5]

In August 1968 the deputy minister of the Ministry of Labor and Employment announced that "the public sector undertakings have been asked to fill vacancies carrying a monthly salary of less than Rs. 500 through the local employment exchanges. The recruitment to higher posts has, however, to be made on an all-India basis in order to attract the right type of talent. Local people, possessing the required qualifications will, of course, be eligible and shall be considered for all such posts."

The government further explained that gazetted posts within the government—the higher-salaried, more senior positions in the administrative services—would continue to take place through the Union Public Service Commission, but that recruitment for the lesser nongazetted positions would be made through the local employment exchanges. The Labor ministry also announced that the government had asked the all-India Organization of Employers to use their good offices to ensure that their constituents would implement the recommendations of the National Integration Council concerning the employment of local persons. State Labor ministers were also instructed to persuade private sector employers to take similar actions.

One Labor minister replied that in his state the private employers seldom made use of the employment exchange machinery, and he raised the issue of whether more pressure couldn't be put on private employers to hire locally through the exchanges. Some raised the question of whether the act could be amended so that employment through the exchanges would be made compulsory.[6]

The central government was unwilling to amend the legislation. The National Commission on Labor, which considered the proposal, expressed a reluctance to give up the notion that a citizen of India should be able to secure employment in any part of the country, even as it pressed employers to give preferences to local people. Article Sixteen of the Indian constitution provides that "there shall be equality of opportunity for all citizens in matters relating to employment . . . ." and that "no citizen shall, on ground only of religion, race, caste, sex, descent, *place of birth*, residence or any of them, be ineligible for or discriminated against in respect of any employment . . . ."

The commission noted, too, that ordinarily industry preferred to employ local people but that "certain regional groups have traditionally specialized in particular jobs." Dock workers in Bombay, for example, tend to be Telugus, and construction workers are often from Rajasthan. The commission reported that "because some groups have been identified as suited to particular types of work, employers have shown preference for them" and that in any case, there were advantages in having a homogeneous labor force. While the commission concluded that there was a need, nonetheless, to shift employment to local people, they were evidently reluctant to press for a policy that would break up these traditional employment patterns.

The commission recommended that in the case of unskilled and semiskilled workers, clerks, and other nontechnical staff, preferences should be given to local people, but that as the skill requirements increased there was a need to seek recruits from a larger area than covered by a local employment exchange. Hence, middle-level technical and nontechnical posts (known as Class I junior scale in the government of India) should be recruited on an all-India basis, even by the private sector. The same considerations seemed to the commission to be relevant for higher nontechnical posts, e.g., top general management, etc., and for the higher technical posts where, concluded the commission, "the best qualified persons will have to be recruited, either by advertisement on an all-India basis or by personal contact."

Finally, the commission members evidently recognized that whatever employment procedures were required for the private sector—such as the compulsory use of employment exchanges—would have to be applied to the public sector as well, and that such a change in policy was likely to be opposed by the nationally minded Union Public Service Commission.

Alternatively, the commission recommended that a variety of new employment procedures be adopted both by public and private sector firms to increase the possibility that qualified local persons would be given preference over equally qualified persons from other areas, including the establishment of special recruitment committees with a nominee from the state government within which the firm is located, and through regular reporting procedures by the firm to the state government.

Government policy calling for the employment of local people in both private and public sector jobs, therefore, provided no sanctions. There were no penalties against employers who failed to notify employment exchanges of vacancies, and there was no requirement that anyone had to hire through the exchanges for any level of jobs. Moreover, the directives of the central government were not always explicit about whether locality referred to city, district, or state, or whether "local" meant place of birth, length of residence, or ethnic origin. To the extent that the central government was explicit, however, "local" meant birthplace and residence, never ethnic origin, a definition at variance with the thinking of most state political leaders.

Nonetheless, it would be a mistake to conclude that the vagueness of the notion "local" and the absence of legal penalties indicates that the policies discussed here served only the symbolic purpose of assuaging the demands of local people for more employment. As far as the government of Assam was concerned, they were quite clear as to what they meant by "local," nor was the state government without any powers to enforce its policy objectives.

The *explicit* policy of both the central and state government was to slow the pace of migration into a state by giving preferential employment to local people. For the government of Assam there was another objective: to increase the *ratio* of employment of Assamese to *local* Bengalis. While none of the legislation or directives to employers explicitly distinguished between Assamese and locally born but ethnically non-Assamese, the government of Assam clearly did not intend to provide job preferences for Bengalis born in Assam. The actual *intent* of the policy was set forth by the Employment Review Committee appointed by the Assamese state legislature to review the status of Assamese employment in the state:

> in the absence of any clear-cut definition of the term "local people," the Committee has had to base its analysis as place of birth in Assam being the yardstick of local people. This yardstick is palpably inadequate and misleading and a clear understanding should be there in government and all others concerned in the matter as to what is meant by the term "local people".[7]

But the committee was evidently legally restrained from providing its own "clear-cut definition" of the term "local people."

There are many ways in which a determined state government can press employers—particularly in the private sector—to implement such a policy. Private firms need the support of the state government in their dealings with central government ministries over licenses for imports, exports, the purchase of rationed raw materials, etc. There are also innumerable ways in which the state government can harass uncooperative employers, involving the enforcement of labor laws, the factory acts, and taxes. Finally, there is always the threat that young street gangs will burn, loot, and vandalize shops, warehouses, and factories owned by alien entrepreneurs who do not pay sufficient attention to local demands over hiring.

Migration Policies

An act of the Indian Parliament passed in 1950 entitled the Immigrants (Expulsion from Assam) Act to remove "infiltrators" who had entered the country illegally after 1947, and a bill passed by the Assam legislature shortly after independence declaring squatter settlements illegal were both important instruments for controlling the Bengali Muslim population. Bengali Muslims were fearful that these two acts might be used to force earlier migrants (many of whom held land illegally, and a few of whom could prove that they had migrated before 1947) to leave the country. It is not surprising, therefore, that Bengali Muslims declared that their mother tongue was Assamese, that they accepted the establishment of primary and secondary schools in Assamese for their children, and that they supported the government against the Bengali Hindus on the issue of an official language for the state and the university.

In neighboring Tripura, a state dominated by Bengali Hindus, the Immigration Act was enforced, resulting in a substantial return migration of Bengali Muslims to East Pakistan between 1961 and 1971, as reflected in an absolute decline in the Muslim population from 230,000 in 1961 to 103,000 in 1971. But in Assam, where the Bengali Muslims proved to be politically supportive of the Assamese Hindus, the Muslim population of Assam continued to grow between 1961 and 1971 at more or less the national rate; indeed, the earlier 1961 census indicated that the Muslim population in Assam had increased by a quarter of a million more than could be accounted for either through natural population increase or migration of Muslims from other states. This surplus may be taken to reflect illegal migration from East Pakistan.

POLICY EFFECTS

Our analysis of the policies adopted by the state government in the areas of education, employment, and migration has led us to conclude that the government's objective was to increase the share of employment in the state by the local Assamese-speaking population, and to win the support of Bengali Muslims for such a policy. In assessing how effective this policy has been it is important to distinguish between the outcomes that were sought, direct and visible, and those outcomes that were unintended, which were often indirect and even invisible to the policymaker and to the public. The former, to which we turn first, can be measured by changes in the composition of the labor force, while the latter requires a broader look at a number of economic, social, and political changes in the region.

Direct, Intended, and Visible Effects

In 1968 the government of Assam established an Employment Review Committee to conduct a survey of employment and report their findings to the Assam Legislative Assembly.[8] Over a period of forty-one months, from May 1969 to December 1972, the committee studied twenty-eight firms, both public and private, located in the Brahmaputra valley. A questionnaire was completed by each of these firms providing data on their labor force—their place of birth, mother tongue, occupation categories, wages, duration of service, and educational levels. Some of the data proved to be unusable for our purposes, partly because each company devised its own format on some categories, the standard job classification schema was not followed, and information on procedures for recruitment was only sporadically collected. Within these limitations, however, the survey provides us with an unusually rich source of information concerning the relationship between ethnicity and employment in one region of India, and makes it possible to examine how this relationship has been changing.

In one sense it may be premature to look at the impact of government policy on employment, for the central government did not issue detailed directives until 1968, and the survey was conducted within only a year or two after the policy was formally put into effect. However, the government of Assam has been pressing firms to give preferences to local people at least since the early 1960s. Moreover, labor turnover for many of the low-paying manual occupations is quite high so that changes in the ethnic composition of the labor force are possible within a brief time period. One can, therefore, discern some trends by examining recent recruitment.

These firms employed 29,537 persons in a total labor force in the organized sector of 722,000. Excluded from this latter figure are those employed in agriculture, the self-employed, all who work in establishments in the private sector employing less than ten workers, and members of the defense forces.

The firms surveyed included the major banks, trading companies, transportation, extractive and manufacturing industries, and a research laboratory. Eighteen of the firms are privately owned, though several are partially owned by the government of Assam, and ten are wholly in the public sector. Ten of the firms operate exclusively in Assam (e.g., the Sarda Plywood Factory, the Woodcraft Plywood Factory, the Assam Oil Company, the Assam Railways and Trading Company, Everest Cycles), while eighteen are branches or divisions of a firm outside Assam (including the banks, Indian Airlines, the Fertilizer Corporation, the Ford Corporation, India Carbon, Indian Refineries, Oil India, the Oil and Natural Gas Commission, and the Regional Research Laboratory). These are among the largest firms in

Assam. They are all highly visible, and most of them have a substantial white-collar force.

Not included in the survey were tea plantations, central, state, and local government services, and education which together employ nearly three-quarters of the labor force in the organized sector. The survey, therefore, represents a sample of the industrial sector in which about 183,000 persons were employed.

ASSAMESE AND NON-ASSAMESE EMPLOYMENT

Approximately one-half of the employees in the survey (14,367 or 49 percent) were born in Assam. Nearly three-quarters of these (10,469 or 73 percent) report Assamese as their mother tongue. In other words, slightly more than a third of the labor force in the survey (35 percent) are Assamese "sons of the soil."

The Bengalis constitute the second-largest ethnic group. Of all employees, 23 percent (6,713) were Bengali, with slightly less than half of these (46 percent) born in Assam. No other indigenous ethnic group has such a large proportion of its members born in the state.

Hindi speakers were a close third, with 21 percent (6,183) of all employees. But most of these (94 percent) were born outside of the state. The remaining 21 percent of the labor force whose mother tongue was neither Assamese, Bengali, nor Hindi were almost entirely migrants. Of these, 43 percent spoke Nepali, 31 percent Telugu, 8 percent Punjabi, and 6 percent Malayali. Of this group, 93 percent came from outside of the state.

It should be noted that the indigenous tribal population, though constituting 6 percent of the total population of the state, account for less than 1 percent of the employees in the firms surveyed.

Were there a typical firm that perfectly reflected the ethnic distribution of the labor force, it would look like this: for each 100 workers forty-nine are born in Assam, of whom thirty-five are Assamese, eleven are Bengali, one speaks Hindi, one is a local tribal, one speaks another regional language; fifty-one are migrants, of whom twelve are Bengali, twenty are Hindi, eight are Nepali, six are Telugu, one is a Punjabi, one is a Malayali, and three speak other regional languages.

These figures only partially reflect the ethnic distribution in urban areas. As noted earlier, in the Brahmaputra valley (where all the firms surveyed were located) the Assamese constituted 33 percent of the urban population, Bengalis 38 percent, Hindi speakers 13 percent, and 16 percent spoke other languages. The Hindi speakers thus held a disproportionate share of jobs in industry, as do speakers of other minority languages. But it should be noted that these groups are primarily migrants and that therefore a larger proportion are members of the labor force than are locally born Bengalis and Assamese.[9] The "underrepresentation" of the Bengalis probably reflects the fact that many Bengalis work in government services, in the professions, or in smaller firms not included in this survey. Nonetheless, it is interesting to note that the Assamese in the urban areas are proportionately represented in industrial employment.

Who employs the Assamese, and for what kinds of jobs? How does the pattern of employment for Assamese differ from that of the non-Assamese? And what kind of firms hire few Assamese?

First, the public sector firms, with the notable exception of the banks (which were nationalized in 1969), tend to hire Assamese to a greater extent than do the private firms. The seven large public sector firms in the survey, employing nearly 12,000 persons, were 51 percent Assamese, 15 percent Bengali, and 17 percent Hindi. Among sixteen private firms employing 15,000 persons, only 23 percent were Assamese, 23 percent were Bengali, and the largest, 27 percent, were Hindi. Five banks, employing about 2,500 persons, were predominantly Bengali, with the Assamese forming about a fourth of the labor force. In short, public sector firms, banks excepted, hire Assamese at more than twice the rate of privately owned firms (Table 1).

Second, two factors, surprisingly, seemed not to be significant determinants of the ethnicity of the labor force: the size of the firm and the location of its head office. There is a slightly higher proportion of migrants employed in the smaller firms than in the larger ones, but the differences are not great. There is not reason to believe, therefore, that the larger firms are more easily affected by government pressures to hire Assamese. And when the head office is located outside of Assam, there is also no tendency for firms to hire more migrants, largely because most recruitment takes place locally.

To assess the reason for the differences between the public and private sector recruitment let us take a look at the recruitment procedures and at the occupational characteristics of the firms that have a high proportion of Assamese and the firms that have a high proportion of migrants or local non-Assamese.

There are fiteen firms whose labor force is less than one-third Assamese (see Appendix 1). One, Indian Airlines, is owned by the government, two are publicly owned banks, and the remainder are private firms. They are primarily low technology industrial firms. Five are plywood and match factories, three are textile mills, one produces cycles, one is a small steel processing factory, one is in

Table 1

Employees in Twenty-Eight Firms: Sector of Activity by Mother Tongue

Mother Tongue	Public Sector excl. banks		Private Sector		Banks		Total	
Assamese	6,073	(51.4%)	3,555	(23.3%)	845	(34.1%)	10,473	(35.4%)
Bengali	1,799	(15.2%)	3,548	(23.3%)	1,366	(55.1%)	6,713	(22.7%)
Hindi	1,998	(16.9%)	4,084	(26.8%)	101	(4.1%)	6,183	(21.0%)
Other	1,939	(16.5%)	4,062	(26.6%)	167	(6.7%)	6,168	(20.9%)
Total	11,809	(100.0%)	15,249	(100.0%)	2,479	(100.0%)	29,537	(100.0%)

N.B. Table refers to mother tongue of employees, *not* migrant status (place of birth) as in some later tables. Many Bengali speakers, for instance, are not migrants.

Table 2
Occupation Classification of Employees by Place of Birth

	Place of Birth		
Occupational Classification	Assam (non-migrants)	Outside Assam (migrants)	Total
1. managerial	652 (39.0%)	1,021 (61.0%)	1,673 (100.0%)
2. clerical/ supervisory technical	2,810 (59.4%)	1,916 (40.6%)	4,726 (100.0%)
A. WHITE COLLAR	3,462 (54.1%)	2,937 (45.9%)	6,399 (100.0%)
3. skilled*	5,750 (57.4%)	4,261 (42.6%)	10,011 (100.0%)
4. unskilled	5,153 (39.3%)	7,971 (60.7%)	13,124 (100.0%)
B. MANUAL	10,903 (47.1%)	12,232 (52.9%)	23,135 (100.0%)
C. TOTAL	14,365 (48.6%)	15,169 (51.4%)	29,534 (100.0%)

*includes subordinates in banks

carbon, one in oil, another in railway shipping. A large part of the labor force in these factories are low paid, unskilled, or semiskilled workers.

As we look at the characteristics of the labor force of each of these fifteen firms and the process by which recruitment takes place, the following emerge. First, a number of these firms use, or once used, labor contractors to import unskilled laborers from other states. Even when labor contractors are no longer used, laborers are often recruited from among the friends and relatives of those who already work in the factory. In either event the results are a well established chain migration between Assam and the Hindi speaking areas, particularly from nearby Bihar.

Second, some firms hire "at the gate." As labor is needed each day, especially when there is considerable absenteeism of migrant workers who have returned home, employers hire from among those who appear at the gate in the morning. Wages for such workers are initially very low—often as little as Rs 1.50 per day. Those who remain for three months or longer are then given higher wages. Since the initial wages, and even the wages after three or six months, are

Table 3
Employees in Eight Firms:* Mother Tongue of Nonmigrants by Occupational Classification

Occupational Classification	Mother Tongue		
	Assamese	Non-Assamese	Total
1. managerial	80 (44.0%)	102 (56.0%)	182 (100.0%)
2. clerical/ supervisory technical	653 (48.1%)	704 (51.9%)	1,357 (100.0%)
A. WHITE COLLAR	733 (47.6%)	806 (52.4%)	1,539 (100.0%)
3. skilled**	322 (58.6%)	227 (41.4%)	549 (100.0%)
4. unskilled	315 (43.6%)	407 (56.4%)	722 (100.0%)
B. MANUAL	637 (50.1%)	634 (49.9%)	1,271 (100.0%)
C. TOTAL	1,370 (48.8%)	1,440 (51.2%)	2,810 (100.0%)

*8 firms are: Assam Hardboards
Assam Railroads and Trading Co.
India Airlines
National Grindlays Bank
Punjab National Bank
State Bank of India
United Bank of India
United Commercial Bank

Note the high proportion of banks—this may bias the sample because the banks have a reputation for employing non-migrant Bengalis.

**includes "subordinates" in banks

often below what Assamese earn in the countryside (but higher than agricultural laborers can earn in Bihar or U.P. when there is no employment at all) few Assamese seek such jobs.

Third, migrants hold jobs at both ends of the occupational spectrum. In the twenty-eight firms surveyed, 79 percent of the jobs are manual compared with 21 percent that are white collar. The majority of the manual jobs (53 percent) are held by migrants. In the white-collar positions, only 39 percent of the managerial positions are held by persons born in Assam, and 59 percent of subordinate clerical or technical positions (Table 2). But a large proportion of these jobs are held by locally born Bengalis, not Assamese. Unfortunately, data on mother tongue were available for only eight of the twenty-eight firms. Among the *locally born* in these eight firms 44 percent of the managers are Assamese speakers, 48 percent of the clerical and technical workers; 68 percent of the skilled workers, and 49 percent of the unskilled workers. In short, even among the locally born less than half are Assamese speakers (Table 3).

For the higher status managerial jobs, therefore, the Assamese compete primarily against migrants; for the clerical and technical positions, the Assamese lose out to locally born Bengalis and then secondarily to migrants; and in the low-skilled positions, the Assamese compete—to the extent that they are interested in these jobs—against migrants.

In what respect do these patterns differ in firms that hire a larger proportion of Assamese? We have already noted that public sector firms tend to hire few migrants and more Assamese than private firms: 51 percent of the workers in seven public sector firms are Assamese compared to only 23 percent of the sixteen private firms in the survey (Table 1). But the differences are not in the categories of managerial or clerical personnel. In these categories, in fact, public sector firms hire proportionately more migrants than do private firms: 69 percent of the managers and 53 percent of the clerical staff in the public firms are migrants, compared with 53 percent and 45 percent respectively in private firms (Tables 4a and 4b). In the public firms, senior jobs are advertised nationally and job interviews are ordinarily held outside of Assam. Many of the senior positions are held by men who have been transferred from other parts of the country by the same firm.

It is at the level of the employment of manual workers that local people do substantially better in the public sector firms. Migrants make up only 36 percent of the manual labor force in the public sector as against 65 percent in the private sector (for descriptions of four public sector firms that employ large numbers of Assamese see Appendix 2).

Several of the public sector firms have made a special effort to seek locally qualified personnel for jobs in the lower clerical positions. One company, for example, has a selection committee with a liason officer from the government of Assam seeking local people for such positions. At the more senior administrative and technical levels, the public sector firms all recruit nationally, that is, they hire personnel through national advertising and through the Union Public Service Commission with interviews in Delhi, Calcutta, and Madras and almost never in Gauhati.

Table 4a
Employees in Public Sector Firms by Occupational Classification and Place of Birth
(excluding banks)

Place of Birth

Occupational Classification	Assam (non-migrants)	Outside Assam (migrants)	Total
1. managerial	266 (31.1%)	590 (68.9%)	856 (100.0%)
2. clerical/ supervisory technical	563 (46.8%)	640 (53.2%)	1,203 (100.0%)
A. WHITE COLLAR	829 (40.3%)	1,230 (59.7%)	2,059 (100.0%)
3. skilled	3,801 (65.9%)	1,966 (34.1%)	5,767 (100.0%)
4. unskilled	2,420 (60.8%)	1,558 (39.2%)	3,978 (100.0%)
B. MANUAL	6,221 (63.8%)	3,524 (36.2%)	9,745 (100.0%)
C. TOTAL	7,050 (59.7%)	4,754 (40.3%)	11,804 (100.0%)

Table 4b
Employees in Private Sector Firms by Occupational Classification and Place of Birth

Place of Birth

Occupational Classification	Assam (non-migrants)	Outside Assam (migrants)	Total
1. managerial	216 (47.0%)	244 (53.0%)	460 (100.0%)
2. clerical/ supervisory technical	1,128 (54.6%)	939 (45.4%)	2,067 (100.0%)
A. WHITE COLLAR	1,344 (53.2%)	1,183 (46.8%)	2,527 (100.0%)
3. skilled	1,508 (42.1%)	2,073 (57.9%)	3,581 (100.0%)
4. unskilled	2,733 (29.9%)	6,413 (70.1%)	9,146 (100.0%)
B. MANUAL	4,241 (33.3%)	8,486 (66.7%)	12,727 (100.0%)
C. TOTAL	5,585 (36.6%)	9,669 (63.4%)	15,254 (100.0%)

In considering why public sector firms have been more successful in hiring local people for the lower-paid, less-skilled jobs than have the private firms, a number of differences should be kept in mind: wages are generally higher in the public sector; there is no practice of initial low-wage apprenticeships; there is no daily wage-labor recruitment at the gate; conditions of work are generally preferable in public than private sector firms; a higher proportion of the manual work force is engaged in jobs requiring some skills; and there is more security and less turnover in public sector jobs. These factors may explain why Assamese are more likely to seek recruitment in the public than private sector firms.

CHANGING PATTERNS OF EMPLOYMENT

What changes have taken place in the pattern of employment for various types of jobs, and to what extent can these changes be attributed to government policy?

There have been only modest increases in employment in the organized sector in Assam in recent years. The industrial slowdown that has affected the entire country since the late sixties has affected Assam as well. Private sector employment actually declined slightly between 1964 and 1969. Much of the new employment, especially in the private sector, represents replacements rather than expansion. There has been some increase in employment by the banks since they were nationalized. Some of the public sector firms are themselves relatively new and have recruited their labor force since 1960. It is interesting to note that the older firms (pre-1947) have a higher proportion of both unskilled (70 percent) and skilled (55 percent) workers who are migrants as compared with firms started after 1960 (where 46 percent of the unskilled and 39 percent of the skilled workers are migrants, Table 5).

Comparisons of place of birth of employees recruited within the last four years of the survey compared with the remainder of the labor force reveals a number of trends (Tables 6a and 6b):

1. There has been an overall decline in the proportion of migrant employment.
2. The decline has been primarily in manual jobs. Migrants make up 55 percent of recently employed unskilled workers as compared to an overall figure of 67 percent for those with more than four years of service.
3. The proportion of migrants among white-collar employees has not significantly changed, although there has been a slight increase in

Table 5

Employees by Occupational Classification, Migrant Status, and Founding Date of Firm

FOUNDING DATE OF FIRM

Occupational Classification	Pre-1947			1947-1959		
	Total Employees	Migrant Employees	% Age Migrants	Total Employees	Migrant Employees	% Age Migrants
1. managerial	445	230	51.7	330	176	53.3
2. clerical	1,736	653	37.6	1,523	471	30.9
A. WHITE COLLAR	2,181	883	40.5	1,853	647	34.9
3. skilled	2,146	1,175	54.8	754	301	39.9
4. unskilled	6,995	4,915	70.3	1,242	816	65.7
B. MANUAL	9,141	6,090	66.6	1,996	1,117	56.0
C. TOTAL	11,322	6,973	61.6	3,849	1,764	45.8

(continued on next page)

Table 5
(cont'd.)

FOUNDING DATE OF FIRM

Occupational Classification	Total Employees	1960-- Migrant Employees	% Age Migrants
1. managerial	898	615	68.5
2. clerical	1,467	792	54.0
A. WHITE COLLAR	2,365	1,407	59.5
3. skilled	7,111	2,785	39.2
4. unskilled	4,887	2,240	45.8
B. MANUAL	11,998	5,025	41.9
C. TOTAL	14,363	6,432	44.8

the proportion of migrants holding managerial positions.
4. The patterns are somewhat different between the public and private sector firms. In the public sector there has actually been an increase in the employment of migrants for white-collar positions, both managerial and clerical (75 percent and 65 percent respectively among recent appointments compared with 68 percent and 52 percent for all appointments in these categories, Tables 7a and 7b). In contrast in the private sector there has been an increase in the employment of local people for managerial positions, but not clerical workers (Tables 8a and 8b).

Among manual workers, there has been relatively little change in the public sector where local people have always been more numerous, but in the private sector 40 percent of the recently employed manual workers are locals, compared to 35 percent for the entire privately employed manual labor force.

Table 6a
Occupational Classification of Recent* Employees by Place of Birth

Occupational Classification	Place of Birth		
	Assam (non-migrants)	outside Assam (migrants)	Total
1. managerial	414 (35.6%)	750 (64.4%)	1,164 (100.0%)
2. clerical/ supervisory technical	1,263 (59.2%)	872 (40.8%)	2,135 (100.0%)
A. WHITE COLLAR	1,677 (50.8%)	1,622 (49.2%)	3,299 (100.0%)
3. skilled	3,446 (61.5%)	2,156 (38.5%)	5,602 (100.0%)
4. unskilled	3,039 (45.1%)	3,695 (54.9%)	6,734 (100.0%)
B. MANUAL	6,485 (52.6%)	5,851 (47.4%)	12,336 (100.0%)
C. TOTAL	8,162 (52.2%)	7,473 (47.8%)	15,635 (100.0%)

*refers to employees with 0-4 years length of service, save in cases of:

Oil and Natural Gas Commission	0-5 years
Sarda Plywood Factory	0-3 years
Woodcraft-Mariani	—
Punjab National Bank	0-2 years

There are three factors at work which encourage an increase in the employment of nonmigrants at both ends of the occupational spectrum apart from government policy. One is that there has been a substantial increase in the proportion of agricultural laborers in rural Assam, from 3.8 percent in 1961 to 10 percent in 1971, so that a larger number of rural Assamese are available for unskilled, low-wage occupations than previously. One test of this hypothesis is whether there is an increase in the movement of Assamese from the countryside to the city. In the past the rate of urbanization of the Assamese was considerably below that of the rest of the country. There is some preliminary evidence that this rate is changing, though we shall know better when detailed migration data are available.

A second factor is the increase in higher paying, low-skilled jobs in the public sector that are attractive to rural Assamese. To the extent

Table 6b
Occupational Classification of Employees with more than Four Years*
Service by Place of Birth

Place of Birth

Occupational Classification	Assam (non-migrants)	Outside Assam (migrants)	Total
1. managerial	238 (46.7%)	271 (53.3%)	509 (100.0%)
2. clerical/ supervisory technical	1,547 (59.7%)	1,044 (40.3%)	2,591 (100.0%)
A. WHITE COLLAR	1,785 (57.6%)	1,315 (42.4%)	3,100 (100.0%)
3. skilled	2,304 (52.3%)	2,105 (47.7%)	4,409 (100.0%)
4. unskilled	2,114 (33.1%)	4,276 (66.9%)	6,390 (100.0%)
B. MANUAL	4,418 (4019%)	6,381 (59.1%)	10,799 (100.0%)
C. TOTAL	6,203 (44.6%)	7,696 (55.4%)	13,899 (100.0%)

*save for cases listed in previous table where
length of service is above the limits previously
indicated

that wages in these positions have become competitive with wages in
the rural sector, we can expect Assamese to move at a greater rate
into the industrial labor force.

Third, there are now more educated Assamese available at the
clerical and managerial levels than ever before. Even without a
system of preferences we should expect some changes in the composition of this section of the labor force.

Undoubtedly, government pressure on employees to hire more
local people has made some difference. Public sector firms, most of
which are newer than the private firms, do not use labor contractors
and explicitly seek to hire local people. Private firms, responsive to
pressures, have made a greater effort to hire local people, especially
Assamese, for the more visible staff positions. But it is important to
note that policy is supportive of trends that are in any event already
at work. For a policymaker the politically most attractive policy is
one which requires individuals to do what they might do anyway, and
which the electorate welcomes. One is reminded—though perhaps
the analogy is too strong—of the comment of the king in St. Exupery's

Table 7a
Recent Employees in Public Sector Firms by Occupational Classification
and Place of Birth
(excluding banks)

Place of Birth

Occupational Classification	Assam (non-migrants)	Outside Assam (migrants)	Total
1. managerial	161 (24.7%)	491 (75.3%)	652 (100.0%)
2. clerical/ supervisory technical	254 (34.6%)	479 (65.4%)	733 (100.0%)
A. WHITE COLLAR	415 (30.0%)	970 (70.0%)	1,385 (100.0%)
3. skilled	2,502 (68.4%)	1,155 (31.6%)	3,657 (100.0%)
4. unskilled	1,620 (54.7%)	1,339 (45.3%)	2,959 (100.0%)
B. MANUAL	4,122 (62.3%)	2,494 (37.7%)	6,616 (100.0%)
C. TOTAL	4,537 (56.7%)	3,464 (43.3%)	8,001 (100.0%)

Table 7b
Employees in Public Sector Firms with Four or More Years of Service by
Occupational Classification and Place of Birth
(excluding banks)

Place of Birth

Occupational Classification	Assam (non-migrants)	Outside Assam (migrants)	Total
1. managerial	105 (51.5%)	99 (48.5%)	204 (100.0%)
2. clerical/ supervisory technical	309 (65.7%)	161 (34.3%)	470 (100.0%)
A. WHITE COLLAR	414 (61.4%)	260 (38.6%)	674 (100.0%)
3. skilled	1,299 (61.6%)	811 (38.4%)	2,110 (100.0%)
4. unskilled	800 (78.5%)	219 (21.5%)	1,019 (100.0%)
B. MANUAL	2,099 (67.1%)	1,030 (32.(%)	3,129 (100.0%)
C. TOTAL	2,413 (77.1%)	1,290 (22.9%)	3,703 (100.0%)

whimsical tale, *The Little Prince*, that he governs his happy kingdom by ordering his subjects to do what they want to do. In this instance, of course, nativist agitation and public policy combine to encourage employers to do what they can easily do, but which some employers might prefer not to do.

Indirect, Unintended, and Invisible Effects

Whenever policies are intended to single out a social or ethnic group for benefits, especially when these take the form (to use Nathan Glazer's phrase for such policies in the United States) of "affirmative discrimination," there are bound to be wide-ranging effects upon the behavior of those who do not benefit from the policy. Employers are asked to hire some people whom they might not have otherwise hired. Local people who do not belong to the preferred ethnic group fear that they are being discriminated against and members of the preferred ethnic group are likely to be angry at employers who do not satisfactorily adhere to the government's policies. There are many consequences of the policy that are not easily measurable or observable: the fears and anxieties of the minorities over employment and job promotions, and the educational and employment prospects of their children, fears of violence, and above all, a sense that their personal prospects rest not on their individual behavior and educational attainments, but on the prospects of the ethnic group to which they belong. When the objective of government is to change the income and status of one ethnic group in relation to another, one of the central effects of policy is that it reinforces ethnic group identities.

In the 1960s and early 1970s a number of major economic, political, and social changes took place in Assam that were reinforced by these policies. In one instance, as we shall see, the absence of change may also be partially related to these policies. One would be ill advised to say that each of these changes (or lack of change) was exclusively the consequence of government policy towards migrants. Indeed, most Assamese, including government policymakers, would deny any relationship between these policies and some of the trends described here, particularly when these trends were unwelcomed. The striking feature of the indirect effect of these policies is how difficult it is for either policymakers or citizens to perceive how policies intended to effect employment might influence the patterns of investment, or citizen loyalties, or any of a number of indirect and sometimes undesirable consequences. The "goods" of policy were visible; the "bads" were not.

Table 8a
Recent Employees in Private Sector Firms by Occupational Classification
and Place of Birth (excluding banks)

Occupational Classification	Place of Birth		
	Assam (non-migrants)	Outside Assam (migrants)	Total
1. managerial	143 (51.8%)	133 (48.2%)	276 (100.0%)
2. clerical/ supervisory technical	305 (56.9%)	231 (43.1%)	536 (100.0%)
A. WHITE COLLAR	448 (55.2%)	364 (44.8%)	812 (100.0%)
3. skilled	680 (42.3%)	928 (57.7%)	1,608 (100.0%)
4. unskilled	1,481 (38.6%)	2,356 (61.4%)	3,837 (100.0%)
B. MANUAL	2,161 (39.7%)	3,284 (60.3%)	5,445 (100.0%)
C. TOTAL	2,609 (41.7%)	3,648 ((58.3%)	6,257 (100.0%)

Table 8b
Employees in Private Sector Firms with Four or More Years Service by
Occupational Classification and Place of Birth
(excluding banks)

Occupational Classification	Place of Birth		
	Assam (non-migrants)	Outside Assam (migrants)	Total
1. managerial	73 (39.7%)	111 (60.3%)	184 (100.0%)
2. clerical/ supervisory technical	823 (53.8%)	708 (46.2%)	1,531 (100.0%)
A. WHITE COLLAR	896 (52.2%)	819 (47.8%)	1,715 (100.0%)
3. skilled	828 (42.0%)	1,145 (58.0%)	1,973 (100.0%)
4. unskilled	1,252 (23.6%)	4.057 (76.4%)	5,309 (100.0%)
B. MANUAL	2,080 (28.6%)	5,202 (71.4%)	7,282 (100.0%)
C. TOTAL	2,976 (33.1%)	6.021 (66.9%)	8,997 (100.0%)

Industrialists: Investment and Employment. In a society in which labor is not free to move from one locality to another, investors may consider the *quality* of the *local* labor force as an *additional* element in the determination of *where* to invest. Where capital is mobile, but labor is not, investors may be reluctant to invest in areas where there are excessive restrictions on the recruitment of manpower.

Whether these considerations have in fact slowed the pace of investment in Assam is difficult to discern. The remoteness of the region from the large urban markets, the difficulties in transportation and communication, and the lack of infrastructures that exist in some of the more developed states are all factors which affect the rate of investment. Some Marwari businessmen with investments in Assam, especially those who have experienced violence at the hands of street mobs, have said that they are reluctant to expand their investments in the state and have instead invested elsewhere in the country. Assam has not apparently succeeded in attracting any major new private investment. None of India's major industrial investors have entered the state. And in the central government there are some officials with the power to influence public sector locational decisions who view with concern the intense nativist sentiment, or as they put it "parochial" tendencies that have prevailed in Assam.

There is no conclusive evidence that the attacks against Marwari shopkeepers, the clashes between the Assamese and the Bengali Hindus, or the protectionist labor policies of the government, have actually slowed the rate of investment in the state. Even in the absence of these developments there are few incentives for private investment in Assam. At a minimum we can say only that these developments are among the factors which investors consider as they make their locational decisions.

Indigenous Minorities: Political Loyalties and Separatism. Since independence there has been a growing disaffection of indigenous non-Assamese toward the Assamese-dominated state government. When India became independent, Assam (as we noted earlier) included a number of districts outside the Brahmaputra valley in which non-Assamese predominated. The surrounding hill districts were populated by indigenous tribal peoples who were increasingly hostile to what they saw as a policy of Assamization on the part of the state government. The prescription of Assamese as an official language of administration, the movement toward the use of Assamese as the medium in the schools and colleges, and the system of employment preferences for Assamese, all tended to strengthen sentiment within the tribal population for separation. Separation seemed feasible to the tribals since most of them live in homogeneous, contiguous areas outside the valley. Moreover, since these regions border on neighboring countries—the NEFA regions to the north touches Tibet, the Garo and Khasi hills touch East Pakistan (now Bangladesh), the Mizo hills border on both Burma and East Pakistan, and the Naga Hills is next to Burma—the central government feared that separatist sentiment could be converted (by enemy arms) into secessionist movements—as indeed it was among the Nagas.

Sentiment for political separation increased in direct proportion to the growth of Assamese nationalism. Government efforts to spread the teaching of Assamese in the schools, to increase the proportion of ethnic Assamese in the administrative services, and to press for job preferences for Assamese were intended primarily to strengthen the position of the Assamese in relation to the Bengali Hindu community, but they also sharpened the cleavages between the Assamese and other indigenous peoples in the state. The result was that by 1963 the rebellious Naga tribes had successfully persuaded the central government to grant them their own state of Nagaland. The Garo, Khasi, and Jaintia tribes were given autonomous status as Meghalaya which was converted into a separate state in 1972. The Mizo hills district was separated from Assam in 1971 and was constituted as the union territory of Mizoram. And the North East Frontier Agency (NEFA) was converted into a union territory, then into the state of Arunachal Pradesh in 1972.

Migrant Settlers: Public Assimilation. The indirect effect most welcomed by the Assamese has been the increasing identification of some migrant communities with the political interests of the Assamese. As we indicated earlier there has emerged a symbiotic relationship between Bengali Muslims and Assamese Hindus. Fearful of losing their land or even being repatriated, many Bengali Muslims sought political protection by allying themselves with the Assamese-dominated Congress party. This alliance is quite striking in view of the historic antagonisms between these two communities prior to 1947.

The Bengali Muslims have provided more than political support in elections and in the legislatures. They have also publicly embraced the Assamese language. Though the law provides for the creation of primary schools with the mother tongue of the students as the medium, if requested by parents, Bengali Muslims have not objected to the establishment of Assamese medium schools in their localities.

Similarly, the tribal tea plantation workers who originate from southern Bihar and Orissa, have not objected to the government's school language policy. Even the adults in both communities have asserted that they have "switched" languages. The 1961 census reported an increase in the proportion of Assamese speakers and a decline in the proportion of Bengali speakers and tea plantation laborers who speak either tribal languages or Hindi. According to census officials, almost all of the 2.2 million Muslims of Bengali origin reported Assamese as their mother tongue. And among the estimated 1.5 million tea plantation workers and their families, only 275,000 reported a tribal language as their mother tongue.[10] Both groups, however, apparently continue to speak their own languages at home and within their own community. By supporting the Assamese Hindus in their anti-Bengali Hindu policies, other migrant communities, especially Bengali Muslims, have won protection from the government in the form of exemptions from potentially threatening policies.

CONCLUSION

From the middle of the nineteenth until well into the twentieth century a constant stream of migration into Assam from other states transformed its social structure and political life. The Assamese found themselves behind in the areas of education, urbanization, and industrialization, second (or third) to one or another migrant groups. As Assamese nationalism grew before independence, one of their greatest political problems was how to increase their numbers in the face of this influx. Since the Assamese could neither control the migration nor increase their own population, they looked upon boundary changes as a means of effecting their numerical ratio. Thus the redrawing of boundaries in 1874, 1905, 1912, 1947, and in the early 1970s were critical events for the Assamese. Most crucial of all, a turning point in the political life of the Assamese, was the partition of Assam in 1947 at the time of independence which reduced the Bengali population and thereby assured the Assamese Hindus of control over the government.

Once in political power the Assamese consolidated their control over the administrative apparatus, extended their domination of the educational system, and then sought to reach into the labor market for a larger share of employment in the modern, urban, organized sector.

Unable to close its borders and expel the migrants and their descendants as have done many sovereign states, the government of Assam turned primarily to educational, language, and employment policies as a means of reversing the status of those groups, most especially the Bengali Hindus, who held a dominant position in the modern, urban, organized sectors of the economy.

In recent years the position of the Assamese has improved, but primarily in unskilled jobs and only secondarily in the clerical and managerial positions sought by the growing Assamese middle classes. To what extent these changes are more than marginally the effects of government policy is problematic for there are economic and educational changes at work that point toward a larger role of the Assamese in the urban and industrial sectors. In any event, the change in *proportion* of jobs held by Assamese should be seen in the context of a low rate of investment in the state, only small increases in the size of the labor market, and growing overall unemployment. Government policy has affected—if it has had any effect on employment at all—only the *share* of jobs acquired by the Assamese within the organized sector. Unless the organized sector itself expands, the opportunities for an increasingly educated and urbanized Assamese labor force are likely to remain limited.

But perhaps the most important impact of the policies described here has been not on the migration process, or even on the economic opportunities of the nonmobile local population, but rather on the process of *incorporation* of migrants, their descendants, and of the non-Assamese local tribal people. The latent function of these policies has been nothing less than that of transforming social relationships among ethnic groups so as to give the hitherto numerous but economically and socially subordinate Assamese a larger role in the economic order, the occupational structure, and in the social hierarchy. The older notion of a social system made up of discrete ethnic groups, each functioning with its own economic sphere, each pursuing its own distinctive cultural life, in a hierarchal social order in which the local Assamese population was by no means at the top, has given way to the notion that the Assamese should be politically, economically, culturally, and socially elevated, and that other communities must modify their public behavior to accommodate themselves to the supremacy of the Assamese. The policies described here are unmistakable signals to those who would migrate to the state, as well as to those minorities who reside in the state, that the Assamese have redefined the conditions under which they can remain. As a result some potential migrants may not come, a few may leave, some may become separatists, but most of the minorities will have little choice but to adapt themselves publicly to the new Assamese notions of integration.

APPENDIX 1
FIRMS THAT ARE LESS THAN ONE-THIRD ASSAMESE

Assam Railways and Trading Co., founded in 1881, has the lowest percent of Assamese (9 percent) of the twenty-eight companies. A large English-owned firm employing 4,633 workers, it has tradition-ally recruited a substantial portion of its unskilled labor force from among Nepalis and Telugus (from Andhra). This pattern continues. During the year prior to the survey the firm hired 537 workers, 447 of whom were born outside of the state. Its administrative personnel are almost all non-Assamese.

Woodcraft-Mariani employs 538 workers, all but a handful of whom (19 percent) are migrants. The workers come primarily from East Pakistan, Bihar, West Bengal, and U.P. (in that order). Thirty-six percent of the workers are Hindi speakers, 35 percent Bengali, and only 18 percent are Assamese. None of its workers have been hired through the employment exchanges although, like other companies, it notifies the employment exchange of openings.

Indian Airlines Corporation is one of a handful of public firms (apart from banks) that employs few Assamese. Only 11 percent of its small staff of 175 are Assamese. Forty-four percent are Bengali, many of whom were born in Assam, though the largest number are from East Pakistan. There are frequent transfers of employees to Assam from other states following a practice of centralized recruitment and trans-fers. More than a fifth of the staff (22 percent) is neither Assamese, Bengali, nor Hindi speaking, having been recruited from all over the country.

The Sarda Plywood Factory employs most of its laborers from among the Hindi-speaking (59 percent) migrants from Bihar, U.P., and Rajasthan, hired at the rate of Rs 2.75 a day through labor contrac-tors. The firm employs 190 workers and has a high turnover. The head office is located in Calcutta.

Assam Hardboards, with 359 workers, is another low technology, traditional firm with a high turnover and a large migrant labor force.

More than half of its employees (57 percent) have been in Assam less than five years: most come from Bihar or U.P. In the best-paid office jobs with salaries ranging from Rs 500 to 749, only 25 percent were born in Assam.

Woodcraft Plywood Factory-Joypore is another small factory with 346 workers, more than half of whom are drawn from Bihar and U.P. Like many of the plywood factories, this factory also hires its workers through labor contractors. Some of its manpower needs are seasonal. Workers are paid a minimum wage of Rs 2.75 a day. The government employment exchanges are not relied upon for hiring workers. Like Sarda Plywood, its head office is in Calcutta.

The Assam Oil Company, founded in 1900, employs 4,018 workers and has a low turnover rate compared with the companies thus far described. No contract labor is employed. However, more than half of the labor force is migrant, and of those who were born in Assam (44 percent), only a little more than half (56 percent) are Assamese. Nearly a third (31 percent) of the labor force in this company is Bengali, half of whom are locally born. A substantial portion of the labor force is also imported from Nepal.

India Carbon, a small, private firm employing 267 persons with its head office in Calcutta, largely employs Hindi-speaking workers from Bihar and U.P. Originally the manual laborers were engaged through labor contractors but this practice is no longer followed. The firm currently has a low labor turnover rate, even, surprisingly, among the unskilled laborers where 65 percent have held their jobs for five to ten years. The firm reports that none of its employees from outside Assam was recruited by direct advertisement or through the employment exchange.

The United Bank of India, a nationalized bank employing 857 workers with its head office in Calcutta, has comparatively few migrants (30 percent), but most of its locally recruited labor force (61 percent) are Bengalis. Many of the migrants are Bengalis, born in East Pakistan, long-time residents in Assam, many of whom worked elsewhere before joining the bank. Of its 857 employees, only twenty-five were recruited through the employment exchanges.

Everest Cycles is another firm hiring unskilled manual workers from Bihar, U.P., and Rajasthan. Sixty percent of its labor force are migrants, almost all from the Hindi-speaking states. The director reported that the casual and unskilled labor are recruited at the gate. "Local people do not want to stick to such jobs," he said, explaining why the unskilled workers are not Assamese.

Steelworth-Gauhati is one of three branches of this firm in Assam, the others being in Tezpur and Tinsukia. They each employ a few hundred workers (255 at Gauhati), with their unskilled workers from the Hindi-speaking states. Almost all of the Assamese-speaking workers are paid under Rs 250 a month. The Bengali workers, many of whom have the higher paid jobs, tend to be hired locally (nineteen out of its twenty-two Bengali workers).

Associated Industries, a company with a chemical unit and a textile spinning mill, employs 717 workers in its two plants. Two-thirds of its workers (66 percent) are migrants. The migrants appear to be hired locally "at the gate." The firm hires workers as apprentices. They are paid Rs 1.50 per day for three months, then Rs 2.00 per day, and after six months, Rs 2.50. Few Assamese apply. Among the skilled workers, too, migrants predominate (72 percent).

The Punjab National Bank, a nationalized bank with regional head-quarters in Calcutta, employs only 101 workers. Its national head-quarters used to be in Lahore, but then it subsequently moved to Delhi. It is an old bank founded in 1896. Its staff, mainly clerical and administrative people, are about half from Assam and half from outside. Nearly a third (32 percent) are Assamese, about another third (31 percent) are Hindi speakers, mainly from Bihar, and about a quarter (26 percent) are Bengalis, more than half of whom are locally born. It is interesting to note that this is the only bank with a large Hindi-speaking staff. Most of the other banks have a larger Bengali staff, and a correspondingly smaller Hindi staff (usually less than 10 percent Hindi mother tongue), reflecting their closer connections with Calcutta.

Assam Match Company, another lumber-based industry employing Hindi-speaking manual laborers, has its head office outside Assam, and has few Assamese-speaking people in the top pay scales. An unusual feature of this firm, however, is that it employs a large locally recruited Bengali labor force. More than a third of its 1,790 workers (35 percent) are Bengali speakers, and the bulk of these are from Assam. The remaining Bengalis are largely migrants from East

Pakistan. This firm does no labor contracting, but it has a continuous stream of workers from Bihar who constitute nearly a quarter of the work force.

Assam Cotton Mills employs migrants for two-thirds of its 750 workers. The firm also uses an apprenticeship system. New workers are paid Rs 1.54 a day for three months, with increases thereafter. Workers are recruited directly from Bihar or U.P. rather than through employment exchanges. About a third of the workers are local-born, almost all Assamese. The Bengalis who hold the higher paid clerical and administrative jobs are almost all from West Bengal. It should be noted that all four of the company directors live in Calcutta.

APPENDIX 2
PUBLIC SECTOR EMPLOYERS OF ASSAMESE

The Oil and Natural Gas Commission, with 3,788 workers, employs 68 percent of its labor force locally, almost all (96 percent) being Assamese. But of those born in Assam, 95 percent are in the lowest wage categories, earning less than Rs 250 per month.

The Regional Research Laboratory, under the Council of Scientific Industrial Research, employs 59 percent of its small staff of 259 locally, and of these 95 percent are Assamese, but again almost all are in the lowest wage group. Only 18 percent of its executives were born in Assam.

The Fertilizer Corporation of India, an employer of 2,035, is 62 percent locally recruited, 88 percent of whom are Assamese speakers. This firm has made a special effort to hire its technical work force locally. More than half of its technical personnel (52 percent) are Assamese. At the managerial level, however, the staff is still predominantly nonlocal. Only 16 percent of the class-1 (managerial) jobs are held by personnel born in Assam recruited in the last year of the survey, and only 6 percent who have been with the firm for two to four years. Again, Assamese predominate at the lowest income positions.

The Food Corporation of India is more than half Assamese (52 percent) and a quarter (26 percent) Bengali, with a comparatively small Hindi labor force (11 percent). The reason for the high proportion of Bengalis and Assamese is that more than two-thirds of its labor force

(68 percent) is recruited locally. While much of the senior staff is recruited outside of Assam, the middle-level positions are predominantly from Assam. One reason is that many of the employees of the Food Corporation are on deputation from the government of Assam. Since state government employees are recruited locally and are more likely to be Assamese than Bengali, this is reflected in the composition of the Food Corporation. Ninety-seven percent of the locally recruited staff is either Assamese (75 percent) or Bengali (22 percent).

NOTES

1. I wish to acknowledge with gratitude the assistance of Martin Slater and Robert Berrier, both graduate students in the Department of Political Science at M.I.T., for preparing the preliminary statistical analysis presented in this paper. I should also like to acknowledge with appreciation the Ford-Rockefeller Foundation Research Program on Population and Development Policy and the National Institute for Child Health and Human Development for funding this study.

2. *Economic Characteristics of Population, Selected Tables*, Census of India, 1971, Series 1-India, paper 3, 1972.

3. Employment data from *Employment Review, Assam State*, the Directorate of Employment and Craftsman Training, Research and Statistical Cell, Gauhati, Assam, March 1974.

4. *Report of the National Commission on Labour*, Government of India Ministry of Labour, Employment, and Rehabilitation, New Delhi, 1969. The recommendations of the commission on the demands of "sons of the soil" can be found on pp. 74-78.

5. *National Integration Council Proceedings*, New Delhi, March 20, 1969.

6. According to figures published by the Labor ministry, nearly sixty percent of the notifications of vacancies to the exchanges resulted in direct placements. In 1968, for example, 3,161,000 persons were registered in the country's 405 exchanges; 551,000 vacancies were notified and 319,000 placements were effected. In Assam, however, only 3,751 placements were made for 8,623 vacancies, a placement/vacancy record of 43 percent. Only 6 percent of those registered found jobs through the exchanges in Assam that year, as compared with 10 percent nationally. *Report of the National Commission on Labour*, Appendix 1.

7. *Report of the Employment Review Committee*, Third Report, 1973 (Assembly Secretariat, Gauhati, Assam, December 1973), p. 357.

8. *Report of the Employment Review Committee*, vols. 1, 2, and 3 (first, second, and third reports) 1973.

9. The high migration rate into Assam's urban areas is reflected in the sex ratio. The sex ratio of Assam's urban areas (in 1971) was 665 women per thousand males, while in Gauhati, Assam's largest city, only 39 percent of the population was female. *Census of India, General Population Tables*, Series 3 — Assam, Part II-A, 1971.

10. The 1891 census reported 1.4 million Assamese speakers in the state.

In 1961 there were 6.7 million. Had the Assamese speaking population increased at the same rate as the Indian population as a whole, the Assamese population in 1961 would have been 2.8 million. The difference — 3.9 million — represents a crude figure as to how many people may have switched to Assamese, if not at home, at least for public purposes.

PART II
CONTEXTS OF POLICY

6

POLICY IN CONTEXT:
THE INTENDED AND UNINTENDED IN MIGRATION POLICY IN THE THIRD WORLD

Joel S. Migdal

Politics and population have been intertwined throughout history, and numerous examples abound of rulers who have influenced or attempted to influence the size and location of their populations. Legislated minimal marriage ages or the requirement of lords' permission for serfs to marry has significantly affected fertility in numerous societies.[1] The Old Testament tells us of the alarm of the Egyptian pharoah over the population growth of the Israelite slaves and the legislation to kill all male Israelite babies.[2] Movements of entire populations were stimulated by war and conquest. More selective migration was the aim of policies enacted by the rulers of Muslim cities who carefully balanced the ethnic composition of their cities by controlling in- and out-migration. These rulers jealously guarded their power by rendering to urban living a state of temporariness and by maintaining ethnic fragmentation which prevented the formation of coalitions against them.[3]

In certain cases policies were directly intended to affect the size and location of populations, but historically populations were most changed by policies which had unintended population effects, what have been called indirect policies. As John D. Montgomery says in the opening paper of this volume, what is peculiarly modern in current population policy is the transformation of these unintended population effects into immediate objects of political scrutiny, problems that demand head-on political action. In the Third World particularly during the last generation a sense of political crisis has begun to surround issues of fertility and migration,[4] and hosts of policies have been generated to cope with population issues.

Policy scientists have often tended to analyze and formulate population policies for Third World societies in a political vacuum, focusing on techniques and ignoring the political context within which policies are first formulated and later implemented. The contention in this paper is that for the policy sciences to begin to understand past policy failures in the realm of population issues, policy scientists must look beyond organizational mechanics. There must be an examination of policy histories in a framework that accounts for the particular political problems and challenges faced by Third World countries in the twentieth century. Specifically, this essay will explore a set of political problems and obstacles that are related to the ability of Third World states to "affect" their societies with migration policies in the direction intended by their governments. It will be argued that certain political preconditions for effective population policies have not been met in much of the Third World resulting in "countereffects" and other unanticipated and undesired outcomes.

Of course, Third World states vary tremendously among themselves, and there even has been a move to differentiate categorically between economically developing or emerging states (Third World) and poorer or nondeveloping states (Fourth World). Nevertheless, there are political problems and challenges in the twentieth century that are common to a broad range of states. At the risk of overgeneralization, then, and fully cognizant that the conclusions of this essay will apply to some countries much better than to others, I will go on to build a framework which outlines some of the political realities shared by many countries in Asia, Africa, and Latin America.

APPROACHES TO MIGRATION AND MIGRATION POLICIES: PERSONAL MOTIVATION AND SOCIAL STRUCTURE

Migration has grown in importance to policymakers and scientists as its visibility has grown. With the shift from predominantly rural-to-rural migration patterns to rural-to-urban ones and with the growth in the overall rate of migration, numerous large cities in the world have been surrounded by mushrooming shantytowns. The populations of these sprawling tin-hut neighborhoods have posed new demands on very scarce resources. Often the patterns and results of migration in the Third World have differed tremendously from past patterns in Western countries.[5] Urban migration, for example, has not represented the same intensity of break with rural society as had occurred in many parts of the West. First, movement to cities has not resulted in a depopulation of rural areas. High rates of natural increase in the rural areas have meant that the societies are still predominantly rural even though, paradoxically, cities are often growing at twice the rate of nineteenth century European cities. Second, new urban dwellers have often been maintaining kinship and other ties in their former villages. Acceptance of so-called urban values in such cases has been much more tentative than one might otherwise have expected.[6]

Many of the studies on the process of voluntary migration have shared two characteristics in the direction of their research. First, much of the focus of concern has been on the micro-level. Studies of motivational factors have been numerous in both international and internal voluntary migration. G. Beijer writes that the factors which stand out in motivational research are: ambition, better job opportunities; hope, better future for the children; courage, for a new beginning, or zest of adventure; and better economic opportunities.[7] Migration to the cities has not been characterized by down-and-outers who lack means, skill, and education. More frequently it is the young person not from the bottom rungs of the community who chooses to make the big move.

Second, in cases where such micro-level research has been joined to that on the macro-level, the concern has been preponderantly for economic variables. The individual has been seen as economic man and his rationality in choosing among various economic alternatives is a prime assumption in such works.[8] For example, Stouffer, in a widely quoted article, developed the concept of "intervening opportunities," stating that "the number of migrants is directly proportional to the number of opportunities in the distance, inversely proportionate to the number of intervening variables."[9] When other social structural variables have been used, they often are linked to both the motivational micro factors and the economic opportunity macro variables. Calvin Goldscheider, for example, writes, "The importance of the economic motive in both internal and external migration is well established. It is no less true for Africa. Nevertheless, we have specified the mechanism that ties the economic motive to the social structure, particularly the role of knowledge of opportunities, the relationship to education, and the pattern of chain migration . . . ."[10]

Policy scientists have utilized these motivational and economic characteristics of migration research as a starting point for their own works stressing governmental action. Their studies have started with the assumption of a rational economic man weighing various alternatives and have emphasized that policies must intervene in the social structure so as to change the calculus of economic incentives. The differential inducements of the areas of origin (often rural) and the areas of destination (often urban) as well as the complex of intervening obstacles have been singled out as points of reference for policymakers.[11]

To intervene in the migration process, then, has come to mean to accept the economic motivation of the individual as a given and to use policy as an instrument to change the relative economic attractiveness of various locations. Attractiveness might be enhanced objectively through such policies as selective investment programs or subjectively by such campaigns as public relations programs which increase knowledge about existing opportunities. Purely restrictive measures on movement are often condemned for not dealing with the "heart" of the matter, the link of motivation to economic opportunities. It is assumed that policies which do not confront rational economic motives and rely on restriction or coercion will face unrelenting resistance and subversion. In addition, there is the disturbing moral element involved with selective restrictions on people's movement. Stanislaw H. Wellisz writes of Asia that "what causes migration is the difference between rural and urban livelihood opportunities (real or expected). The fact that migration into urban areas continues shows that there is a continuing difference between levels. If restrictive measures were taken to slow down migration, the potential migrants would be condemned to a lower living standard."[12] Despite these sentiments, bulldozing still seems to be the major method used to deal with the problems generated by growing shantytowns.[13]

THE IMPORTANCE OF POLITICAL VARIABLES

Of late there has been some questioning of widely accepted assumptions, particularly if continuing urban migration is really always explained by differences in living standards between those of the rural cohorts from which in-migrants to the city come and those of urban dwellers.[14] Viewing individual motivation solely on the basis of economic gains and losses leads to oversimplification. A purely economic analysis of motivation glosses over the host of other personal values and environmental constraints which *combine* with economic factors in influencing human behavior and shaping personal choices and preferences.

The emphasis on motivation in primarily economic terms, for example, may obscure the crucial role of political variables, both in the migration process itself and, more importantly, in the realm of migration policy making. To give an obvious illustration, economic opportunities have long been associated with voluntary international migrations. Between 1846 and 1924, it has been estimated, fifty million people emigrated from Europe.[15] Economic motivation notwithstanding, it would be impossible for a similar percentage or even a similar number of the African, Asian, or Latin American populations to emigrate today because of *political* barriers that restrict their entry into other countries.[16] Conversely, political factors may induce migration even when economic factors act in the opposite direction. This has been the case, for example, in many of the international population shifts in the Middle East since World War II.

The emphasis upon motivation on the micro-level and economic structure on the macro-level in studies of migration has in many cases had the unfortunate effect of excluding political variables from the theoretical focus. Many analyses have greatly underemphasized the complex political environment within which policies are devised and then implemented—particularly in the context of the political problems facing many Third World states. The political milieu, the macro-level structure and substance of states, has a decisive effect upon the micro-level day-to-day programs and planning of governments, but the connections between these levels has remained analytically vague and relatively unexplored.

After almost two decades of assuming that social modernization and political development would be coming to Third World states through some undefined evolutionary process, social science theoreticians have begun to doubt their own assumptions and to call into question the very terms they had employed. Instead of modernization and development, we find talk of negative development,[17] decay,[18] dysrhythmic processes,[19] and enduring neopatrimonialism.[20] Although there have yet to be any comprehensive theoretical attempts to explain this unexpected unfolding of events, we can identify some of the key failures. On the political level, two distinct but sequentially related processes had been seen as the key to successful development. First was a process of centralization. This process involves a concentration of power in the state, stripping lords, *caciques*, corporate villages, tribal chiefs, and others of the ability to perform key political functions autonomously and claiming sole jurisdiction of the functions for the institutions of the state.[21] Such tasks include everything from running the postal service to collecting taxes to controlling the means of violence (the military and police). Centralization, in short, means that the state defines and applies a uniform system of justice or a set of preferred outcomes[22] within its boundaries. Performance of political functions and public administrative tasks depends solely on one's connection to the state.

Second was a process of political integration. Here the state uses its new concentrated (centralized) powers to incorporate the participation of ever increasing numbers of its population into its array of institutions. Integration involves participation of the population in the state's organizations and procedures as well as an acceptance, in broad terms, of the values or preferred outcomes put forth by those institutions. It implies the demise of sectors challenging the central values of the state and the elimination of the distinction between the Great Tradition and the Little Tradition.[23] Also implied is the weakening of other primordial ties such as those based on ethnicity, kinship, or locale.

Other simultaneous processes in the society were thought to be extant which would stimulate centralization and integration. Economic change and Westernization, for example, were seen as powerful forces weakening the old local political entities and easing the path to centralization. Social mobilization meant the breaking of old value commitments and thus, it was thought, opening people to the commitments, i.e., the preferred outcomes, put forth by the institutions of the state.[24] Social mobilization and modernization were seen to be mutually reinforcing, as well, and their simultaneous growth was thought to presage political centralization.

For better or worse, depending on one's value standpoint, few states in the Third World have had unequivocal success in achieving the scenario of the social scientists. Bureaucracies have grown but, as Fred W. Riggs writes, political organs are weak and there is a "lack of balance between political policymaking institutions and bureaucratic policy-implementing structures."[25] Some functions have been appropriated by the state while many others effectively have not. Old political forces, from local bosses to "archaic" kinship groups, have proved exceedingly resilient and adaptable. And, even more startling, some such local forces have *gained* in strength, and *new* ones have arisen. Forces as diverse as local moneylenders[26] and tribal groups[27] have found that the changes of the twentieth century may work to their advantage instead of spelling their demise. They have continued to establish power bases autonomous of those of the state and to perform a variety of political functions independently of state control.

Political integration at a state level has been even more elusive than centralization.[28] Participation in the state's organizations and procedures has been partial and intermittent, in most cases, and acceptance of the values or preferred outcomes of the state has been on a superficial, expressive level, at best. Many Third World states, then, have come to be characterized by relative weakness because of their inability to displace other internal political forces and because of their failure to make their values the accepted values of the society.

The existence of such a political environment is important not only at an abstract, theoretical level but has vast implications on a concrete policymaking level for issues like migration, as well. In the next section, we shall look at the repercussions of the failure of political centralization and integration and their relations to various policy sequences. The major hypotheses are that the absence of the precondition of centralization means that the state lacks necessary autonomy and coherence in policymaking and is hampered in coalition building; and the absence of the precondition of extensive political integration affects social response, resulting in maldistributions in the outputs of policies and uneven participation in the components of government programs.

THE POLICYMAKING CONTEXT

Policymaking takes place within a highly politicized environment. It demands choosing a particular direction for action when various groups in the society might prefer action in different directions while other groups want no action at all. In terms of migration, it means trying to influence the rate, direction, or content of population movement—which translates into getting people to do things they otherwise would not have done. Policymaking is thus a direct stimulant to political mobilization. For example, a program designed to precipitate migration to an area short of industrial manpower might call for an investment in housing, education, and other services in that area. That program might be supported by industrial employers from that area and by representatives of the most mobile ethnic groups in the country but simultaneously might be opposed by industrialists in other areas who seek programs oriented towards their needs, by the dominant ethnic group in the area which seeks to maintain its numerical advantage, and by rural landowners who fear losing portions of their labor force. Effective policymaking, then, requires the power to overcome newly mobilized oppositional forces as well as the inertial forces against which the policy is designed to "intervene."

Two interrelated sources of such power can be identified. The first is the degree of autonomy and coherence the state has, indicating the extent to which it can devise and enact policies *in the face of varying constellations of social forces over different issues*. Second is the coalition of supportive social forces which can be mobilized by the state *on any particular issue*. And yet these are precisely the elements in the promotion of policies which may be sorely lacking in Third World countries.

Autonomy and coherence of the state are qualities gained in the process of political centralization. Both result when forces in the society are reduced from competitors over the jurisdiction of political functions in the society to competitors over the distribution of values in particular policy areas, *once the jurisdiction is recognized as that of the state*.[29] In a centralized state, policies are not isolated phenomena. The administrative expansion that accompanies direct political policymaking into new areas of political concern for the state is an integrated process. That is, there is a high intercorrelation among successful and effective policies in different spheres (see fig. 1). They are enacted and administered by various agencies that all draw their strength, not only from their own organizations and resources, but from the power already concentrated by the state, from the legitimacy accrued to the state, and from the tie of agencies to each other as related arms of the state's will. All these elements add up to the coherence of the state. Direct policies call for a variety of accompanying and overlapping services.

The greater the success of prior programs, the more of a reservoir of services, personnel, and machinery the new policy has to draw upon; and then the smaller the likelihood of a constellation of social forces blocking any particular policy. The autonomy of the state indicates the ability of its institutions to function independently of a particular array of social groupings.

Administrative expansion that comes without the precondition of sufficient political centralization, as has occurred in many Third World countries, leads simply to swollen bureaucracies rather than to a process of increasing autonomy and coherence. Larger bureaucracies or adoption of new administrative techniques in and of themselves do not supply a source of power leading to consistently successful policy interventions in key social processes.

Figure 1

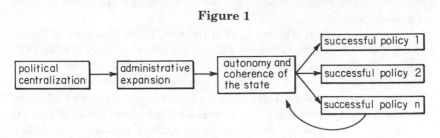

(Although there are a number of feedback loops in this process, I have chosen to depict just one because of its particular importance; that is, the more the state achieves success in its programs, the more its goals can be pursued increasingly independent of other social forces with different goals.)

Besides increasing autonomy and coherence of the state, the second source of power drawn upon to devise and implement policies is the supportive coalition of forces which the state can muster. Coalition building in Third World societies, however, may be particularly difficult. When one speaks of the process of coalition building, one usually makes a major pluralistic assumption that there is a host of overlapping interests among groups and that these interests are felt in varying degrees of intensity. It is further assumed that conflict over particular interests is mitigated by shared values in other areas and that there are numerous avenues of social contact for individuals and groups to learn of both their areas of conflict and areas of consensus with others.

No matter how valid one may consider these assumptions for highly industrialized societies, there are reasons why they are invalid for many Third World societies. First, the rapid social structural change that has been occurring in many of these societies during the last generation or more may leave societal groups without institutional nexuses to foster contact with one another. For example, instead of a single national market in which all participate fully and which creates a common set of symbols familiar to all, there may be fragmented markets consisting of a major national market but also of local peasant markets with only tangential ties for the peasants to the national market. In other areas as well, institutional discontinuities may create gaps in social communication and in material interests between groups as diverse as desert bedouins and urban industrialists.[30] Discontinuities may be particularly severe in the political realm where lack of centralization results in separate islands of political communication with extremely limited structural ties among the islands. Such gaps make it nearly impossible to build bridging coalitions.

Second, the social fragmentation in some countries among tribal groups, ethnic communities, linguistic groups, etc., may simply preclude extensive coalition-building which is based on *interest* formation. Existing mobilization systems may tend to accentuate communal lines of cleavage only. Although there may be some instances when this is of use to the state in coalition-building, it can also turn out to be a veto power for communal groups against the state's organizations that are attempting to forge a single society while they simultaneously must deal with issues such as fertility and migration, having vast cross-communal implications. Communal fragmentation simply exacerbates the difficulties of a political environment already characterized by structural discontinuities. All this is not to say that existing coalitions are always ethnically based. It is simply that interest-based coalitions are rare because of the nature of the social structure.

To summarize briefly, we have seen that the political and social conditions existing in many Third World countries may make it more difficult to promote public policies than in more politically centralized states. The political context inhibits sequential processes involving the development and implementation of effective and far-reaching direct population policies. Coalition-building in the promotion of policies is exceedingly difficult in societies with great institutional discontinuities stemming from rapid change and in societies plagued by communal fragmentation. Although governmental elites may be small in number and homogeneous in background, they frequently face real difficulties in mobilizing other societal elites in support of their programs. Actual application of a policy once formulated also suffers in states without significant autonomy and coherence. Devising and implementing effective policies are possible when the state has access to sufficient sources of power—and the precondition for such access is a significant degree of political centralization.

In addition to political centralization, political integration has been noted as another of the fundamental political challenges facing many Third World countries. Difficulties in achieving desired social goals through governmental policies are intimately involved with a faltering process of political integration as well. One aspect of the difficulty in achieving political integration is that mass participation in the state's organizations and procedures is incomplete and intermittent. As a result, social response to governmental policies may become extremely problematical. First, there may be huge differentials among groups in their regular contact and interaction with state institutions which means that the outputs of governmental programs will be distributed unevenly within the target population.[31] Rates of acceptance in terms of behavioral modifications and adoption of policy norms among groups will tend to be highly skewed.

Once again, in highly fragmented and delicately balanced politics, such variations in social response to governmental programs may create a tremendous strain.[32] Due to their past participation in state organizations, groups already high in status are usually in the best position to take advantage of the services and benefits stemming from new policies. In Bogotá, Colombia, for example, the Department of Planning of the Special District of Bogotá sought to deal with the problems stemming from *tugurios* and *barrios clandestinos*, the shantytowns in and around the city. The result, however, was that the urban renewal programs ended up benefitting the elites and the upper middle classes through new luxury housing, a clean-up of the central city blight, and escalating land values in the central business district.[33]

Those who are best placed also stand to gain most from policies aimed at stimulating migration to a frontier area. Tension can result among resentful have-not groups which lack immediate access to information about services and amenities and thus do not benefit as much as other groups. In Israel, for instance, population dispersal to previously uninhabited territory was accomplished by the establishment of new *moshavim* (sing., *moshav*) for new immigrants to Israel. These were cooperative agricultural villages that gave the small-holder members opportunity to own their land. Much bitterness and factionalism emerged in the 1950s as groups, particularly those composed of immigrants from other Middle Eastern countries lacking political connections or knowledge, felt they were assigned much worse village lands than those assigned to European immigrants. Another example is in India where we find tensions close to the surface concerning policies that lead indirectly through population movements to a change in the ethnic composition of the local population.[34]

A second difficulty connected to a lack of integration is that *aspects* of policies may be utilized by the population but the overall goals of the policies are nevertheless subverted. Certain policies, for example, may be designed to precipitate migration to an area in order to stimulate local and outside investment and permanent settlement in the area. Migrants, however, may maintain their primary commitment to their extended families who remain at "home" and migrate only as a means to gain short-term rewards. Cash, for example, may immediately be sent back to the family in the area of origin.[35] Thus, policy objectives may ultimately be subverted by an outflow of capital from precisely that area in which the government sought investment. And there might be a resultant counterstream of migration toward the flow of money sent "home."[36] Of course, all governments face difficulties in implementing programs because the values embodied in the programs differ from individuals' goals (in the United States, one immediately thinks of Prohibition). Success of any policy depends on compatibility between a significant segment of the target and interested population and the main elements of the policy. It is the wide divergence in basic values between large segments of the population and states in the Third World that undermines many governmental policies.

THE MIX OF DIRECT AND INDIRECT POLICIES: THE ADMINISTRATIVE COUNTEREFFECT

As already suggested, the political milieu that characterizes many Third World states—particularly the low levels of political centralization and integration—does not necessarily preclude policymaking on population issues. On the contrary, policies *are* formulated and implemented but with often unexpected results because of the weakness of the state vis-à-vis local political forces and the nature of political participation in state institutions. This section will analyze the nature of some of the unintended and undesired effects of migration policy, particularly what I call the "administrative countereffect."

It is well known that the complexity and unwieldiness of state organizations may result in the state's simultaneously pursuing contradictory goals. Policies of one agency may inadvertently come into conflict with policies of another. Clusters of policies may attack a problem not only in a single direction but may clash as different directions are taken. The Zambian case provides a telling example of such a clash of policies. Robert H. Bates and Bruce W. Bennett have attempted to assess the effects of governmental programs on rural to urban migration in Zambia. They found that government expenditures on agriculture and, even more importantly, on rural health facilities, have small but significant retarding effects on urban migration. They write, however, that "on balance, it is likely that the government, despite its goals, has done more to promote the exodus than to stem it by concentrating its expenditures so heavily in the urban zones in Zambia."[37]

A related administrative countereffect may be generated by changing conditions in the rural areas themselves. In states attempting to increase their impact on outlying areas, one of the possible results of sending new personnel to such areas to deal with issues of new political concern is the transformation of such personnel into new patrons.[42] After the 1952 revolution in Bolivia, for example, the Nationalist Revolutionary Movement (MNR) laid the basis for new syndical organizations among peasants. What emerged was a situation in which the secretary-generals of the syndicates became increasingly like the displaced *hacendados*.[43] In postrevolutionary Mexico as well, *caciques* (local autocrats) have wielded considerable arbitrary power partly due to their own client relationship to party or government functionaries. Lack of coherence of a state's machinery translates itself on a concrete level into the absence of adequate supervision of bureaucrats and other functionaries in local areas and a proliferation of corrupt practices. The resources and sanctions that such personnel control enable them to make demands on the local population.

Although such a situation exists in many urban areas as well, the remoteness of rural areas often makes them even more susceptible to unregulated personnel sent from the capital city. A result might be, then, that the very people who are supposed to administer programs stemming urban migration are making the rural areas less secure through their capriciousness. One of the constant themes echoed by peasants in Latin America and Asia is the insecurity of participation in the organizations and procedures that are challenging the old lords and patrons.[44] To such peasants, lack of coherence on the part of the state does not only mean different agencies working in opposite directions. More importantly to them, it means bureaucrats working at cross-purposes with the policies they are assigned to administer or creating a political milieu in which the realization of the policy goals becomes impossible. In India, for example, the government adopted a policy to sell fertilizer on a limited basis to peasants at below-market prices. The aim was to make fertilizer available even to the poorest farmers in the village. In interviews with me, poor peasants related how, in practice, bribery and kickbacks resulted in those best able to afford fertilizer receiving the rations of those least able to afford the market prices.

The entry of the state into new arenas of political concern formerly relegated to particular social institutions, such as the family, may create a whole array of unintended outcomes. As the state succeeds in stripping these institutions of their former functions, a process of social disintegration takes place. There are fewer reasons for individuals to maintain their old commitments anymore.[45] A migration policy intended to stem population movement, then, may be part of an administrative expansion that is breaking down old commitments and thus causing social disintegration. Goldscheider has noted, however, that there is an inverse relationship between social integration and migration.[46] Thus a policy designed to *curb* migration also becomes part of a process causing a decline in the level of social integration which is associated with *increased* migration.

This administrative countereffect of social disintegration is particularly serious because, as we have seen, the breakdown of old forms of integration does not necessarily presage their replacement with new statewide forms. The result is that the state succeeds in breaking old commitments, but it thereby unleashes social processes that make its own desired political integration even more improbable. New waves of urban migration related to the breakdown of old institutions create new demands on the state with which it has difficulty coping, and this works against its establishment of the new political community. The higher rates of migration and growth of cities that Third World countries are experiencing today compared to those in Europe in the nineteenth century mean they are facing heavier demands and pressures in terms of building centralized states with integrative capabilities.

Without integration on the state level and with the weakening of some of the old integrative mechanisms, people turn to local or regional institutions and to old ones that have successfully adapted to changing conditions. As examples of fairly autonomous local and regional integrative institutions, we have already referred to the increased prominence of tribal and linguistic communities as well as to the patron-like roles of political functionaries in the rural areas. Whether they are tribal leaders, bureaucrats, or *caciques*, local powerful leaders often establish themselves as brokers between the local community and the state. Their ability to institutionalize their roles stems, to a large degree, from the new roles and policy orientation of the state. The state has intruded itself into new areas and weakened old institutional loyalties but it has frequently been incapable of following up that intrusion by creating a "social whole," a coherent set of statewide institutions.[47] Leaders of local or regional groups, then, may use their roles as brokers to distribute resources designated by the government for particular programs. That distribution, however, may be according to criteria very different from those intended by government leaders.

These new brokers and local integrative mechanisms may also cause unintended effects in the specific realm of migration. Communal groups that become institutionalized on a supra-local level (as opposed to the old institutions which were much more likely to be purely local) provide important links for migration. Chain migration is a process whereby migrants follow an established path charted by those preceding them. In many countries, the new migrant finds organizations of kin, former neighbors, coreligionists, etc., created by those who preceded him. These organizations ease his transition into his new environment and many even help the new migrant find a job. Their exclusive and supra-local qualities may provide incentives to migrate even when, looked at from a macro-level, there is no clear economic incentive to motivate individual migration to an area.

Less familiar than clashes of different policies, however, is the problem of a single policy creating contradictory effects. In other words, the administrative and political processes involved in policy formulation and implementation may create "noise." Direct policies, in such cases, generate additional unintended effects (and thus become indirect policies) fostering events contrary to expressed goals.

Such effects may be inherent in any government's programs, but the rapid expansion of bureaucracies in the Third World may make them particularly susceptible to this mix of contradictory direct and indirect components in the same policy. Their increased concern with issues that were never before explicitly political introduces a situation of administrative expansion into areas previously untouched by state machinery.[38] The administrative expansion itself has specific effects on a society regardless of the content of the particular policies being pursued, and in certain cases these effects will run counter to the goals of the specific policies. Although the results of administrative expansion on social behavior have not been systematically studied, several effects can be cited which may have a significant influence on the history of migration policies.

Administrative expansion into new geographic areas is often preceded by bureaucratic growth in the main political centers. Agencies and departments must be created and enlarged to oversee such processes as budgetary control of the new programs as well as distribution and supervision of field personnel. These processes may have a two-pronged effect running counter to a policy designed to stem urban migration from rural areas and from smaller urban centers. First is the economic effect, the creation of new jobs in the civil service as well as the spinoff opportunities that derive from the added income to the city. The bureaucratic expansion itself demands either a greater shift of resources towards these large centers through the imposition of new taxes or the requirement for greater productivity in the cities. A shift in resources creates administrative countereffects, unintended incentives working against the expressed goal of slowing the rate of urban migration to the large centers.

A second effect of the creation of new and enlarged agencies and departments is on a political level. The assumption that voluntary migration stems from a purely economic motivation may have to be modified to a degree to allow for another motive to migration, personal security. On an explicit level, war and other violent disorders are often major causes for migration, particularly internationally.[39] Even in situations of relative peace, however, security may be an element in voluntary internal migration as well. In Western countries, for example, differentials in crime rates and capabilities of authorities in dealing with crime may be an important element in migration patterns. Third World states may find the element of personal security closely related to differentials in capabilities of administrative regulation and control.[40] Some areas within states may be much better regulated than others in such areas as limiting interest rates, controlling prices, and supervision of police behavior. Governmental regulation and control through administrative organs serve to minimize whimsical use of power by local powerful men, thus giving more predictability to the realm of interpersonal relations. Such predictability or security in the expectations of the behavior of others is a prime political commodity. In part, such personal security is an intervening variable between economic motivation and migration, but in part, it is independent of economic considerations.

In Palestine during the late nineteenth century, for example, the population was located primarily in the major towns, such as Jerusalem, Nablus, and Jaffa, and in the hilly and rocky terrain on the west bank of the Jordan River. The most fertile valleys in the Galilee and along the coastal plain were nearly deserted and were left mostly fallow. Security was the main reason for this population distribution. By this period, the slowly dying Ottoman Empire was barely exercising any political control in its provinces and that which was exercised during its last attempt at reform was limited almost solely to the towns. Many peasants were willing to walk long distances to their fields in order to reside in towns where a semblance of political order existed. Others withdrew to villages atop rocky hills and mountains to avoid the predations of Bedouin tribes that wandered unmolested in the plains and valleys.

In short, twentieth century states may be finding that an administrative countereffect of the proliferation and enlargement of bureaucratic agencies and departments in the largest cities is to make those cities more attractive as areas of destination in migration processes. The outgrowth of a policy to *limit* urban migration might thus be to augment a stream of migration into the cities. Not only do public services come to be disproportionately dispensed in cities that serve as administrative centers, but also there may be a perception of a growing gap in administrative regulation and control between these areas and outlying areas. People might then migrate to cities because of the sense of increased political control there accompanying administrative expansion. In Zambia, for example, it was found that urban migration was related to new governmental policies aimed at development in rural areas and to the bureaucratic foibles which characterized these policies in remote areas.[41] In the Dominican Republic, as Glaessel-Brown indicates in another paper in this volume, Trujillo's establishment of his unofficial headquarters in San Cristobal undermined his policy of limiting in-migration to that city.

These structures can aid in explaining the risk-taking propensity of many urban migrants even when a pure economic calculus would suggest against migration. They may provide opportunities, services, and social security to members of their group that are simply unavailable to the nonaffiliated migrant. Also, brokers can use their ties to state organizations in order to attempt to concentrate state resources in their hands. Their distribution of these resources to their own constituencies may foster a chain migration into their domains even when government population policy is in a contending direction.

Administrative countereffects and other unintended aspects of policies are not limited solely to migration policies but also apply to policymaking in many other realms of social life. Each type of policy has its own substantive elements that combine with the political characteristics of the state and the nature of the policymaking processes in different ways. We would therefore expect that the intensity and direction of administrative countereffects and other unintended effects would vary considerably by issue-area.[48] Until there is a body of policy histories that begin to analyze some of these differences, there is little that can be said about which policy areas will generate the most intense, contradictory, unintended effects. We can, however, briefly note several of the special characteristics of the migration issue that might make it particularly susceptible to administrative countereffects.

Migration is a dual population process. Unlike fertility and mortality, which involve one population process, migration involves leaving one population and entering another.[49] Influencing the process of voluntary migration means changing the relative attractiveness of an area vis-à-vis numerous other areas. Policies designed to intervene in the process of internal migration may be especially susceptible to affecting unintentionally *both* the area of origin and the area of destination. The result may then be that the relative attractiveness of a single area is little changed or even changed in the opposite of the intended direction.

Also, migration is a selective process with certain categories of people more likely than others to migrate in certain circumstances.[50] Policies designed to stem migration may, in fact, inhibit certain categories of people from migrating but may simultaneously stimulate others. Or policies designed to increase migration to an area may lure certain groups but also may create a counterstream or return migratory flow of other groups. For example, a land reform policy intended to stem the urban migration of landless peasants may simultaneously stimulate the urban migration of landlords and all those who earned their living by rendering services to the landowners. Since we have so few conclusive generalizations about which categories migrate under which circumstances (the age variable being the major exception), it is particularly difficult to judge whom policies will affect and the nature and intensity of the counterflows that the policy will stimulate.[51]

CONCLUSION

The major argument put forth in this essay is that there are certain political preconditions for a state to develop effective social policies. A significant degree of political centralization and integration is a necessary prerequisite for states to develop sufficient autonomy and coherence and for their governments to muster strong supportive coalitions. Without such preconditions, governments' interventions in social processes lead to unintended and unexpected results. Attempting to analyze the nature of these unintended results is quite problematical because of the paucity of policy histories that could be used as data. We have tried to specify to some degree, however, what the nature of such unintended effects might be in the realm of migration policy. Administrative countereffects, the indirect and contradictory effects of direct policies, have particularly important ramifications on the overall direction and intensity of social policies of many Third World states.

Migration analysis and policymaking are extremely difficult in many Third World countries because of these countries' unusual degree of heterogeneity and fragmentation. Differences among geographic areas in the same country may be very high not only in terms of socioeconomic indicators but also in terms of proximity to various symbolic configurations of values.[52] Most developed countries have a highly dominant configuration of values, but many Third World countries, due to their lack of centralization, have numerous, competing configurations with different strengths in different areas. Such differences may combine with variations in levels of socioeconomic indicators in unexpected ways. For example, a migration stream toward the capital city might exist even if economic opportunities are relatively poor there because some people might want to be as close as possible to the locus of secular, "modern" values. Or, conversely, there may be counterstreams and return migratory flows from a capital city even when it has clear economic advantages because some people find unexpected personal "losses" in being so removed from the loci of "traditional" values. Once again, the selectivity of the migration process must be taken into account to understand the many facets of motivation for relocating.

When and why people will migrate within a country characterized by high variability within its borders, then, is problematical because different elements attract or repel different segments of the population. Intervening in a process of voluntary internal migration runs into difficulty because it means changing the relative attractiveness of an area vis-à-vis other areas for diverse segments of the population with different value preferences. International migration may be more amenable to policymaking by weak states simply because the policy must deal with only half of the equation—either the area of origin or the area of destination. In changing conditions in either half, the government need not worry to the same degree about ramifications on the other half outside the borders of the country. The contradictory effects that their policies generate are much easier to control in international migration than in internal migration where what occurs in both the area of origin *and* the area of destination greatly affects the ability of the state to achieve its most basic goals of survival and statewide integration.

NOTES

1. See William L. Langer, "Europe's Initial Population Explosion," *The American Historical Review*, 69 (October 1963) pp. 1-17.

2. Exodus 1:9-10: "Behold, the people of the children of Israel are too many and too mighty for us; come let us deal wisely with them, lest they multiply ..." Also, see Exodus 1:15-22.

3. See Ira Marvin Lapidus, *Muslim Cities in the Later Middle Ages* (Cambridge, Mass.: Harvard University Press, 1967); and G.E. von Grunebaum, "The Structure of the Muslim Town" in *Islam: Essays on the Nature and Growth of a Cultural Tradition* (2nd ed., London: 1961).

4. Donella H. Meadows et al., *The Limits to Growth* (New York: Universal Books, 1972); and Mihajlo Mesarović and Eduard Pestel, *Mankind at the Turning Point* (New York: Dutton, 1974).

5. See M.A. Qadeer, "Do Cities 'Modernize' the Developing Countries? An Examination of the South Asian Experience," *Comparative Studies in Society and History*, 16 (1974) pp. 266-283; and T.G. McGee, *The Urbanization Process in the Third World* (London: Bell, 1971).

6. See Alex Inkeles and David H. Smith, *Becoming Modern* (Cambridge, Mass.: Harvard University Press, 1974), pp. 216-229.

7. G. Beijer, "Modern Patterns of International Migratory Movements," in *Migration*, J.A. Jackson (ed.), (Cambridge: Cambridge University Press, 1969), p. 48.

8. J. Isaac wrote, "The decision to emigrate may obviously result from a number of motives which may differ in each individual case. But ... the desire to become better off, has been predominant." Quoted in ibid., p. 12. Also, see United Nations, *Determinants and Consequences of Population Trends*, ch. 6.

9. S.A. Stouffer, "Intervening Opportunities: A Theory Relating Mobility and Distance," *American Sociological Review*, 5 (1940) pp. 845-927.

10. Calvin Goldscheider, *Population, Modernization, and Social Structure* (Boston: Little, Brown, 1971), p. 219.

11. The language comes from Everett Lee, "A Theory of Migration," *Demography*, 3 (1966) pp. 49-52.

12. Stanislaw H. Wellisz, "Economic Development and Urbanization," in *Urbanization and National Development*, Leo Jakobson and Ved Prakash (eds.), (Beverly Hills: Sage Publications, 1971), p. 44. Of course, migration to urban areas does *not* show that there is a continuing difference between levels unless one already accepts Wellisz's premise of what causes migration.

13. See William Mangin, "Latin American Squatter Settlements: A Problem and a Solution," *Latin American Research Review*, 2 (Summer 1967) pp. 65-98.

14. N.H. Lithwick, "The Growth of Urban Populations: Two Patterns," paper presented at the 3rd World Congress of Engineers and Architects in Israel, Tel-Aviv, December 17-24, 1973. Also, see Shahid Javed Burki, "Migration, Urbanization, and Politics in Pakistan," in *Population, Politics, and the Future of Southern Asia*, W. Howard Wriggins and James F. Guyot (eds.), (New York: Columbia University Press, 1973), pp. 147-89.

15. Quoted in Beijer, p. 49.

16. On some of the major international migrations since the fifteenth century, see W.D. Borrie, *The Growth and Control of World Population* (London: Wiedenfeld and Nicolson, 1970), ch. 5. Current international migration from Southern to Northern and Western Europe has been compared to European migrations to the United States. C.P. Kindleberger, "Mass Migra-

tion Then and Now," in *World Migration in Modern Times*, Franklin D. Scott (ed.), (Englewood Cliffs, N.J.: Prentice-Hall, 1968), ch. 26.

17. Fred W. Riggs, *Administration in Developing Countries* (Boston: Houghton Mifflin, 1964), p. 42.

18. Samuel P. Huntington, "Political Development and Political Decay," *World Politics*, 17 (April 1965) pp. 386-430.

19. C.S. Whitaker, Jr., "A Dysrhythmic Process of Political Change," *World Politics*, 19 (January 1967) pp. 190-217.

20. S.N. Eisenstadt, "Traditional Patrimonialism and Modern Neopatrimonialism," *Sage Studies in Comparative Modernization* (1973).

21. This, of course, does not mean that the state cannot decentralize by assigning the performance of political functions to particular groups or agencies. The key, however, is the state's new jurisdiction, which is literally the *power* of declaring and administering law or justice.

22. Harold D. Lasswell, "Population Change and Policy Sciences: Proposed Workshops on Reciprocal Impact Analysis," in *Policy Sciences and Population*, Warren F. Ilchman et al. (eds.), (Lexington, Mass.: D.H. Heath, 1975), pp. 117-18, gives a framework to enumerate a society's preferred events.

23. Robert Redfield, *Peasant Society and Culture*, Phoenix Books (Chicago: University of Chicago Press, 1960), pp. 42ff.

24. Karl W. Deutsch, "Social Mobilization and Political Development," *American Political Science Review*, 60 (September 1961) pp. 493-514.

25. Fred W. Riggs, "Bureaucrats and Political Development: A Paradoxical View," in *Bureaucracy and Political Development*, Joseph LaPalombara (ed.), (Princeton, N.J.: Princeton University Press, 1963), p. 120.

26. On Thailand, for example, see *New York Times*, October 15, 1975, p. 12. Also, see Guy Hunter, *Modernizing Peasant Societies* (New York: Oxford University Press, 1969).

27. For example, see J. Clyde Mitchell, *The Kalela Dance*, The Rhodes-Livingstone Papers, no. 27, Manchester University Press.

28. Donald G. Morrison and Hugh Michael Stevenson, "Integration and Instability: Patterns of African Political Development," *American Political Science Review*, 66 (September 1972), 902-26, for example, relate the high rate of African instability to lack of political integration.

29. Reinhard Bendix, "Centralization, the State, and Political Cleavage," in *Class, Status and Power*, Seymour M. Lipset and Bendix (eds.), (2nd ed., New York: The Free Press, 1966), p. 81.

30. Nirmal Bose writes of Calcutta that it is "the scene of a major confrontation between the enduring institutions of old India — her caste communities and diversity of ethnic heritages — and the pressures and values arising from the urbanization that presages India's industrial revolution." Quoted in Burki, p. 152.

31. For example, public services in many Third World countries are disproportionately concentrated in the largest urban centers. We would expect, then, that participation in organizations and procedures of the state, which is often a condition for access to such services, is also disproportionately high in such centers.

32. Myron Weiner sees the migration process in India as one with contradictory effects. "At one level of society, interstate, intercultural migration

is an integrating force which brings together men and women of diverse cultures and languages who share common occupations and common membership in modern institutions. At another level of society, such migration is economically and culturally threatening." "Socio-Political Consequences of Interstate Migration in India," in Wriggins and Guyot.

33. William T. Flinn, "Rural and Intra-Urban Migration in Colombia: Two Case Studies in Bogota," in *Latin American Urban Research*, vol. 1, Francine F. Rabinovitz and Felicity M. Trueblood (eds.), (Beverly Hills, Calif.: Sage, 1971), p. 91.

34. See Weiner. Also, greater utilization of urban opportunities in Lebanon is part of the background of the Lebanese civil war.

35. West Bank Palestinian Arabs often have a son migrate temporarily to Kuwait as a means to stimulate a cash flow back to the extended family. Also, see Joel S. Migdal, "The Role of the Family in Relation to the Tension of Societal Change," *International Journal of Group Tensions*, 4 (June 1974) pp. 184-207. On return migratory flows, see George R. Gilkey, "The United States and Italy: Migration and Repatriation," and Susan Geiger Rogers, "Emigration and Return of the Chagga," both in Scott.

36. James M. Beshers mentions "the phenomenon of the young males seeking employment in other areas yet returning at regular intervals in hopes of resettling in their native villages." *Population Processes in Social Systems* (New York: The Free Press, 1967), p. 140.

37. Robert H. Bates and Bruce W. Bennett, "Determinants of the Rural Exodus ih Zambia: A Study of Inter-Censal Migration, 1963-1969," *Cahiers d'Etudes Africaines*, 14 (1974) p. 559.

38. New problems arose for European states, as well, when they first began to pass legislation which "touched a wider range of human activities (for example religion) than that of medieval states." Joseph R. Strayer, *On the Medieval Origins of the Modern State* (Princeton, N.J.: Princeton University Press, 1970), p. 102.

39. See, for example, Borrie, ch. 5.

40. For some graphic material on banditry in nineteenth century China, see Kung-chuan Hsiao, *Rural China* (Seattle: University of Washington Press, 1960).

41. See Robert H. Bates, "Rural Development in Kasumpa Village, Zambia," *Journal of African Studies*, 2 (1976) pp. 333-62.

42. On Southeast Asia, see James C. Scott, "Patron-Client Politics and Political Change," Paper presented at the American Political Science Association meetings, Los Angeles, Calif., September 8-12, 1970.

43. Dwight B. Heath, "New Patrons for Old: Changing Patron-Client Relationships in the Bolivian Yungas," *Ethnology*, 12 (January 1973) pp. 75-98.

44. Joel S. Migdal, *Peasants, Politics, and Revolution* (Princeton, N.J.: Princeton University Press, 1974), esp. ch. 9.

45. Deutsch.

46. Goldscheider, pp. 322-23.

47. F.G. Bailey, *Politics and Social Change* (Berkeley: University of California Press), p. 219.

48. On the concept of issue-areas, see James N. Rosenau, "Foreign Policy

as an Issue-Area," in *Domestic Sources of Foreign Policy*, Rosenau (ed.), (New York: Free Press, 1967), pp. 11-50.

49. Goldscheider, p. 49.

50. Ibid., p. 300.

51. One crude differentiation is that between "innovating" migration and "conservative" ones. See William Petersen, "A General Typology of Migration," *American Sociological Review*, 23 (June 1958) pp. 258.

52. See Edward Shils, *Center and Periphery* (Chicago: University of Chicago Press, 1975).

7

UNIFORM POPULATION POLICIES AND REGIONAL DIFFERENCES IN THE SOVIET UNION

Nancy Lubin

A vast country with great ethnocultural diversity, the USSR has exhibited unchanging demographic aims since the beginning of the Soviet era. A traditional emphasis on labor-intensive rather than capital-intensive development has meant an undeviating goal of promoting greater fertility among the Soviet population, and the traditional emphasis on "russification" and the Great Russian nationality has implied a desire to effect this rise particularly among the Slavic nationalities.

In spite of these desires, fertility in the Soviet Union as a whole has steadily declined. Moreover, because of birth rate differentials among nationalities, the Slavs have also comprised a steadily decreasing proportion of the Soviet population. The severe decline in the rate of population growth that came with the 1960s, as well as the widening disparities between the growth rates of the different nationalities, has recently made the problem acutely apparent to Soviet leaders. Not only do population trends portend a more rapidly aging population for the next few decades—a prospect which can only exacerbate an already existing labor shortage and endanger future economic development; the trends also suggest increasingly widening disparities between the growth rates of the different ethnic groups—with the least productive and most culturally alien sectors of society comprising a steadily increasing proportion of the total population.

Soviet history has witnessed repeated alterations, shifts, and reversals in population policy.[1] Abortions were legalized in 1920, made illegal in 1936, greatly expanded in 1944, and then sharply cut back in 1947. Divorce laws were changed dramatically from perhaps the world's most liberal in the 1920s to probably the world's most severe twenty years later. And while legislation regarding female employment has changed little since 1917, implementation of the law has changed a woman's position from one of the world's most "liberated" to among the world's most confined.

The number of reversals indicates the long-standing Soviet awareness of her population problem. This essay will discuss some of the contraints that have hindered effective population policymaking throughout Soviet history. Although the Soviet Union has indeed witnessed an exceedingly large number of demographic catastrophes which have had profound effects upon the size and composition of her population, the failures of her population policies are as much a product of her political and social system as they are of her demographic composition.

Economic, ideological, and bureaucratic constraints have hampered the efficacy of population policy at every stage of its development. In the initial stages of problem identification and information gathering, the constraints of bureaucratic centralization, coupled with those of an ideology which refuses to verbally recognize political differences among the various nationalities, have left Soviet policymakers with loosely defined goals and inadequate data for determining the means of achieving them. While the nature of Soviet society and her population problem have grown more complex with time, economic and ideological constraints have continued to impede the formulation of policies to deal with these complexities. And equally fundamental, constraints arising from the inability of the Soviet bureaucracy to administer its policies in the implementation stage have further crippled the development of an effectual approach to population problems. The effects of these constraints on population policy suggest profound implications for the future of Soviet society, domestically and internationally, as well as providing useful demographic models for the world.

DEMOGRAPHIC BACKGROUND

Although the USSR, with 7 percent of the world's population, ranks third in population size after China and India, it has experienced a steadily declining rate of population growth since the turn of the twentieth century. From forty-four per thousand in 1926, the birthrate fell to twenty-five per thousand in 1959, and then to 17.4 per thousand in 1970 (see Table 1). This decline was initially offset by a concurrent drop in the national mortality rate, but a leveling off of the death rate in the 1960s brought with it an even more severe decline in the overall rate of population growth. In the ten years between 1959-1970, the percent of natural increase was only half that of the previous ten years, dropping from 1.74 in 1959 to only .92 in 1970. Soviet officials have calculated the "optimal net reproduction rate" to be 1.21; the actual rate, however, has dropped from 1.7 in 1926, to 1.3 in 1959, and 1.1 since the mid-1960s.

Economically, the implications of such a downward trend are especially severe for a country which in the past has stressed labor-intensive rather than capital-intensive development. Since the beginning of the Soviet era, the economy has been endowed with ample human resources. Because of the steady decline in the birthrate, however, the population as a whole has been aging; consequently, the proportion of new entrants to the labor force relative to total population has been decreasing, and the proportion of aged dependents increasing. While the proportion of people of retirement age or older, (aged fifty-five and older for females, sixty and older for males) in 1926 and 1939 fluctuated around 7 to 8 percent of the total population, this figure had increased to 10.4 percent by 1950, 12.4 percent in 1960, and 15.0 percent in 1970; present projections suggest that this proportion could very well reach 21 percent by the end of the century.[2] At the same time, while the number of those in the work force still increased during the period 1958-1974 (by about 740,000 workers per year between 1958-1965, 1.6 million per year between 1966-1970, and 2.57 million per year between 1971-1974), calculations now indicate that the trend will dramatically reverse itself after 1974, and if the birthrate remains at the level of recent years, there will be no increase whatsoever in labor resources during the last five years of the century. Unless changes can be effected elsewhere, the trend

Table 1
Population Growth in the USSR
(per 1,000 population)

Year	Birthrate	Deathrate	Net Increase
1926	44.0	20.3	23.7
1930	39.2	20.4	18.8
1940	31.2	18.0	13.2
1950	26.7	9.7	17.0
1960	24.9	7.1	17.8
1964	19.5	6.9	12.6
1968	17.2	7.7	9.5
1969	17.0	8.1	8.9
1970	17.4	8.2	9.2

Year	Birthrate	Deathrate	Percent of Increase
1930	39.2	20.4	1.88
1959	25.0	7.6	1.74
1961	23.8	7.2	1.66
1969	17.0	8.1	0.89
1973	17.6		

Source: *Narodnoe Khoziaistvo SSR v 1970 g.*, p. 47.

forebodes only a long-term worsening of an already growing labor shortage in the Soviet economy, and an increasingly heavy burden of nonworkers for the economy to carry.

Politically and economically, the Soviet Union's population problem has been further compounded by the vast disparities in the growth rates of different nationalities—particularly by the fact that a disproportionate share of births are attributable to women of the Turkic-Muslim nationalities of the Caucasus and Central Asia. At present, about three-fourths of the Soviet population is comprised of Slavs: the Russians, the Ukranians, and the Byelorussians. The second most numerous peoples, and by far the most rapidly multiplying, are the Muslim Central Asians, followed by the peoples of the Caucasus. Predominantly rural and characterized by a certain Muslim cultural unity, these groups contrast markedly in values, way of life, and level of economic development with the Slavs. During the past sixty years the composition of the various national groups in the total population has changed dramatically, as the fertility level of the Balts and Slavs has hovered around replacement level while that of the Central Asians has remained extremely high. According to the 1970 Soviet census data, the birthrate is now between two and two and a half times greater in Central Asia than in the RSFSR (which contains 82.8 percent of all Russians), while the proportion of Slavic peoples as whole in the total population has declined from a total of 76.3 percent in 1959 to 74 percent in 1970. The Russians themselves comprised 51 percent of the population in 1970 and today are in minority status.

In short, projections indicate that if the rate of increase that occurred between 1959 and 1970 continues, the fourteen million Turkic-Muslins will double their population in about twenty years. Between 1980 and 1990, almost three-fourths of the net increase of the total Soviet work force, not considering migration, will occur in Central Asia, Kazakhstan, and the Transcaucasus. Central Asia alone will account for about 40 percent of the increase in the total Soviet work force between 1980 and 1990 when the number of new entrants to the work force will increase by two million in Central Asia and decline by about two million in the USSR as a whole.[3] Thus, as the size of the total Soviet work force diminishes, a rapidly growing proportion of those workers will be of non-Slavic nationality.

THE INITIAL STAGES OF INFORMATION GATHERING AND PROBLEM IDENTIFICATION

An awareness of a population problem and the call for increased population growth are not new to Soviet society. Lenin's indictment of "neo-Malthusianism,"

> this tendency for the philistine couple, pigeon-brained and selfish, who murmur fearfully: May God help us to keep our own bodies and souls together, as for children, it is best to be without them,[4]

was only echoed in the words of Khrushchev three decades later:

> He who founds a family is a good citizen. Our country will become stronger the larger the population. Bourgeois ideologies have adopted cannibalistic theories, among which is the theory of overpopulation . . . . Among us, comrades, the problem is completely the opposite. Out of 200 million, if we were to add another 200 million, even that would not be enough.[5]

And the same is repeated today.

> One may call "optimal" that level of reproduction under which the economic and social development of the country will be relatively quick . . . . To have the optimal pure coefficient at 1.2, for every 100 families we must have 320 births . . . . We must aim for at least 3-children families.[6]

As will be illustrated, early legislation was formulated with the explicit aim of increasing the population. Since the past two decades have witnessed not only an even more marked overall birthrate decline, and more pronounced regional variations as well, it is clear that population has become an ever-imperative policy problem.

In spite of the dimensions of the problem, political, bureaucratic, and ideological constraints have hindered both information gathering and a problem definition. Demographic study in the USSR is heavily enmeshed with questions of domestic and foreign policy, and both the amount and type of data collected tend to depend very much on the political preferences of the central government. For example, despite the apparent renewed emphasis on demographic research in the 1960s, Soviet censuses have become markedly less comprehensive,[7] and the types of questions asked in surveys seem to be carefully chosen so as to obscure certain deficiencies in Soviet society.[8] At the same time, the absence of coordination among demographic social scientists, data-gathering organs, and policy formulators within the central leadership has also impeded fruitful discussion and more precise defining of population problems. As a result of rivalry between demographers and the data-gathering sources of the USSR (primarily the Central Statistical Agency) and because of the fact that there is no central organ in the Soviet political structure that deals specifically with problems of population, policymakers confront a unique problem of "centralization of funds and poor access to data."[9]

Other ideological and political factors have magnified the information-gathering and problem-identification problem at regional and national levels. Soviet planners have become increasingly wary of the widening disparities between the population growth rates of the different nationalities. During the Stalin era, considerable concern was expressed about "pan-Moslem and pan-Turanian tendencies."[10] Today, Cohn has pointed to the "centuries-old fear of the Asians" that plays a major role in Soviet political thought.[11] Soviet planners would ideally hope to narrow the gap between the population growth rates of the different nationalities, while simultaneously raising fertility for the Union as a whole. Inferential evidence suggests that they hope to raise the fertility level of the Slavic peoples, while promoting a gradual birthrate decline among the Turkic-Muslim Central Asians.

But Communist ideology inhibits the recognition of the Soviet people as anything but a homogeneous unit. Official identification of the problem in regional or ethnic terms is politically impossible. Although ideology acknowledges the great disparities in cultural attitudes and traditions, in the Soviet Union each national group is valued in theory as being an integral and important part of the nation. Hence, in theory at least, a high rate of increase among the Muslim Central Asians, for example, should indeed represent a *positive* sign to Soviet planners as a counterbalance to the more severely declining rate of growth for the Union as a whole. Politically, moreover, the fact that the USSR shares a long common border with China, and the fact that the Soviet peoples are already greatly outnumbered by their Chinese neighbors, should make the maintenance of a high rate of population growth desirable particularly in the Central Asian areas.

Soviet leaders today appear to be unofficially pursuing policies to promote the migration of Slavs to the Central Asian areas, irrespective of the high rate of population growth among the indigenous peoples of that region. Such a policy, if fully implemented, would keep the border population large while equalizing the Slavic/non-Slavic imbalances in the Central Asian region. But such a policy, if officially articulated, would also have such severe ethnocentric overtones that it would be irreconcilable with official Soviet ideology.

Some Soviet demographers have obliquely referred to the necessity of moderating ideology when the demographic needs of the country require it. Even should ideological constraints be somewhat tempered, however, and official aims defined as a lowered birthrate among the Central Asian peoples, the Soviet Union could be faced with still more far-reaching political repercussions. As Feshbach sugggests, a differential policy of encouraging birth control among the Moslem population in Central Asia could fan resentment not only in the areas affected but also in countries of the Third World with similar cultural and economic characteristics.[12]

Thus the Brezhnev and Kosygin leadership continues to define the population problem, officially, at least, in the same words as their predecessors. Official demographic aims reflect only the need for increased population growth among the population as a whole. The highly centralized approach toward problem identification and the lack of precise, clearly defined target groups, coupled with the very vagueness of officially propounded demographic goals, increasingly have served only to complicate the already complex stages of formulating and implementing an effective population policy.

EARLY LEGISLATION

Until the advent of World War II, Soviet population policy reflected a series of shifts and reversals in response to changing demographic and political situations of the USSR. The initial years of the Communist regime saw loose official morals and extremely liberal family legislation: unregistered marriages had the same validity as registered ones; divorce was granted merely upon the request of either spouse; no distinction was made between the illegitimate child and the child born in wedlock; abortions, although discouraged, were legal. The Constitution of 1918 established the obligation of every citizen to work, regardless of sex, but it also provided certain protective measures for women, such as the prohibition of female employment in night work, overtime work, or war, detrimental to a woman's health, and offered working mothers and pregnant women special benefits as well, such as paid maternity leaves and extra work breaks, along with allowances for nursing mothers after they had resumed work.

With the rapid urbanization, industrialization, collectivization, famine, and general decline in living standards that came with the late 1920s-1930s, population policy was reevaluated and changed. Although official aims remained unaltered, the existing legislation was deemed to have encouraged a "light-hearted attitude toward the family," increased family instability, and encouraged smaller families. With the general political and bureaucratic tightening that occurred in all spheres of Soviet society, therefore, legislation was reversed in 1936: abortions were made illegal; the unregistered marriage was discouraged; and divorces were made more difficult to obtain. A new aura of victorianism was established, while family research as a discipline was largely stamped out. And to reconcile the two goals of increased family stability and greater fertility, illegitimacy was encouraged, provided its incidence reflected "a desire to have and raise one's own children" and not "sexual looseness" and a "dissolute" and "casual attitude."[13] Likewise, while women were still considered an integral part of the work force, direct family allowances were added to the benefits of motherhood.

Toward the end of World War II, the need to restore the population was more urgently recognized, and 1944 saw an intensification of the 1936 legislation. Divorces were made extremely time-consuming and costly to obtain; the unregistered marriage was abolished; the prohibition of abortions was reaffirmed; and although the regime undoubtedly preferred to have children born in wedlock, illegitimacy was actively encouraged, rather than passively condoned. Greater proportions of women were required to participate in the labor force; but along with the intensification of the 1936 family laws, the system of family allowances was greatly expanded as well.

While the 1944 legislation introduced the Soviets' first all-out effort to raise fertility, however, it also first illuminated the major constraints inhibiting such an effort. The financial demands of the family allowance policy—especially if the policy were to keep pace with inflation—were recognized as posing too great a strain on the government purse; the Soviet budget had traditionally emphasized heavy industry and investment greatly at the expense of consumption, and the ravages of war now presented only a greater need to divert funds in that direction. Similarly, while abortions remained illegal, the incidence of illegal abortion was apparently very high. The divorce rate declined dramatically, and it soon became clear that a couple's inability to dissolve a marriage did not necessarily imply higher fertility, or the promotion of happy, more stable marriages. By officially removing the stigma attached to illegitimacy, and by praising the unwed mother and offering financial support for the illegitimate child, the legislation paradoxically made the fact all the more glaring. And in light of the extremely harsh divorce laws, that fact that a man was legally permitted to enter into sexual relations without fear of moral or financial repercussions may indeed have discouraged a significant number of men from marrying in the first place.

Thus with the 1940s came the growing awareness that higher fertility in the USSR could not be encouraged by economic incentives alone, nor could it be fostered by purely legalistic and procedural measures affecting abortion, marriage, divorce, and illegitimacy. The former, to be effective, demanded too much in the way of financial allocation for the country as a whole. The latter, on the other hand, were merely reflections of a desire on the part of the populace to limit fertility, not direct incentives or disincentives in themselves. The following period, therefore, saw a moderation of all Soviet policies, including a reduction of family allowances, with the result that their effects were rendered meaningless.

In 1947 allowances were halved, and the sums allotted for mothers with many children cut back so much that they lost their incentive value for increasing childbearing. Eight years later, in 1955, abortions were once again legalized under certain conditions. In 1964, legislation regarding illegitimacy was altered so that paternity could be either voluntarily admitted by the father or determined by the court. And in 1966, divorces were made easier to obtain: divorce procedure was simplified, and publicity was no longer required. "Population policy" was pared down to negligibility, and the economic priorities and ideological victorianism which the leadership had inherited, and which had been firmly reinforced by industrialization and the "tightening of family responsibilities" in the 1930s, offered little to fill the vacuum.

THE 1960s: ECONOMIC AND IDEOLOGICAL CONSTRAINTS

The more pronounced birthrate decline that became apparent with the 1960s again demanded direct intervention to reverse the trend. Yet as the population problem was brought into sharper focus, so, too, were the constraints of policy formulation. An allowance system without value (both with respect to the average wage and with respect to the proportion of women and families receiving such aid), poor housing, and a woman's lack of free time (due both to the economic necessity for almost full female employment and to the low level of the consumer industry to alleviate their "second working day" at home) were prime factors contributing to a lowered fertility rate. But their resolution demanded substantial financial resources: new daycare centers and more and better labor-saving appliances and everyday services were required to permit women to combine work and childbearing. Taking women out of the work force, fully or partially, and providing them with the necessary financial means to stay home and have children represented not only a significant addition to government expenditures, but also implied a net loss in production. Adequate housing was required to accommodate individual families. And continued emphasis on the family allowance policy as a means of encouraging greater childbearing also demanded financial allocations that would keep pace with both inflation and the rising needs and wants of an increasingly sophisticated population. As indicated by a comparison with other countries, at least a substantial amount more than the Soviet government had allocated was required if allowances were to be effective, and even then, results were by no means assured.

The 1960s-70s did in fact see a rise in government expenditures in all of the above areas. Indeed, growth rates for investment and consumption narrowed to an average of 6.9 and 5.1 percent respectively throughout the sixties,[14] and the ninth five-year-plan (1970-1975) marked the first time targets for consumption were set higher than those for investment. But as in 1947, it was soon evident that economic priorities lay elsewhere. Although targets for consumption had been set higher than those for production, they repeatedly were unmet and plans were consistently cut back. Consumer goods remained in short supply: by 1972, the availability of personal services, such as laundries, repair services, and barber facilities were still miniscule, the total amounting to a mere 20 rubles per person per year. Although the number of children enrolled in daycare centers nearly doubled over the decade, daycare centers still had not kept pace with demand.[15] By the beginning of the 1970s, Soviet citizens were still "the most poorly housed of any major country in Europe—and poorly housed also by comparison with the government's standard for health and decency."[16] And the slight, incremental changes that occurred had not improved the worth of family allowances.

Gradually, the mid-1970s witnessed a reversion back to the traditional priorities of industry, investment, and defense. The gap between growth rates for industry and consumption once again began to widen, averaging 7.0 and 3.8 percent per year respectively by the mid-70s;[17] the recent tenth five-year-plan (1976) once again set targets for industry higher than those for consumption. Today, 72 percent of all women, among the highest proportion in the world, is engaged in the urban work force, while the number of daycare centers is still limited. Only 38 percent of all Soviet families has refrigerators, only 11 percent has vacuum cleaners, and diaper services, clothes driers, and dishwashers are virtually nonexistent to alleviate the burden of the "second working day."[18] Discussion has increasingly focused on the total abolition of family allowancss. And as Tatiana Yevgenevna writes to Pravda, "I and my five children are crowded into fifteen square meters without communal conveniences or even a kitchen . . . ."[19] In short, economic constraints of the past decade have continued to prevent the Soviet government from even minimally keeping pace with the rising needs and demands of a larger and increasingly sophisticated population.

The 1960s also began to see increasing attempts to fit the population's desires to the economic limitations of the government. By the beginning of the 1960s, and especially towards the end of the decade, Soviet planners were trying "to mold public opinion in favor of the optimal number of children in the family,"[20] rather than trying to provide the economic conditions that would have an optimal influence on the birthrate. Once again, procedural changes were made in family laws: the 1969 Kodeks on Marriage and the Family established the marital age at eighteen, presumably as an encouragement for earlier marriages rather than as a response to demand, while abortions were still legal, legislation of 1966 somewhat restricted the right to abortions on nonmedical grounds. But in addition, with the renewed emphasis particularly on family research, more attention was turned in the official arena toward sex education and general education and propaganda as a means of shaping people's sociocultural attitudes toward the family and toward the question of increased childbearing. In 1963, the first book on the subject of sex (*Boy and Girl*) was published in Moscow "to mold views in young people that will make the creation and maintenance of a happy family and the rearing of healthy and comprehensively developed children a part of the concept of civic duty, along with an honest and conscientious attitude toward labor, the defense of the homeland, and public obligations."[21] A few years later, S.I. Golod completed a study of sexual mores in Leningrad—the only such study published in the postwar period.

Here, too, however, attitudes were not eradicated so easily, and deep-seated Russian "victorianism"—a factor quite separate from the economic sphere—ended up being a major constraint of policy formulation as well. When it came time, for example, in 1968 for Golod to defend a thesis dissertation on the subject of sexual mores he was not permitted to do so: "Much of the social-psychological interest, particularly sexual relations, is simply taboo as a subject of research."[22] And *Boy and Girl* turned out to present more Communist dogma and morals than it did sexual information. As the book concluded, for example,

> Young people should not indulge in casual sexual affairs, for this is how venereal infections are spread. Young men who measure their manliness by the number of girls they have seduced will never make good communists.

On a broader level, while Soviet officials apparently hoped to temper the high rate of abortion with more and better contraceptives, their "verbal puritanism" greatly hampered the formulation of birth-control policies, and the need for increased production, availability, and education on contraceptives was largely ignored. Soviet legislation never mentioned family planning since that was considered to be an "absolutely private matter for each married or unmarried woman."[23] And although a small start has recently been made towards establishing a marriage counseling clinic in Leningrad, the organization is not officially recognized and consists only of volunteer physicians, psychologists, and sociologists. Although women's consultation clinics have sprung up in different parts of the country, sexual advice and instruction lies primarily in the hands of doctors; and the "deep fear of sexuality which is so much a part of official Russian culture"[24] makes it particularly difficult for doctors to act in this sphere. It is now estimated that every third Soviet marriage is destined to end in divorce. As of 1970, 15 percent of thirty-year-old men and 23 percent of men in the twenty-five to thirty age group were unmarried.[25] As of 1972, the average age of bridegrooms was estimated between twenty-seven and twenty-nine, and of brides twenty-four and twenty-five[26]—the highest average age in Soviet history, and high by comparison to the United States and other Western countries as well. And 10 percent of all children born are illegitimate. Although in practice morals may be loose, the birds and the bees still have little place in official Soviet parlance.

REGIONAL EFFECTS

Because of economic and ideological constraints, Soviet population policies formulated up to and throughout the 1970s have had little impact in establishing either the financial preconditions or the social attitudes necessary to increase fertility. In assessing the total formulation process of Soviet population policies, however, one cannot ignore their effects on the second aspect of the USSR's population problem, the widening disparities in population growth rates among the USSR's different regions and among her different nationalities. Given the vast disparities both in levels of economic development and in cultural heritage, particularly between the Central Asians and the Slavs, standard, centralized policies invariably have differing effects in different regions and among different nationalities—whether these policies be economic or ideological in orientation. In light of the low level of economic development and the Turkic-Muslim cultural framework of the Central Asian peoples, moreover, policies directed indiscriminately toward the population at large may indeed have diametrically opposite effects in one region as compared to another. Hence, while the 1959 and then 1970 censuses may have brought the widening disparities in regional and national growth rates more acutely to the attention of Soviet leaders, the same population policies discussed above have often exerted not merely a negligible impact, but an impact directly counter to official demographic aims.

For example, while it is admirable that allowances, in perfect congruence with ideology, were formulated to apply equitably toward the population at large, the benefits of the Soviet allowance policy have by no means been equally distributed among the regions and nationalities. As illustrated above, the prime target group for the past 28 years has been the large Soviet family. Hence, despite original goals of raising fertility primarily among the Slavic population, large disparities between nationalities in both desired and actual family size, (see Table 2) have meant that the prime beneficiaries of the family allowance policy have been the Central Asians—in particular, the Tadzhiks, Uzbeks, and Turkmen. Whereas in 1975 the average desired number of children per family in Central Asia was five or six, the number was 1.6 in Moscow and 1.8 in Latvia and Estonia—below even the minimal number of children required to receive allowance benefits.

David Heer has computed for each republic the number of mothers of ten or more children per million population who received heroine-mother awards in 1962-1963.[27] Relative to total population, mothers of ten or more children represented eighteen per million population in the USSR as a whole.

In the predominantly Moslem republic of Azerbaijan the proportion was eighty-two per million. The lowest rate in a predominantly Moslem republic was that in Uzbekistan, thirty-nine per million. The

Table 2
Average Number of Members per Family, by Nationality and Urban and
Rural Residence, 1959

Nationality	Total	Urban	Rural
Tadzhik	5.2	5.1	5.2
Uzbek	5.0	4.9	5.0
Turkmen	5.0	4.7	5.1
Azerbaijan	4.8	4.6	4.9
Armenian	4.7	4.4	5.0
Kazakh	4.6	4.7	4.5
Kirgiz	4.5	4.3	4.6
Georgian	4.0	3.8	4.1
Moldavian	3.9	3.6	4.0
Belorussian	3.7	3.4	3.7
Russian	3.6	3.5	3.7
Lithuanian	3.6	3.4	3.6
Ukrainian	3.5	3.3	3.6
Latvian	3.1	3.0	3.2
Estonian	3.0	3.1	3.0

Source: USSR, 1959 Census

only non-Moslem republic with a higher proportion than Uzbekistan was Armenia, where the rate was forty-six per million population.

According to his computations, 27 percent of all the mothers receiving awards for having ten or more children came from the five predominantly Muslim republics of Azerbaijan, Kirghizia, Tadzhikistan, Turkmenistan, and Uzbekistan—which together comprised only 9 percent of the total population of the USSR. Moreover, according to the 1959 census, Muslim nationalities constituted only 39 percent of the population of Kazakhstan; yet in 1962-63, two-thirds of the mothers receiving heroine mother awards in Kazakhstan were of Muslim nationality.

The statistics show that the total number of heroine mothers since 1959 has decreased from about eighteen per million to thirteen per million in 1970. But given the continued regional and national disparities in birthrate and the differences in both actual and desired family size, it is likely that the proportion of mothers-with-many-children of Muslim nationality has changed little.

Along with the numbers of recipients of awards for large families, income differentials between republics are also vast—a fact which

Table 3
Average Number of Heroin Mothers per Million of Total Population
(1962-63) and Percentage of Total Population of Moslem Nationality (1959)

Area	Average Number of Heroine Mothers per Million Population, 1962–63	Percentage of Total Population of Moslem Nationality, 1959
USSR	18	11.9
Ukrainian SSR	8	0.2
Estonian SSR	9	0.1
Belorussian SSR	11	0.1
Latvian SSR	12	0.1
RSFSR	14	6.3
Georgian SSR	19	12.4
Kazakh SSR	33	39.1
Lithuanian SSR	33	0.1
Moldavian SSR	38	0.0
Uzbek SSR	39	81.5
Armenian SSR	46	7.6
Kirgiz SSR	52	60.3
Turkmen SSR	54	78.8
Tadjik SSR	64	83.5
Azerbaijan SSR	82	72.1

makes the family allowance payments, if of value at all, of more value to the Central Asian family than to its Russian or Baltic counterpart. Not only does the Central Asian receive on the whole greater benefits for having a larger number of children, benefits represent a greater percentage of the Central Asian's average income than a corresponding amount would for the Slavic family. Alec Nove recently suggested some of his own findings with reference to regional breakdowns in the average per capita income.[28] According to Nove, the Central Asian Republics have shown little change in per capita income since 1960, remaining relatively static in proportion to the national average. With the average for the USSR at 948 rubles per capita, Estonia, Latvia, and Lithuania are all way above the national average, (with 1316, 1406, and 1239 rubles per capita respectively). The average per capita income in the Russian Republic is about 950 rubles. "Way at the bottom of the heap" in per capita income are Central Asia and Azerbaijan.[29] With a greater value placed on large numbers of children, a predominance of larger families, and a lower per capita income, the Central Asian, one might expect, would far more readily regard a family allowance as a positive incentive for continued childbearing, or as a significant income supplement, than would the average Slavic or Russian citizen.

Thus, despite its original intent to direct itself equitably toward the population at large, the Soviet family allowance policy in fact has chosen as its target group the large, low-income family—in particular, perhaps, the average Muslim family of Central Asia and Azerbaijan. In so doing, if not actively encouraging a higher birthrate in Central Asian areas at least perpetuated a high birthrate among the Muslim Central Asians, while value with respect to the average Slavic family has been negligible or nil.

This development has become of increasing concern to Soviet policymakers, as illustrated by repeated pronouncements—although guarded—on the need for some decentralization in the family allowance policy. As Perevedentsev has written,

> In establishing a system of "family increments" we must carefully consider such questions as the size of the payments and to whom they should go, and try to forecast in which parts of the country and among which groups they will be effective.[30]

Repeated suggestions to change the target group to the small family—for example, to formulate a system whereby larger sums would be given for the third child, with decreasing allowances for the fifth, sixth, and each subsequent child—have profound regional and national implications. But since a mother must have two or three children before she has five, and since ideology dictates that measures be centrally designed and directed indiscriminately toward the population at large, such a policy could place only greater financial demands upon the Soviet budget.

Other policymakers have suggested more blatant decentralization of population policy, calling for an intensification of child allowance and other pronatalist policies in the Russian and Slavic republics while reducing or eliminating the family allowance policy in the Muslim and Turkic republics. The overt racial implications of the latter suggestion, however, could still not be fully reconciled with official ideology at the present stage of its development. And conversely, given the financial burden associated with childrearing, particularly in urban Slavic areas, elimination of the allowance policy altogether (however small allowances may be) would also represent a direct disincentive for childbearing. Because, then, of the same economic and ideological constraints of policy formulation, the Soviet Union seems left with a policy which is exerting a negligible effect upon the average Russian family, but is conceivably having a positive, directly pronatalist effect on the average Central Asian family.

Although perhaps not as sharply the same constraints of policy formulation seem to be illustrated by other Soviet population policies also governed by economic considerations. On a regional level, effects of Soviet policy formulation vis-a-vis the consumer industry may also in fact be twofold. Because of the wide disparity in economic development between the different regions of the USSR—the fact that while some regions are highly developed others are still underdeveloped and just beginning the modernization process—greater availability and quality of consumer goods and housing will have very different, if not diametrically opposite effects in different regions.

While in the Slavic urban areas an increase in consumer goods and services appears to be a necessary precondition for the birthrate to rise, in less developed areas an increase in the consumer industry generally occurs as a concomitant of the modernization process, and is therefore generally associated with a decrease in fertility.

Theoretically, then, formulation of a policy to promote a uniform rise in the quantity and quality of consumer goods and services throughout the Soviet Union should create the conditions for the birthrate to rise in Slavic areas, and for fertility to decline in the non-Slavic areas. Yet according to several sources, the housing situation is even worse in the countryside and rural Central Asian areas than it is in the cities. Technical amenities of modern civilization are still scarce (e.g., many villages are still without electricity, running water, sewage systems, and piped gas). Creches and daycare centers are fewer in number and "not as stable as in the cities."[31] Thus the fact that consumer goods and services and quality housing have remained scarce throughout the country has a double-barreled effect: on the one hand, it may be discouraging greater fertility in the already highly developed areas of European Russia; on the other, by prolonging the modernization process in the less developed areas of the USSR, it may also be perpetuating the high birthrate among the non-Slavic peoples, and encouraging the wide growth rate disparities between different nationalities. Soviet policies formulated to eradicate "family instability," loose morals, the rising age or decreasing incidence of marriage, high divorce rates, or to eradicate the high rate of illegitimacy, are generally irrelevant in Central Asia. Problems of family instability are rare in those areas where the large, extended family is still a highly valued and deeply ingrained foundation of life. Likewise, references to problems of pre- or extramarital sex are anachronistic when Muslim society prizes virginity before marriage ard stresses loyalty after marriage.

Similarly, while the average age of marriage has risen throughout the USSR to a national average of 29.1 for bridegrooms and 26.5 for brides (1967),[32] greater proportions of Central Asians marry at a very early age. According to the 1959 census, whereas in Byelorussian cities and towns 8 percent of the females aged eighteen or nineteen were married, in the Turkimenian rural areas 54 percent of the women of that age group were married. Today, while the national average age of a bride is twenty-four, close to one-tenth of Uzbek brides are eighteen or younger.

As a rule, moreover, marriage as an institution is fundamental to Muslim society: the prophet Mohammed has been quoted as requiring every Muslim to marry, and indeed unless a Muslim does marry, his funeral is not legitimized.[33] Furthermore, although divorce may be common in certain Central Asian areas, societal pressures tend to work against the dissolution of marriages, and most divorcees soon remarry. Illegitimacy is not at all acceptable in Central Asia, and is indeed considered a curse in Islam.[34]

But ideological constraints of policy formulation still demand that policies be directed toward the population as a whole. Thus, although no statistical breakdown is available by region on the incidence of abortion, a policy of encouraging later marriages or abortion in those areas of the country where the birthrate is high is impossible if abortions or a high age of marriage officially are regarded with disfavor elsewhere in the USSR. This situation has led to a process of policy formulation wherein what policymakers say with one breath, they must qualify with the next:

> Reduction of the average age of marriage holds a tremendous potential for an increase in the birthrate . . . Needless to say, I am not talking about early marriages in general. The fact that marriages of people under twenty are becoming more rare is good from all standpoints, including a demographic one.[35]

Just as economic policies became diluted when extended throughout the country, so, then, have ideological policies become diluted with qualifications designed to make a central policy applicable to the population at large. Perhaps what is most needed in these areas for the birthrate to decline are, again, more contraceptives, family planning, and general sex education. Yet traditional reticence of the Soviet government, to formulate policies that include increased attention toward family planning and sex education, has only compounded the problem of lowering the birthrate in Central Asia as much as it has compounded the problem of raising the birthrate in Slavic areas. The fact that family planning is almost universally absent from the Central Asian areas, the fact that contraceptives are rarely available, if at all, and the poor prospects for family and sex education again imply that social policies as they are formulated in the USSR will have little impact on reshaping attitudes toward the family in Central Asia, or consequently, on narrowing the gap in the growth rates between the nationalities.

CONCLUSION

Any major change in policy could now fundamentally undermine the very economic, ideological, and bureaucratic foundation of the Soviet system. The requisite amount of financial resources to provide better housing, services, and day-care centers, or to free women from the labor force, would demand a major redirection of economic priorities, far beyond the slight redirection of the 1960s. Policies designed to shape sociocultural attitudes would demand major changes in a heritage of Soviet social thought, while policy decentralization would demand the dispensation of a fundamental tenet of Soviet ideology. The changes required to make policy implementation more effective could ultimately demand a major overhauling of the entire bureaucratic and administrative structure. All of the above pose threats to the existing bureaucratic elites and the existing balance of power. Thus Soviet population policy as it exists today— centralized, vacillating, loosely defined, and poorly implemented— holds little promise of altering "undesirable" population trends in the USSR, while in many ways it is indeed directly encouraging the very perpetuation of these trends.

The population problems elaborated above are not unique to the Soviet Union. But the consequences of the constraints operating within the Soviet context are quite different from those in other countries. Unlike France or Hungary, the Soviet Union is not faced with the threat of negative population growth. Nor is it, as is India, threatened with the prospect of being unable to meet the barest subsistence requirements of a rapidly growing population. The consequences of ineffective policies in the Soviet Union are far more political than they are evolutionary, and could far more directly threaten the very foundations of the Soviet system than its physical capacity to survive—to feed itself, or to reproduce itself. Although one can only speculate as to their implications, demographic trends and the effects of Soviet policies seem to indicate more far-reaching social and economic repercussions than an aging population or a potentially severe labor shortage alone might suggest. The fact that there is considerable fertility potential in Central Asian and other non-Slavic areas, even if the birthrate declines (since, for example, over 50 percent of the Central Asian population was under age fifteen in 1970), only heightens the demands that may be placed upon the Soviet leadership.

Present trends foretell a rise in ethnic stratification and ethnic tensions, together with a decline in the productive capacity of the nation as a whole. Russian domination of both the urban work force and of the country's social, economic, and political life may be challenged within the next decade or two. The already perceptible influence of the different nationalities on Soviet foreign policy may only become more pronounced. Major administrative, economic, social, and ultimately political adjustments may soon be demanded in Soviet society and its relations to the world.

NOTES

1. Where "population policy" refers to that compilation of direct and indirect policies which affects the size, quality, and location of the Soviet people.
2. U.S. Dept. of Labor, "Population of the USSR, 1950-2000" p. 64.

3. Robert A. Lewis and Richard H. Rowland, "East is West and West is East . . . Population Redistribution in the USSR and its Impact on Society," unpublished manuscript, p. 29.

4. H. Sigerist, *Socialized Medicine in the Soviet Union* (NY: Norton, 1937) p. 244.

5. Alfred Sauvy, "La Population de l'Union Sovietique," *Population*, II(1956):475.

6. Viktor Perevedentsev "We're 250 Million," *Molodoj Kommunist*, 3(1973):90

7. For example, while the 1926 census comprised fifty-seven published volumes, the 1970 census reduced the number to seven, Helen Cohn, Lecture at the Harvard Population Center, March 19, 1976., despite the apparent renewed emphasis on demographic research in the 1960s.

8. In the 1970 census, for example, questions on housing were omitted. See Feshbach, "Observations on the Soviet Census." *Problems of Communism*, (May-June 1970):63. Cohen states that a sample fertility study in 1960 was not publicized, much less discussed, for several years.

9. Cohn.

10. J.F. Besemeres, "Population Politics in the USSR," *Soviet Union*, (1975):68

11. Cohn.

12. Feshbach, p. 62.

13. David and Vera Mace, *Soviet Family* (Garden City, New York: Doubleday, 1963), p. 241.

14. Hodgman, *Soviet Industrial Production, 1928-1951* (Cambridge: Harvard University Press, 1954), p. 50.

15. "A Demographic Problem: Employment of Women and the Birthrate." Discussion. *Voprosy Ekonomiki* (May 1969): p. 158.

16. Gertrude E. Schroeder, "Soviet Economic Growth and Consumer Welfare: Retrospect and Prospect," *Soviet Economic Prospects for the Seventies*, Washington, 1973, p. 9.

17. Hodgman, p. 50.

18. Schroeder, p. 8.

19. D. Novoplyansky, "Should Soviet Women Have More Children?" *Current Digest of the Soviet Press*, 24(Dec 27, 1972):7.

20. D. Valentei and G. Kiseleva, "Remedies Sought for Sagging Demographic Curve," *Current Digest of the Soviet Press*, 21(October 29, 1969):11.

21. Peter Stafford, *Sexual Behavior in the Communist World*. (New York: The Julian Press, 1967), p. 246.

22. Wesley A. Fisher, "Soviet Family Research." Paper presented at the 1975 Annual Meeting of the American Association for the Advancement of Slavic Studies, Atlanta, Georgia, October 8-11, 1975, p. 16.

23. Anita Glassl, "Soviet Citizens Voice their Sex Problems," *Review of Soviet Medical Sciences*, vol. 7, no. 2, 1970, pp. 28-32.

24. I would like to thank Mark Field for suggesting this point.

25. V. Perevedentsev, "Some Factors in the Falling Birthrate," *Current Digest of the Soviet Press*, 27(September 3, 1975), p. 3.

26. Ibid.

27. David Heer, "Family Allowances and Fertility in the Soviet Union." *Soviet Studies*, 28(October 1966): 158.

28. A. Nove, from a lecture given November 1975 at the Harvard Russian Research Center. It should be noted that, as Nove stated, "the figures may be distorted, as the Russians in a republic generally earn much more than the indigenous population . . ." Such a distortion would only make the national disparities even more acute, however, and intensify the above assertions.

29. A. Nove and J.A. Newth, *The Soviet Middle East* (NY: Praeger 1967), pp. 42-43, offer statistics concerning the disparity between RSFSR and the Asian republics. The authors feel that "the disparity may actually be increasing in recent years because of differences in population growth rates."

30. V. Perevedentsev "Demographer Calls for Earlier Marriages," *Current Digest of the Soviet Press*, vol. 24, Oct. 11, 1972, pp. 1-3.

31. Interview with a Soviet Emigre, Boston, October 1975.

32. V. Shlyapentokh "Pravda Says No to Marriage Bureaus," *Current Digest of the Soviet Press*, 23(July 13, 1971):10.

33. Interview, Sabiha Syed.

34. Ibid.

35. V. Perevedentsev "Marry Early," p. 36. See note 30.

8

SEASONAL LABOR MIGRATION ON HISPANIOLA: A POLICY OF CONVENIENCE[1]

Eleanor E. Glaessel-Brown

The Caribbean island Hispaniola presents an unusual case for population policy-watchers. Similar to neighboring islands, its area is limited: population size, composition, and distribution represent legitimate public concerns. Unlike other islands in the West Indies, Hispaniola is shared by two very different sovereign entities: Haiti and the Dominican Republic. An issue that links the two countries directly and shows how demographic situations and population policies in neighboring countries affect each other is the Haitian seasonal labor migration to the Dominican Republic.

This form of labor mobility has counterparts in many areas of the world, where traditional economies supply labor to more industrialized neighbors. Other examples in the Western Hemisphere include Mexican, Central American, pre-Castro Cuban, and other Caribbean migration to the United States and Colombian migration to Venezuela and the United States. These cases have several features in common: they involve massive migrations; the workers assume jobs at the lowest pay and skill levels of the receiving nation; the greatest proportion of migrant workers enter or remain in the country illegally; they are employed despite high native unemployment; and although there is considerable opposition to the migration on the part of organized labor groups or from a racial and ethnic standpoint, little has been done to stop it.

This paper addresses the question of why the Dominican Republic has adopted an ostensibly contradictory policy officially outlawing labor migration from Haiti, while allowing significant seasonal mobility to occur: a case of policy articulation vs. policy practice. Both the policy and the practice are accommodations to convenience, revealing a seasonal symbiosis based on an intricate interplay of demographic, economic, political, and cultural realities.

Demographically, Haiti is overpopulated (in terms of the ratio of livelihood opportunities to population) in both rural and urban areas. Surplus labor migrates to the Dominican Republic where, although unemployment exceeds 20 percent, there is a chronic shortage of field workers. The economic disparity between the two countries makes the low-paying, insecure jobs shunned by Dominican labor acceptable to the Haitian worker who does slightly better than he would at home while earning a cash income. Conversely, since cheap labor is available, the Dominican agricultural wage scale remains depressed. Sugar production costs are reduced in the Dominican Republic while Haiti reaps foreign exchange. There are political gains to be made in both countries by ignoring official policy. The Dominican government does not have to be responsible for the welfare of its illegal aliens, while the Haitian government benefits from a population pressure release, helping to free both governments to concentrate on programs of aggregate economic growth. Finally, Haitian and Dominican cultural differences make the foreign workers more readily visible in the Dominican Republic and, spurred by historical antipathy between the two nations, this distinction helps to perpetuate their illegal status.

The paper also contends that, if present trends continue, the interdependent relationship will be strengthened. Certain aspects of Dominican development have triggered internal rural-urban migration and international emigration patterns that will perennialize Dominican dependence on foreign field workers, while Haiti will continue as a steady source of labor.

HISTORICAL PERSPECTIVE

Immigration and migration policy have played a major role on

Hispaniola since the Spanish arrived almost five centuries ago and laid the foundations for the present demographic, economic, political, and cultural situations.[2]

The conquistadors drafted Hispaniola's indigenous population into heavy labor in the construction of the city of Santo Domingo and as miners and domestic servants. Within a short time the Indian population plummeted in size as illnesses for which they had no immunity, aggravated by poor conditions and fatigue, overwhelmed them. In 1494 about 130,000 Indians were enumerated around the new settlement; by 1518 there were only 11,000 left. The Spaniards then turned to the surrounding islands which they systematically depopulated in their greed for forced labor. Soon those Indians also succumbed to the alien conditions. By 1502 the demise of the native island populations became the catalyst for a flourishing African slave trade to provide an alternate work force for the developing labor-intensive sugar industry.

The Spanish population remained small and isolated. Indians killed the few men left by Columbus after his first voyage, and diseases ravaged subsequent groups of Spaniards. There were few Spanish women, and although concubinage was common, marriage with Indian and Negro slave women was not, so that the higher fertility associated with family units awaited the arrival of settlers in later decades. The population was still so sparse in 1526 that emigration was forbidden "on pain of death."

During its early colonial years, the island enjoyed economic and political prominence as the administrative capital of the Indies, but that era ended abruptly as Havana gained in importance and reports of greater riches lured skilled workers and merchants to the South and Central American mainland. This marked the first substantial emigration from Hispaniola, severely depressing the economy and reducing those who remained to a livelihood of piracy and contraband traffic. Such illicit activities caused the Spanish crown to force the population to concentrate around Santo Domingo. The deserted hinterland then allowed French pirates and settlers to become established on the western end of the island where they were able to develop large sugar plantations unchallenged. In 1697 the western third of Hispaniola was ceded to France and a small white ruling elite developed "hayti" into one of France's wealthiest colonies based on sugar production and slavery.[3] In contrast, the Spanish two-thirds of the island continued to decay.

In the eighteenth century Haiti became the first Western Hemisphere nation to abolish slavery. It declared its independence and expelled most of the remaining white population. Haiti then turned its sights to neighboring Santo Domingo. The poorly administered and sparsely populated Spanish colony succumbed in 1822 to twenty-two years of humiliating Haitian rule that left an indelible mark on the Dominican psyche.

Once reclaimed by Spain and granted a "second independence," a cautious Santo Domingo pursued an active pronatalist policy in search of inhabitants to distribute throughout the country and particularly to settle along the Haitian border. To achieve the desired resettlement, an aggressive immigration policy was also instituted, with repeated invitations extended to Europeans from the Canary Islands. By the end of the nineteenth century many Canary Islanders had settled in Santo Domingo and began to revitalize the sugar plantations and to develop caçao, coffee, and tobacco production. Still relying on immigration, Santo Domingo imported a labor force for the sugar harvest from the British Antilles and from Haiti.

Since that time between 20,000 and 60,000 Haitians have migrated annually to the Dominican Republic in search of seasonal employment. Many of these workers have settled in the western provinces of the Dominican Republic; others have simply remained on the plantations between harvests.

With the worldwide depression of the early 1930s, the price of sugar fell drastically, the Haitian labor migrations to Cuba were suspended, and more migrants than ever flowed into Santo Domingo where unemployment was also severe. In 1933 all work permits were revoked, but the situation was not relieved. As the crisis peaked in 1937, the Haitian migrants apparently became the scapegoat for internal problems and more than 10,000 individuals are reported to have been massacred by order of the dictator Trujillo. During Trujillo's remaining years, the border was heavily guarded and a number of policies to discourage spontaneous migration were implemented. After Trujillo's assassination in 1961, Haitians once again spilled over the border. President Joaquin Balaguer disclosed that between 1961 and 1966, 300,000 Haitians entered the country. Both Port-au-Prince and Santo Domingo tried to control the movement, and finally in 1966 a formal agreement between the Balaguer and Duvalier governments allowed for the entrance of between 10,000 and 20,000 temporary workers annually. The agreement stipulated that the migrants had to secure work permits, that they were to be adult males only, and that they were to work exclusively in the sugar harvest, leaving the country once it was over.

Over the years Dominicans have made it eminently clear that they are opposed to the Haitian migrations and particularly to the continuing tendency of the migrants to remain in the country. Finally in 1971 the agreement of 1966 was superceded by a law absolutely prohibiting the influx of Haitian cane cutters. Yet despite this explicit policy, thousands of Haitians continue to cross the border. There are reports of active recruitment as well as the use of Dominican military vans to transport the workers.

CONTEMPORARY DEVELOPMENT

Contemporary economic and demographic patterns shed further light on the nature of the relationship between Hispaniola's two nations.

Sugar has remained the principal export product in the Dominican Republic accounting for about 48 percent of total exports in 1970. This one-crop economy is precariously vulnerable to purchases made by the United States which buys Dominican sugar under a preferential quota system above world market prices. (The Dominican Republic is presently second only to the Philippines as a U.S. sugar supplier.) Coffee has replaced sugar as Haiti's principal export product. Per capita income in 1970 was approximately $330 in the Dominican Republic and $80 in Haiti, a measure distorted in both countries by uneven wealth distribution. Development prospects for the Dominican Republic are favorable. Increased investor confidence, rising sugar prices, a reorganization of the sugar corporations, new ferronickel and gold mining and oil refining operations have led to what the Inter-American Development Bank views as the "remarkable recovery" of the Dominican economy after the political chaos of the mid-1960s.[4] Average annual growth in GDP during the 1969-1972 period was 10.9 percent, reaching 12.5 percent in 1972. The Haitian economy was totally devastated during the struggles of the nineteenth century, and Haiti continues to be one of the poorest countries in the Western Hemisphere.

Both Haiti and the Dominican Republic have experienced similar stormy political histories, replete with numerous internal revolts, frequent government turnovers, United States receiverships and occupations, and infamous dictatorships. The present governments of both countries are descendents of those of preceding decades; Balaguer in the Dominican Republic was president during the Trujillo dictatorship, and Jean-Claude Duvalier is the son of the late "Papa Doc," Haiti's despotic ruler for fourteen years.

The United States receivership and occupation had a profound demographic impact on the Dominican Republic: rudimentary public health measures were implemented for the first time and mortality plunged as a result. The Dominican population, which had barely sustained growth for four centuries and had relied heavily on immigration, suddenly began to grow through natural increase. Although the Dominican Republic remained the only country in the Caribbean willing to accept immigrants, in a twist of circumstances it was designated by North American population experts as a country in urgent need of a population control program. President Balaguer became one of the first heads-of-state to acknowledge rapid population growth as a national concern, and in 1968 the country adopted an antinatalist policy and implemented a national family planning program. Statistics compiled by the Latin American Demographic Center show the crude birth rate to have declined slightly from 50.1 births per thousand population in 1950 to 45.8 in 1970, while the crude death rate in the same period decreased dramatically from 20.3 deaths per thousand population to 10.9; fertility remained fairly constant while mortality was almost halved. The population enumerated in 1970 was almost twice that reported in 1950.

Haiti's population problem has always been considered more serious because of the late Duvalier's apparent lack of interest in doing anything about it. In 1970 Haiti had a crude birth rate of 43.9 and a crude death rate of 19.7, but exceptionally high infant mortality has kept population growth lower than in the Dominican Republic. Dominicans are nevertheless concerned that Haiti has a slightly larger total population than the Dominican Republic on one-third of the island. Although Haiti has no population growth policy, a family planning program began in earnest in 1971.

Figure 1 traces Dominican and Haitian population growth in millions from 1935 to 1970 and projects growth to 1990 at the current median estimated rates: 3.0 percent per annum for the Dominican Republic and 2.4 percent for Haiti. Urban population is also shown.

A POLICY OF CONTRADICTIONS?

Hispaniola's colonial legacy and contemporary development patterns have influenced the persistence of Haitian seasonal labor migration to the Dominican Republic and the policy that oversees it. Yet how can the apparent contradictions in policy be explained, that is, why does the Dominican policy officially outlaw the entry of Haitian workers while unofficially allowing the migration to occur each year?

Much of what has been written about Caribbean migration focuses on demographic considerations and the density factor: too many people per square kilometer and arable land, in the context of pre-

Figure 1
Population Growth Curves for Haiti and the Dominican Republic, for All
Censuses and Projected to 1990, Total and Urban Population
(in millions)

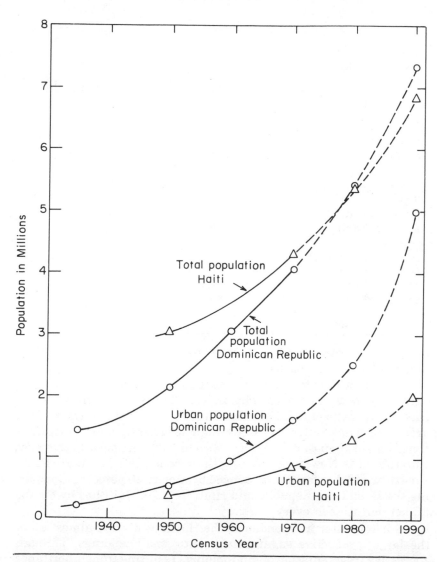

dominantly rural, colonial plantation economies, with limited employment opportunities in industry. Indeed, in the 1970s the Caribbean nations were ten times more densely populated than South

Table 1
Population Densities in the Dominican Republic and Haiti
(population per square kilometer)[6]

	Haiti	Dominican Republic
Total population/ total area	178	86
Rural population/ arable land	154	54
Rural population/ arable land	1161	272
Agricultural labor force/ arable land	579	74

American countries and four times more densely populated than Central American nations.

Haiti, in terms of total population to total land area, has one of the highest densities in the Caribbean. Yet what is most striking about Haiti is the ratio of rural population to *arable* land and the ratio of agricultural labor force to arable land. The latter figure is almost four times higher than that for Puerto Rico in 1950 just prior to the mass emigrations to New York. (During the decade 1950-60, Puerto Rico's agricultural labor force was reduced by almost 40 percent.) Comparing the Dominican Republic and Haiti in 1970, Haiti has by far the higher densities in every category:[5]

Immediately after independence, the Haitians divided almost all of the large, productive sugar estates into small holdings. Through successive fragmentation of landholdings resulting from inheritance laws, as well as serious overcultivation and deforestation, the Haitian countryside has become depleted and unproductive. The only incentive for the Haitian peasant farmer to remain on his land is the fact that he owns it and little else. This landholding system has kept more people in rural areas than would otherwise be possible or, perhaps, wise.

The fact that the major Haitian migration stream is not directed toward other Caribbean islands is not difficult to explain. Since Cuba closed its doors, increasing emigration has taken place to the Bahamas, but most Caribbean islands are themselves islands of emigration. They offer limited opportunities and would hardly welcome large numbers of unskilled immigrants. It would not be accurate, however, to conclude that most Haitians go to the Dominican Republic because it is closest and shares a land border. The flaw in this seemingly reasonable explanation is that with an uncommonly large combined police and military force, patrolling a 190-mile border should not be too difficult—if that were the objective.

What is missing from the exclusively demographic "push" explanation (Haitians forced to flee poverty) are the "pull" factors associated with the Dominican Republic. Andre Corten[7] has observed that since the passing of the explicit law in 1971 prohibiting the immigration of Haitian workers and their employment on sugar lands, the continued entrance of such workers could be cause for political intervention unless an economic function were being served by the immigration. In that case, the activity would be quietly integrated into the sphere of Dominican-Haitian political relations. This is indeed what has happened.

Although unemployment and especially underemployment have been consistently high in Santo Domingo, particularly during the 1960s and early 1970s, Dominicans have always been unwilling to cut their own sugar cane. They consider it demeaning and grossly underpaid work ($1.50 a ton, not all of which is clear income). Furthermore, the harvest season lasts only six to eight months of the year, leaving almost half a year to either look for other work or remain unemployed.[8] The characteristic low wages, low status, poor working conditions, unstable (seasonal, "dead-end") nature, and highly personalized relationship between worker and supervisor have made this precisely the type of work that is relegated to a foreign labor force in many countries.[9]

For the Haitian worker, the benefits of accepting these jobs seem limited at first glance. Most Haitians interviewed by Corten in the Dominican Republic in the 1960s were landowners; they had something to return to. Characteristic of most migrants, they did not originate from among the most destitute and ill-prepared stratum of the population in Haiti. Yet the migrants clearly occupy the bottom rung on the Dominican socioeconomic scale. Conditions they endure in the Dominican Republic are not much, if at all, better than those they left in Haiti. Moreover, while the cane cutter's wage in the Dominican Republic is $1.50 compared with $.50 in Haiti, the higher cost of living in the Dominican Republic reduces the Haitian migrant's real income. Thus the economic gains resulting from migration are somewhat limited.

Then why do so many Haitians subject themselves to what can hardly be considered a beneficial situation? One explanation is that potential migrants are purposely given inaccurate information by Haitian labor contractors who collect a fee per head. But if this were the sole reason it would be difficult to understand why the practice persists year after year, and to explain the consistent emigration from Haiti to other locations over the years as well as the marked fluctuations in the volume of migrants to the Dominican Republic, apparently in response to changes in economic climate and border restrictions. The fact is that employment in seasonal agricultural work in the Dominican Republic offers the Haitian migrant advantages in addition to the moderate income differential (although wages are low, they are better than those in Haiti), including easy access, a low-skill requirement, and a limited time commitment. Since the work is temporary, concerns about job advancement, long-term benefits, and improved working conditions are less important. Thus the disadvantages for local labor are often less relevant for migrant workers who intend to return home after accumulating some savings.[10]

The crucial question is that if the seasonal migrations allow agricultural local shortages in the Dominican Republic to be solved through recruitment of workers from a less developed economy then why is there an explicit law prohibiting the labor transfer? Corten argues that Haitians play a fundamental role in the Dominican social and economic structure and that the entire operation is carefully orchestrated and controlled by the Dominican elite and perpetuated by Haitian middlemen. According to this argument the quota of legal entrants was historically maintained below needs and the migration is now prohibited precisely because the Dominican government and sugar mill owners *prefer to perpetuate the illegal status of Haitian workers to keep wages and costs low*. Rayford Logan writes that in 1937

Some 60,000 poverty-striken Haitians received slighly higher wages on the Dominican side. The Dominican planters welcomed this opportunity to depress the wages they paid to local labour. Here, on an abysmally low scale, was the classic pattern of the exploitation of foreigners to undercut the wages of indigenous workers.[11]

The existing law is simply not enforced. Once in the Dominican Republic, the Haitians have no legal petitioning power to improve their situation and their illegal status makes it easier to deport the workers when they are not needed. Thus labor insecurity is institutionalized.

In a recent article, Arismendi Díaz Santana[12] links the persistence of the sugar industry's mode of production that requires an imported labor force to the Dominican Republic's economic dependence on the United States. He argues that because of Dominican dependency the minimization of sugar production costs has been accomplished in the Dominican Republic by extending the acreage under cultivation and maintaining a large, diffident work force rather than by modernizing the means of production. In that way, fluctuations in market price are absorbed by the foreign labor instead of endangering investments in fixed capital. Aside from depressing wages, the presence of Haitian migrant workers retards the unionization and politicization of the Dominican agricultural work force. Díaz Santana concludes that, in addition to severing dependent relations, the Haitian workers should be fully integrated into Dominican socioeconomic relations.

Yet despite the fact that the Haitian seasonal labor migration is beneficial to certain sectors in both countries and is tacitly supported by both governments, it is the object of political opposition in the Dominican Republic. The most obvious explanation for this is that local wages for agricultural work are depressed by the availability of cheap labor. With per capita income in the Dominican Republic almost four times what it is in Haiti, the Dominican government would find it difficult to get local labor to work at a Haitian wage. But cane cutting has been shown to be unappealing for more reasons than recompense alone. Another explanation for the popular opposition to Haitians' presence on Dominican soil is the apparent animosity Dominicans feel toward the Haitian people because of fears originating from tales of oppressive rule and because of racial and ethnic differences. Hispaniola's cultural legacy has been predominantly

Spanish-European in the eastern section and decidely French-African in the West. Although both countries are now considered racially and ethnically Negro or mulatto by international statisticians,

> Dominicans . . . think of themselves and would like to be known as white and European. The Dominicans thus look down upon the neighboring Haitians whom they consider Negro, African, and uncivilized.[13]

Logan noted that Dominican workers shunned harvest employment because they "considered themselves culturally and racially superior to the Haitians who were competing with them."[14] Apart from the issue of Haitian national origin, Dominican immigration policy for many years was overtly and covertly racist. The invitations to immigrate extended to inhabitants of the Canary Islands during the nineteenth century had the clear intent of increasing the proportion of whites in the nation's population. In 1919 a law prohibited the immigration of workers who were not Caucasian, but a year later the secretary of agriculture found it necessary to issue an order allowing black workers into the country to prevent economic chaos. In 1925, the ministry of agriculture was authorized to grant temporary permits. For a short time during the Trujillo era, the Dominican Republic became a haven for white European refugees who were settled along the Haitian border. Trujillo also levied an extra and prohibitive tax on black immigrants (a curious turn of events since Negroes were originally brought into the country against their will as slaves).

An additional consideration is that Dominicans have always had a poor and guarded relationship with the Haitians. The two cultures are completely different, including what for Dominicans are mysterious differences in religious practices and an unintelligible language. The Dominican public has retained a vivid memory of submission to Haitian rule and is terrified at the prospect of a repeated invasion. Dominicans are well aware of Haiti's uncontrolled population growth and the most vocal opponent of the Dominican national family planning program to this day has been the influential, adamantly pro-natalist Committee for the Defense of the Frontiers which periodically reminds the Dominican public of past problems with neighboring Haitians whom they consider poised for spontaneous emigration into the still sparsely populated border areas.[15]

At the time of Haitian rule a group of free Negroes from the southern United States immigrated to the Dominican Republic, and later another group of English-speaking Negroes, imported from islands in the West Indies to work in the sugar harvest, settled in the country. Many, except for an enclave of U.S. freemen on the Samana Peninsula, were generally assimilated into the Dominican population. The myths, fears, and resentments that surround the Haitians do not generally extend to these *Ingleses*. Nanci Gonzalez writes that West Indians and Haitians have become assimilated into Dominican society in a different manner from other ethnic groups[16] because of locational and class factors. Haitians, in particular, live on or near the sugar plantations and assimilate only in the lower socioeconomic strata. She describes "an extreme prejudice against Haitians ... [that] has become part of the national ideology."[17]

Thus the elements that determine the policy governing Haitian labor migration to the Dominican Republic are initially demographic, laced with economic necessity and political contradiction, and strongly influenced by racial, ethnic, and historical considerations. As long as the present governments stay in power, and as long as it continues to be economically expedient for the elites of both countries, it is reasonable to predict that the situation will remain unchanged: the migration will be officially proscribed but it will continue on a large scale illegally.[18]

INTERNAL MIGRATION AND LABOR DEPENDENCE

The preceding analysis explains most of the contradictions evident in the policy dealing with Haitian labor migration to the Dominican Republic. Yet the question lingers: if the Dominican government were intent on protecting field labor jobs for its citizenry and were willing to press for wages more in line with the Dominican cost of living, would it be difficult to do so? The answer is—probably not. The border could be patrolled and, with sugar prices held artificially above world market prices, higher wages would not cripple the Dominican growers. Perhaps a more appropriate line of inquiry would be: is the local population a reliable future source of labor? With the Dominican Republic's improving economic fortunes has come a change in migration patterns that will increase Dominican dependence on foreign, seasonal labor for the sugar industry.

In predominantly agricultural societies such as Haiti, migration is mostly rural-to-rural in pursuit of field labor jobs. As a country begins to industrialize, the urban labor market expands and the flow to urban areas begins. Greater awareness and higher aspirations filter into the countryside and, as migrants return from forays to large cities, new customs, thoughts, and experiences are diffused.

The Dominican Republic[19] is not yet a highly urbanized country with 60 percent of the population still living in rural areas; nevertheless, population distribution has been undergoing rapid change. In the last decade, 70 percent of population growth has occurred in urban areas; the urban growth rate for the 1960-70 period was a high 5.7 percent per annum. In 1960 there were only seven cities with populations of more than 20,000; by 1970 this figure had doubled.

Haiti has not experienced similar internal migration; the urban growth rate for 1960-70 was a lower 3.8 percent per annum, and the population was only 17.6 percent urban in 1970. One reason for this is that the urban economy is not expanding to an extent that would warrant a substantial migration stream; a second reason is that Haiti's free-holding land tenure arrangement encourages farmers to remain in rural areas. In the Dominican Republic most migrants have nothing to lose and little hope of becoming land owners. With the distinct remnants of a colonial land tenure system, almost half of the best land is given to state-owned sugar production, 57 percent of the remaining arable land is in holdings of less than five acres, and the rest is concentrated in large private estates. When the government reclaimed Trujillo's immense holdings (including twelve of the country's sixteen sugar mills) after his assassination, its plan was to institute land reform. The revolution of 1965 interfered, and when it was over all the land was back in the hands of the government and large private landowners.

General development policies have had, and probably will continue to have, the unintended effect of encouraging migration. New roads facilitate travel, new schools spread awareness and aspirations throughout the countryside, the concentration on sugar production increases unemployment among Dominican peasants and investments in urban services make cities more attractive. Urban growth in the Dominican Republic is also characterized by high primacy (the concentration of population, resources, and economic and political functions in one or two cities). The capital, Santo Domingo, and the second city, Santiago, accounted for approximately 50 percent of the total urban increase during the last two decades. By 1970 every fifth Dominican lived within the National District (capital) area.[20] Haza reports that 80 percent of the people living in Santo Domingo have incomes higher than the national average, and the average income in Santo Domingo is twice that of the rest of the nation. He has summarized economic indices that are concentrated in the National District, including:

a) roughly 60% of total sales (wholesales), from 1947 to 1957; b) two-thirds of the value of construction in the country from 1963 to 1970; c) 22.6% of Government investment in 1970; d) more than two-thirds of housing built or financed by the government from 1962 to 1971; e) 50% of public investment in hospitals in 1940-1954, and approximately one-fourth of public medical care; f) almost half the equity investment in industries; and g) 78.6% of installed electric energy capacity, 75.2% of net energy generation and 60% of electrical billings by the Electric Corporation.[21]

Someone living outside the capital would not be at all incorrect in thinking that the lights are brighter in Santo Domingo.

Other population gains were recorded in the major areas of development outside the National District, but these were also areas surrounding provincial capitals. The fact that four of the six divisions considered as western border provinces have grown only slowly may indicate that Trujillo's policy of encouraging settlement in that area kept more people there than otherwise would have stayed.

The following long-term consequences of internal migration on Dominican rural areas may be anticipated:

1. A reduction in fertility as migrants take their reproductive potential with them.
2. An increase in the dependency ratio with a major section of the labor force leaving the pool.
3. Some increased income as migrants return to the sending communities (or remit cash to their relatives there).
4. An introduction of social change and modern consumer habits through interaction with returned migrants.
5. A lowering of local unemployment, but also a syphoning away of the most enterprising citizens.

The movement of the Dominican population toward urban areas in search of more lucrative employment opportunities will limit the availability of field workers and leave the way clear for foreign labor. The fact that most of the western provinces are again growing slowly and even losing population because of the new migration trends means that Haitian expatriates will continue to encounter little effective resistance to their presence.

These internal migration flows and the high rate of natural increase in the Dominican Republic, however, are not being absorbed entirely by Dominican cities. Emigration to the United States has reached sufficient proportions to make a noticeable dent in national statistics, reflected in the unexpected decline in the country's total population growth and in the urban growth rate between 1960 and 1970. There are estimates of more than 100,000 migrants to the United States during the past decade, making the Dominican Republic the third highest source of immigrants from the Western Hemisphere after Mexico and Canada. Dominicans half jokingly refer to New York as their second city.

This is a highly significant phenomenon: the Dominican Republic is urbanizing in New York City. The obvious parallel is Puerto Rico in the postwar era when time for local development was gained through heavy emigration to the mainland.

> Undoubtedly, emigration has kept the population from growing at the rapid rate indicated by the high rate of natural increase and has made it possible for Puerto Rico to accomplish something that is denied most underdeveloped areas.[22]

Glen Hendricks[23] portrays the unusual socioeconomic links that have developed between New York and a small Dominican town he studied in the early 1970s. More than half of the village households had members living in New York at one time; there was almost daily contact with the northern metropolis as well as an extraordinary dependence on remittances from relatives working there. Emigrants shuttle back and forth to simultaneously maintain family ties in the Dominican Republic and resident visas or jobs in New York. International migration data show that most migrants are between the ages of twenty and thirty-five and originate from the lower-middle income group. Of the more than 140,000 legal Dominican residents in New York in 1970, 48 percent were younger than twenty years old.

This intense emigration has developed only during the 1960s attaining an estmimated average rate of about 2.0 percent per annum between 1960 and 1970. The Dominican government appears to have taken a laissez-faire stance regarding its emigrees and has left the regulation headaches to United States consulates and immigration officials. As in the Puerto Rican, Mexican, and Haitian cases the Dominicans are probably content to let the pressures of unemployed, unskilled labor slowly leave the country. Ironically Dominican labor in the United States often assumes low-paying, nonskilled jobs similar in occupational scale to those occupied by Haitian migrant labor in the Dominican Republic. There is also a large Haitian population in eastern United States cities; however, a higher proportion are skilled laborers and professionals who enter the United States legally. While the Dominican illegal alien often gains entry into the

United States and escapes detection by posing as a Puerto Rican, this deception is much more difficult for a Haitian.

Finally, the following demographic assumptions could influence the perpetuation of the Haitian/Dominican seasonal migration symbiosis:

1. Fertility has been more or less stable in both countries; one might expect a further decline in the Dominican Republic as a result of economic progress and an antinatalist policy accompanied by the availability of family planning. A small rise in fertility followed by a decline may be expected in Haiti.
2. Mortality has declined steadily in the Dominican Republic since 1940 and will probably continue to do so; in Haiti, a considerable decline can be anticipated.
3. Population growth from natural increase will continue to be high in the Dominican Republic, although international emigration will keep the national growth rate down; if there is a marked decline in mortality (particularly infant mortality) in Haiti, a high growth rate is anticipated, which might surpass that of the Dominican Republic.
4. Urbanization and rural-urban migration will continue at a higher rate in the Dominican Republic due to Haiti's lag in economic development.

Haiti's potentially explosive population growth combined with its limited availability of arable land for a predominantly rural-based society, the continued fragmentation of parcels through inheritance laws, and slow economic development retarding urbanization almost assure that a Haitian seasonal labor supply will be available for some time to come.

Aside from the totally unexpected, the situation outlined in this paper could be dramatically altered by changes in two aspects of the sugar industry. First are factors associated with the market, such as price fluctuations and tariff adjustments, or a reallocation of sugar trade quotas in the United States. Second are factors associated with production, such as attempts to mechanize the harvest and to change the form of cane cutting to increase worker productivity (both of these measures are intended to reduce the number of workers required). The reported recent request by Dominican coffee planters for Haitian workers to fill a local labor gap, however, indicates that the basic mechanism of labor dependence holds.

CONCLUSION

Haitian seasonal labor has allowed the Dominican Republic to continue expanding its profitable, labor-intensive sugar industry at relatively low cost, while pursuing a development program based on urban industrialization, resource extraction, and tourism. Rural-urban migration facilitates the industrialization program, while international emigration relieves population pressure in the Dominican Republic. Policies for influencing Dominican internal and international migration patterns are weak; the local population has become increasingly horizontally mobile, thus reducing demands to change the land tenure system and agricultural wage scales and opening the lowest level of agricultural jobs for cheap, transient, less demanding labor. The Haitian migrants are similarly diverted from frustration in their own cities.

Rampant illegal migration has persisted in the face of a clearly articulated policy and popular opposition because of a tremendous inertia built into the system; for both sending and receiving nations, the migration serves as an alternative to basic socioeconomic change. The foreign workers have an illegal status imposed upon them by a law forbidding their entry but which in reality assures a docile labor force that can be readily manipulated or deported. Haiti allows its potentially volatile surplus labor to filter into the Dominican Republic, just as the Dominican Republic exports some of its excess population to the United States. There is no paradox in this policy; it is indeed a convenient arrangement—the only disadvantage is an unfortunately disproportionate accrual of benefits.

NOTES

1. Rolando Alum, Wayne Cornelius, Eduardo LaTorre, George Masnick, David Smith, and Howard Wiarda made helpful comments on earlier drafts of this paper, a more extensive work written in May 1975 which included material from two unpublished papers: "Haitian Migrant Labor in the Dominican Republic," and "Internal Migration in the Dominican Republic: Patterns, Rates and Policy Implications."

2. The following are some of the sources consulted in researching the historical antecedents of labor migration on Hispaniola: Mejico Angeles y Amiro Perez Mera, *Poblacion y Salud: Efectos de la Fecundidad, Mortalidad y Migracion*, Documento Presentado al Seminario Sobre Problemas de Población Celebrado en la UASD del 13 al 19 de Enero de 1975 (Republica Dominicana, 1975); Sherburne F. Cook and Woodrow Borah, *Essays in Population History: Mexico and the Caribbean* (Berkeley, California: University of California Press, 1971) 1, pp. 376-410; Harold L. Geisert, *The Caribbean:*

Population and Resources (Ann Arbor, Michigan: University Microfilms, 1960); Hermannus Hoetinck, "The Dominican Republic in the Nineteenth Century: Some Notes on Stratification, Immigration and Race," in *Race and Class in Latin America*, (ed.) Magnus Morner (New York: Columbia University Press, 1970); Rayford Logan, *Haiti and the Dominican Republic* (London: Oxford University Press, 1968); Aaron Segal, *Politics and Population in the Caribbean* (Rio Piedras, Puerto Rico: Institute of Caribbean Studies, 1969.); Nicolas Sanchez-Albornóz, *The Population of Latin America: A History* (Berkeley, California: University of California Press, 1974); Secretario de Estado de Justicia, *Indice General de la Legislacion de la Republica Dominicana 1844-1936* (Ciudad Trujillo, 1937); Howard Wiarda, *The Dominican Republic* (New York: Frederick A. Praeger, Publishers, 1969).

3. By 1789, nine-tenths of the Haitian population was composed of African slaves, whereas this was true of only one-tenth of the Dominican population.

4. Inter-American Development Bank, *Economic and Social Progress in Latin America*, Annual Report 1973 (Washington, D.C.: IADB, 1973), pp. 184-191; other sources for economic and demographic data primarily in this section include: Angeles y Perez Mera; Emilio Cordero Michel et al., *Seminario Sobre Problemas de Poblacion en la Republica Dominicana* (Santo Domingo: Editora de la Universidad Autonoma de Santo Domingo, 1975); Dirección General de Estadística, *Poblacion de la Republica Dominicana Censada en 1950* (Ciudad Trujillo, 1954); Economic Intelligence Unit Ltd., *Quarterly Economic Review: Cuba, Dominican Republic, Haiti, Puerto Rico*, 1974 through 1976; Oficina Nacional de Estadística, *Censo Nacional de Poblacion y Habitacion: 9 y 10 Enero 1970, Cifras Oficiales Preliminares*, Boletin Censal Nu. 3 (Republica Dominicana, Julio 1970); Oficina Nacional de Estadística, "Comentarios Sobre los Resultados Definitivos del V Censo Nacional de Población," unpublished paper, December 1971; Oficina Nacional de Estadística, "Comentarios Sobre los Resultados Definitivos del V Censo Nacional de Población: Segunda Parte," unpublished paper, March 1972; Oficina Nacional de Estadística, *Estadistica Demografica* (Santo Domingo: ONE, 1963-65, 1967, 1968, 1970); Pan American Union, *Datos Basicos de Poblacion en America Latina 1970* (Washington, D.C.: Department of Social Affairs, 1971); Hernando Perez Montas, "Dominican Republic," *Country Profiles* (New York: The Population Council, 1973); Kenneth Ruddle and Kathleen Barrows, *Statistical Abstract of Latin America 1974* (Los Angeles, California: University of California, Latin American Center, 1974); Sección General de Estadística y Censo, *4 Censo Nacional de Poblacion 1960* (Ciudad Trujillo, 1961); Jorge L. Somoza, *America Latina: Situacion Demografica Alredador de 1973 y Perspectivas Para el Año 2000* (Santiago: CELADE, 1975); United Nations, *Demographic Yearbook* (New York: Council on Social and Economic Development, numerous volumes consulted); United Nations, *Population and Vital Statistics Report: Latest Available Data*, United Nations Statistical Papers, Series A, XXVI (1974); World Bank Staff Report, *Population Policies and Economic Development* (Baltimore, Maryland: Johns Hopkins University Press, 1974).

5. A study of emigration from Dominica (an island in the Lesser Antilles) to Great Britain shows that population density and pressure are not necessary factors of mobility in the Caribbean. Apparently people leave low-density Dominica in numbers equal to more crowded neighbors because (1)

the economy is based on the small-scale exportation of bananas, an easily damaged, high weight/price ratio product; (2) most land is held in large holdings, and the limited available land is financially inaccessible to peasant farmers; (3) there is no farmer credit system; (4) the hinterland marketing infrastructure is highly deficient; and (5) wages on the plantations are unattractively low, even though there are labor shortages during some seasons and when the banana boats arrive. Therefore, despite a low density, opportunities are very restricted for peasant farmers on Dominica and they emigrate. Barbara Welch, "Population Density and Emigration in Dominica," *Geographic Journal* 134 (1968) pp. 227-35.

6. Compiled from: Joginder Kumar, *Population and Land in World Agriculture: Recent Trends and Relationships*, Population Monograph Series, no. 12 (Berkeley, California: University of California Press, 1973); Ruddle and Barrows 1974; United Nations, *Statistical Yearbook 1972* (New York: Council on Social and Economic Development, 1973); World Bank Staff Report 1974).

7. Andre Corten, "La migration des travailleurs Haitiens vers les centrales sucieres dominicaines," *Cultures et Developpment* 2 (Automn 1970) pp. 713-731.

8. It is also possible that the Dominican refusal to do the work has some historical antecedents. In the eighteenth century a proposal surfaced to

... reserve certain occupations for whites ... from now on schools will be closed to Negroes and for *mulatos primerizos* (first generation) who will be destined for agricultural work.

Harry Hoetink, *Slavery and Race Relations in the Americas: An Inquiry Into Their Nature and Nexus* (New York: Harper and Row, Publishers, 1973), p. 25.

9. For a discussion of the dual labor market hypothesis see Michael J. Piore, "Notes on the Conceptualization of Labor Market Reality," A background paper prepared for the National Research Council, January 1975; and Michael J. Piore, "The 'New Immigration' and the Presumptions of Social Policy," Proceedings of the 27th Annual Meeting of the *Industrial Relations Research Association* (December 1974): 350-58. In Michael J. Piore, "The Role of Immigration in Industrial Growth: A Case Study of the Origins and Character of Puerto Rican Migration to Boston," M.I.T. Department of Economics Working Paper No. 112 (May 1973), Piore hypothesizes that

... a continuous stream of migrants from economically backward areas is crucial to the process of economic growth, at least as it has occurred in the Western World, and that the social tensions associated with ethnic and racial minorities which both the United States and Western European nations have been experiencing in recent years are a by-product of this migratory process and the particular way in which it has been organized in modern times.

The evidence in this paper seems to coincide with Piore's hypothesis.

10. The fact that many seasonal migrants prolong their stay indicates that they are able to find work, perhaps in the preparation of the fields for the next crop. Similar to Latin American migrants to the United States, they continue in the country as long as they are occupied and not deported.

11. Logan, p. 145.

12. Arismendi Díaz Santana, "The Role of Haitian Braceros in Dominican

Sugar Production," *Latin American Perspectives* 8 (Winter 1976) pp. 120-32.
13. Wiarda, pp. 75-6.
14. Logan, p. 145.
15. Howard Wiarda writes

> ... the opposition (lies) organizationally in the Committee for the Defense of the Frontiers and, more broadly, in the widespread Dominican fear and resentment of the next door Haitians .... The fact that Haiti's population still outnumbers that of the Dominican Republic by a ratio of about 3:2, that masses of Haitian laborers are brought in every year to cut cane and seldom return to Haiti, and that the total Dominican population is now estimated to be at least 10 percent Haitian give special urgency to the Committee's appeal ... its approach is frankly racist as well as nationalistic ...

Howard Wiarda, "The Politics of Family Planning in the Dominican Republic: Public Policy and the Political Process," in *The Dynamics of Population Policy in Latin America*, (ed.) Terry L. McCoy (Cambridge, Massachusetts: Ballinger Publishing Company, 1974) pp. 308-9.

16. Spaniards, Italians, Lebanese, Canary Islanders, North Americans, Austrian and German Jews, Chinese and Japanese. See Nancie L. Gonzalez, "Social Functions of Carnival in a Dominican City," *Southwest Journal of Anthropology* 26 (1970) pp. 328-42.

17. Nancie L. Gonzalez, "Patterns of Dominican Ethnicity," in *The New Ethnicity: Perspectives from Ethnology*, (ed.) John W. Bennett (St. Paul, Minnesota: West Publishing Co., 1975) p. 112.

18. It is difficult to determine the number of Haitians living in the Dominican Republic. The record of legal Haitian immigration into the country is limited and, since this is basically an illegal process, such data would be fragmentary where they did exist. Border registration data for most of the years during the period 1963-1970 include total Haitian entries into and total departures from the Dominican Republic, but their validity is dubious since hundreds more Haitians left each year than entered. This probably means that some who entered illegally, later departed through official checkpoints. Furthermore, the figures in no way represent the number of seasonal workers in the Dominican Republic. Estimates include:

(1) Border Commission estimate (1968)—200,000 legal and illegal Haitians living in the Dominican Republic; National Planning Office estimate (1968)—100,000; Department of Immigration reports more than 40,000 legal Haitian residents and estimates another 45,000 illegals in 1970 (Díaz Santana, p. 129.)

(2) In mid-1960s, 200,000 Haitians lived in the Dominican Republic. (Nazli Choucri, *Population Dynamics and International Violence* (Lexington, Massachusetts: D.C. Heath and Company, 1974), p. 126.)

(3) About 60,000 to 250,000 Haitians lived in the Dominican Republic in 1970. (From Committee for the Defense of the Frontiers estimate.)

(4) Seventy percent of the workers at Central Romana (Gulf and Western) are Haitian. (Corten, p. 718.)

(5) Total of 50,000 Haitians lived in the Dominican Republic in 1965. (Aaron Segal, p. 73.)

(6) Wiarda has estimated that in 1970, 10 percent of the population was Haitian; considering immigration since the nineteenth century (includ-

ing second generation) probably closer to twenty percent.

(7) Fifty-eight percent of the foreign population originated in Haiti in 1950. (Compiled from Direccion General de Estadistica.)

19. Sources consulted for urbanization and internal migration data for the Dominican Republic and Haiti include: Kingsley Davis, *World Urbanization*, Population Monograph Series (Berkeley, California: University of California Press, 1972); Jorge E. Hardoy, "Políticas de Urbanización y Políticas de la Tierra Urbana: La Situación en Cuba, Haiti, Jamaica, Mexico y la Republica Dominicana," in *Public Policy and Urbanization in the Dominican Republic and Costa Rica*, (ed.) Gustavo A. Antonini, Proceedings of the 22nd Annual Latin American Conference (Gainsville, Florida: University of Florida, Latin American Center, 1972); Walter D. Harris Jr., *The Growth of Latin American Cities* (Athens, Ohio: Ohio University Press, 1971); Luis Orlando Haza, "Urban Growth in the Dominican Republic: A Descriptive Overview," in *Public Policy and Urbanization in the Dominican Republic and Costa Rica*, (ed.) Gustavo A. Antonini (Gainsville, Florida: University of Florida, Latin American Center, 1972); all Oficina Nacional de Estadística publications cited in note 4; Eugenio Perez Montas, "Rural Community Development in the Dominican Republic," in *Latin American Urban Research* 2, (eds.) Francine Rabinowitz and Felicity Trueblood (Beverly Hills, California: Sage Publications, 1972); Ruddle and Barrows 1974; Seccion General de Estadística 1961; Somoza 1975; United Nations, *Demographic Yearbook*, various volumes.

20. Average growth between 1920 and 1970 in Santo Domingo was 6.4 percent compared with 1.4 percent in rural areas. Since it is known that rural fertility and natural increase are higher than urban, internal migration must account for most of the difference. Furthermore, there has been an increase in the primacy index from 3.2 in 1950 to 4.3 in 1970.

21. Haza, p. 241.

22. Geisert, p. 34.

23. Glen Hendricks, *The Dominican Diaspora: From the Dominican Republic to New York City: Villagers in Transition* (New York: Teachers College Press, 1974). See also Nancie L. Gonzalez, "Peasants Progress: Dominicans in New York," *Caribbean Studies* 10 (1971) pp. 154-71.

PART III
POLICY AS PROJECTION

9

PROJECTED INFLUENCES ON POPULATION POLICY IN AUSTRALIA

Phillip G. Clark

This chapter will project three influencing factors on Australian immigration policy, each of which is rooted in the past: economic growth and labor-force considerations, environmentalist interests, and racism. Each factor will be discussed separately and the likely direction of its influence on population policy, independent of other influences, will be outlined. Finally, one possible synthesis of these separate (or component) projections will be set forth, as an approximation of the "cybernetics" of policy decisions now understood as a simplified version of the social feedback system.

ECONOMIC GROWTH AND SIZE OF THE LABOR FORCE

The growth of the Australian economy since federation of the commonwealth in 1901 has required a continuous, though fluctuating, supply of labor (see Fig. 1). Immigrant labor was increasingly in demand in industry and manufacturing, particularly for developing Australia's vast ore and mineral reserves and in the construction and transportation industries. Following World War II, economic growth

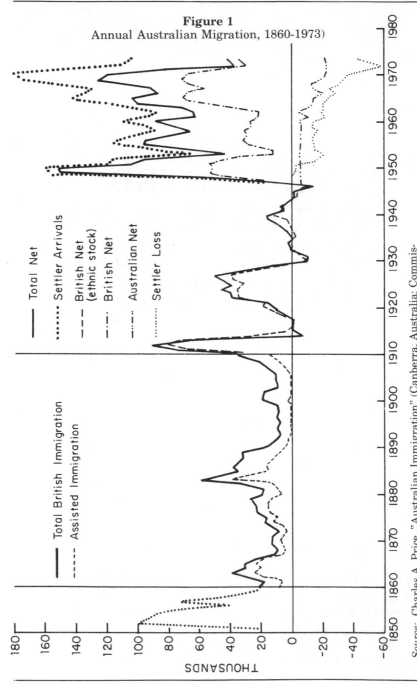

Figure 1
Annual Australian Migration, 1860-1973)

Source: Charles A. Price, "Australian Immigration" (Canberra, Australia: Commissioned Paper No. 6 of the National Population Inquiry, 1973).

Table 1
Increase in the Labor Force Attributable to Post-1947 Immigration

	1947-61	1961-72	1947-72
Male	81.8	68.4	75.5
Female	55.3	39.8	44.6
Total	73.0	52.3	61.2

Sources: Combined from: Committee of Economic Inquiry,
Report (Canberra, Australia: Australian
Government Publishing Service, 1965) and
Charles A. Price, "Australian Immigration"
(Canberra, Australia: Commissioned Paper
No. 6 of the National Population Inquiry,
1973).

and expansion received a renewed impetus from the great new potential for industrial development that the war effort had revealed. The economic growth demand for labor thus generated was supplied by the massive number of new immigrants which entered Australia from 1947 to 1971, particularly during the first nine years of this period (see Table 1).

The 1965 Report of the Committee of Economic Inquiry is still the most comprehensive appraisal of the relationship between economic and population growth available. Its conclusion that "the pursuit of economic growth is of paramount importance" still tends to dominate economic planning in Australia. The 1973 Australian Treasury Economic Paper entitled "Economic Growth: Is It Worth Having?" defending the growth concept may be interpreted as the official position of (at least one branch of) the federal government. This "white paper" defined economic growth as "the process of expanding the options available to realize society's priorities" and argued, in response to criticisms of growth leveled by environmentalists, that it was the ordering of priorities within growth, not the concept itself, that should be challenged. It concluded:

> The process of best achieving the welfare of society from the resources available will normally result in a net growth of the *per capita* output of the economic system as conventionally conceived. This growth will come from better resource alloca-

tion, improved management and skills, technological progress, and net investment. It is an important *effect* because it adds to the resources of the community for meeting future social needs. But in essence the problem of providing more social (environmental) "goods," as against more "economic" goods, is not a growth question at all. There are many problems in achieving satisfactory economic growth, but the pattern of wants of the community, whether these wants are labelled economic or not, is not one of them.[1]

What remains uncertain is whether continued economic growth will demand the high level of immigration of labor experienced in the past.

In 1971 Australia's population was relatively a young one, with a median age of only twenty-eight years, a relatively high proportion (62.7 percent) in the working age groups (fifteen to sixty-four years), and a relatively low proportion (8.5 percent in the aged-dependent sector (see Table 2). By 1971 the population structure had substantially recovered from the impact of the sharp decline in births experienced during the depression years. Through the 1950s and into the mid-1960s, the deficits in entries to the nation's labor force arising both from the natural decrease in the population in the younger working ages and from the rapidly rising educational participation rates had been largely offset by the net gains of immigrants between the ages of twenty and thirty-nine years. A high proportion of these immigrants had been selected and assisted to come to Australia because they had skills that were in short supply.

By the 1960s, however, the perceived need for immigrant labor declined as the first cohorts of the baby boom grew to working age. Moreover, at the same time Australia encountered a rising trend in female participation rates. Over the next fifteen years, even without immigration, the fifteen to sixty-four population age group will grow. But immigration actually rose during 1967-71, producing a net gain of over 500,000. There is every indication that the labor force will be well supplied over the next fifteen years.

The projected immigration level of roughly 50,000 annually until the turn of the century is rather conservative, but it will meet projected labor demands: indeed, there is growing concern over increasing competition for jobs in many sectors of the economy. It is also apparent that migrants are imposing a large economic strain through their demands on productive capital and social overheads. The recent

Table 2

Contribution of Post-1947 Immigration to Australian Population Growth,
1947-73
(in thousands)*

Age Group	0-14	15-24	25-64	65+	Total

Males

(Increase in thousands between 1947 and 1973)

	0-14	15-24	25-64	65+	Total
Natural increase of 1947 population	362	263	316	151	1,092
Post 1947 immigrants and children	587	301	825	34	1,747
Total increase	949	564	1,141	185	2,839
Per cent due to post 1947 immigration	61.7	53.4	72.3	18.4	61.5

Females

	0-14	15-24	25-64	65+	Total
Natural increase of 1947 population	346	226	346	275	1,193
Post 1947 immigrants and children	550	291	691	48	1,580
Total increase	896	517	1,037	323	2,773
Per cent due to post 1947 immigration	61.4	56.3	66.6	14.9	57.0

Total

	0-14	15-24	25-64	65+	Total
Natural increase of 1947 population	708	489	662	426	2,285
Post 1947 immigrants and children	1,137	592	1,516	82	3,327
Total increase	1,845	1,081	2,178	508	5,612
Per cent due to post 1947 immigration	61.6	54.8	69.7	16.1	59.3

*Source: Charles A. Price, "Australian Immigration"
(Canberra, Australia: Commissioned Paper
No. 6 of the National Population Inquiry,
1973), p. 107.

National Population Inquiry accepts the desirability of continued
migration, but recommends that it be smaller and more closely tied to
domestic labor demand.

ENVIRONMENTALISM AND CONCERN FOR THE AUSTRALIAN QUALITY OF LIFE

Until the late 1960s there was little concern over a possible "optimum" population for Australia based on its ultimate "carrying capacity." Theories of the late 1920s and 1930s touched on these issues but were thought to have little relevance in the early 1960s when the main concern in Australian population circles was the decline of the birth rate.

Meanwhile other trends began to affect planning for Australia's future population needs: the danger of depleting mineral reserves following the tremendous expansion of both Australian and overseas investment in the extraction and export of a wide range of mineral ores (iron, bauxite, uranium, and coal); the increasing pollution engendered by industrial concentration and increasing population density in the major capital cities (particularly Sydney and Melbourne); fear of environmental deterioration of coastal recreation areas, estuaries, and native forests by excessive development and use by a growing and increasingly affluent population; and an increasing awareness of the impact of global rapid population growth. These concerns have been voiced with increasing forcefulness by Australian environmentalists and members of the "zero population growth" movement.

The Australian situation is unique in its relatively underpopulated and unpolluted nature, and in being able to plan rationally for the future use of its environmental resources and population levels:

> Australia is the only large country in the world that is still "underpopulated".... All too easily, Australia could in a few years—less time than has elapsed since the First Fleet of settlers arrived—become as obviously overpopulated as India is now or the United States of America will be in thirty years. But Australians have the chance to decide otherwise, and they would be foolish if they did not take it.[2]

The Australian "environmentalists-populationists" tend to identify with the growing world-wide concern over what is termed "the global predicament of mankind," arising from the prospect of at least a doubling of the world's population by the turn of the century. Thus, it is argued, for the benefit of *all* mankind, Australia should act responsibly both in the use of its still vast supplies of natural resources and in its rate of population growth.

Returning to calculations of optimum populations made in the 1920s and 1930s, Australian ecologists began to emphasize the limited "carrying capacity" of the continent's water supply, noting that the interior of Australia is too dry to support dense populations. They anticipate that population growth will continue, as in the past, along the coastal fringes of the south and east (see Fig. 2). Ecologists consider schemes for the irrigation of this region a myth. Rainfall is low over most parts of the country; where heavier it is also more erratic, resulting in highly variable river system discharge. Any major extension of the rural population would have to rely on large-scale irrigation, which would place greater strains on the capacity of river systems. Unforeseeable droughts or floods could be disastrous for areas that have been cultivated or pastures opened to grazing. Estimates for the number of people that could be supported in Australia at a relatively high quality of life, based on present estimates of water resources, range from a low of 28 million to a high of 48 million at American levels, or from a low of 68 million to a high of 277 million at European levels (the actual population at the time of the last census in 1971 was 12.7 million).[3] But it can be argued that even 28 million is too high to maintain the present standard of living. Such a judgment involves a consideration of more environmental variables than just agricultural productivity: open space, freedom of movement, and diversity of landscape are among those things considered. These involve, of course, conceptions of an optimal population and environment.

Those who approach the optimal concept from the perspective of ecological control and conservation seem prepared to offer a definite estimate of population size to be attained as an optimum:

> To determine the optimum population for Australia, we must pay special attention to the vulnerability of the Australian ecosystem. Australian environments are easily abused because they are relatively dry ... and the pattern of rainfall is erratic.... Our optimum population must be an equilibrium population: neither increasing nor decreasing. To maintain an equilibrium it must have a balanced age and sex distribution, which is not easy to achieve (though by planning immigration carefully it could be easier for Australia than for countries which must rely on manipulation of reproductive rates) .... I suggest that a population of twenty-five to thirty million people will be close to an optimal level for Australia, given current environmental considerations, cultural attitudes, and technology.[4]

Figure 2
Australian Population Distribution (June 1971)

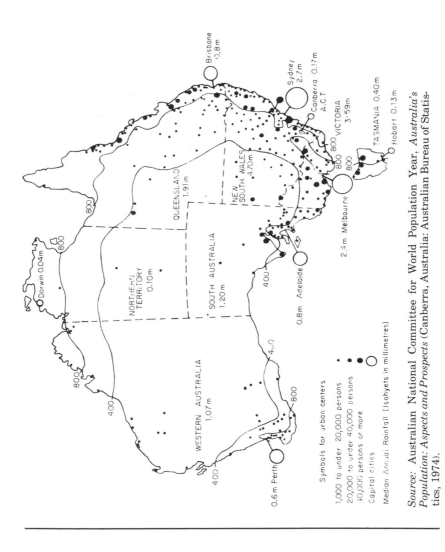

Source: Australian National Committee for World Population Year, *Australia's Population: Aspects and Prospects* (Canberra, Australia: Australian Bureau of Statistics, 1974).

It is interesting to note the central role played by carefully controlled immigration in this author's approach to the achievement of an optimal, equilibrium population.

Others concerned with the concept of optimum have been less eager to define it or to assign it some absolute value. A "desirable" level in terms of less (urban) crowding, more access to the natural environment, preservation of flora and fauna, and the control of pollution seem to be the motivations behind their concern rather than an analytical concept of an optimum. For example, in its submission to the public hearings of the National Population Inquiry, the Institute of Australian Geographers expressed the view:

> It is difficult to contemplate an optimum size for Australia ... simply because accelerating technological advance ... and social attitudes continually change any rules on the basis of which an optimum population might be defined ... However, if an optimum population concept is inappropriate, notions of a preferred distribution of population are not ... Thus specific consideration should be given to optimality in terms of the accessibility to the national population of the national land-space.[5]

On the whole, few in Australia today would revive the rigid concept of an optimum as it was examined in the 1920s and 1930s, both because of the apparent incapacity of physical or social science to predict technological changes or the ultimate availability of resources and because of the growing recognition that a wide range of human activities must be included in any consideration of the "quality of life." The complexity of outlining exactly what is meant by the concept is well set out by Loud:

> An optimal population can be defined as one that is large enough to realize the potentialities of human creativity to achieve a life of high quality for everyone indefinitely, but not so large as to threaten dilution of quality, the potential to achieve it, or the wise management of the ecosystem. The quality of life may be equated with the variety and flexibility of options available, including convenient access to ample and varied material goods and amenities. Adequate diet, attractive living and recreational space, plentiful clean water and pure air, sufficient industrial raw materials, adequate health services and educational and cultural opportunities, and sufficient wilderness to buffer unforeseen imbalances are the minimal terms of the quality equation.[6]

Environmentalists and others concerned with excessive population growth in Australia occupy the position of a "pressure group" on the

Table 3
Population Projection: Age Composition
(figures in millions, with percentage distribution for Table 2 in parentheses)

Year	I Fertility Constant 1968–71 Level			II Fertility Constant 1973 Level			III NRR = 1 by 1975–76		
	No Immig.	50,000 Net Gain	100,000 Net Gain	No Immig.	50,000 Net Gain	100,000 Net Gain	No Immig.	50,000 Net Gain	100,000 Net Gain
Persons 0–14									
1973	3.7(28.4)	3.7(28.4)	3.7(28.4)	3.7(28.4)	3.7(28.4)	3.7(28.4)	3.7(28.4)	3.7(28.4)	3.7(28.4)
1981	4.1(28.4)	4.3(28.6)	4.4(28.7)	3.8(26.8)	4.0(27.0)	4.1(27.0)	3.5(25.3)	3.7(25.5)	3.8(25.7)
1991	4.6(29.2)	5.2(29.3)	5.5(29.5)	4.1(26.3)	4.5(26.6)	4.8(26.3)	3.5(23.4)	3.8(23.7)	4.1(24.0)
2001	5.2(28.3)	5.8(28.5)	6.4(28.7)	4.4(25.5)	4.9(25.8)	5.4(26.0)	3.6(22.8)	4.1(23.1)	4.5(23.4)
Persons 15–64									
1973	8.3(63.2)	8.3(63.2)	8.3(63.2)	8.3(63.2)	8.3(63.2)	8.3(63.2)	8.3(63.2)	8.3(63.2)	8.3(63.2)
1981	9.1(62.8)	9.4(62.8)	9.7(62.8)	9.1(64.2)	9.4(64.2)	9.7(64.3)	9.1(65.5)	9.4(65.5)	9.7(65.5)
1991	10.2(61.6)	10.9(61.8)	11.6(62.0)	10.0(63.9)	10.8(64.2)	11.5(64.4)	10.0(66.4)	10.7(66.6)	11.4(66.7)
2001	11.7(62.9)	12.9(63.2)	14.2(63.5)	11.1(64.9)	12.3(65.3)	13.6(65.5)	10.6(66.9)	11.9(67.3)	13.1(67.6)
Persons 65+									
1973	1.1(8.4)	1.1(8.4)	1.1(8.4)	1.1(8.4)	1.1(8.4)	1.1(8.4)	1.1(8.4)	1.1(8.4)	1.1(8.4)
1981	1.3(8.8)	1.3(8.6)	1.3(8.4)	1.3(9.0)	1.3(8.8)	1.3(8.6)	1.3(9.2)	1.3(9.0)	1.3(8.8)
1991	1.5(9.3)	1.6(8.8)	1.6(8.5)	1.5(9.8)	1.6(9.3)	1.6(8.9)	1.5(10.2)	1.6(9.7)	1.6(9.3)
2001	1.6(8.8)	1.7(8.3)	1.7(7.8)	1.6(9.6)	1.7(9.9)	1.7(8.4)	1.6(10.3)	1.7(9.6)	1.7(9.0)

Assumption I: GRR=1.414, NRR=1.373

Assumption II: GRR=1.211, NRR=1.176

Assumption III: NRR to decline linearly from 1973 level to 1 by 1975–76 and remain constant thereafter at that level

Source: Adapted from: National Population Inquiry, *Population and Australia: A Demographic Analysis and Projection* (Canberra, Australia: Australian Government Publishing Service, 1975), p. 285.

government, rather than a force *within* the governmental structure, although there is now an embryonic Ministry for Environmental Affairs. But they are a well-educated and vocal movement. Their articulate and well-publicized presentation of their case has already been a major factor in encouraging the reevaluation of the growth philosophy in the Australian context, particularly with respect to metropolitan sprawl, pollution, resource use, and the levels of population. This group will doubtless continue to play an important role in evaluating the government's growth policies, though its impact in the next twenty to thirty years will be minimal. The levels of these appear to have already been accepted and are being planned for by various state planning authorities. In the longer run, however, the influence of the "environmentalists and populationists" appears assured, as the limits to growth, however defined, are approached. Population projections, especially when considered in terms of age structure, show a clear need for adjustments in present policies.

An analysis of the three projection models shown in Table 3 shows that the primary demographic characteristics of the Australian population (birth and migration rates, proportionate age composition, and dependency ratios) will change significantly if the volume of migration were fixed in advance, so that the desired growth rates in the total population were attained by adjusting the levels of total fertility. These characteristics, however, will not be affected if the level of total fertility were predetermined and the desired growth rates achieved by supplementing natural growth with net migration. Thus in the first situation, when changes in total fertility are required, the number of births is affected immediately; later, as a result, the entire age structure of the population is influenced. In contrast, with predetermined fixed levels of fertility and varying volumes of net migration, the variation in the age structure of the population and other demographic variables (birth rate, for example) would be less marked, as the annual influx of the immigrants required to achieve the desired growth rate in the total population is well spread out from the beginning over a wide range of age.

A rigid control over the total fertility of the population in order to adjust it to a required level each year to achieve a fixed growth rate in the total population until the end of the century is almost certainly not practicable. But the entry of a required number of immigrants with specified age and sex structure might be achieved by administrative regulation (such as the annual "target" concept) without major new legislation. If the immigration assumptions of fixed net intakes of new settlers of 100,000 or fewer each year are realistic in terms of the immigrant market, total population growth rates cannot aim for much above 1.5 percent a year. There is no evidence that fertility will respond in a way that will provide the needed levels of natural increase. The present trend in Australia seems to be towards a smaller family size among those cohorts that will be bearing children over the next fifteen years. Thus the likely outcome seems to be growth rates that will move below, rather than above, 1.5 percent.

CONSIDERATIONS OF RACISM

The historical background of population policy in Australia has always included an element of racism. The preference for immigrants of British and European background has led to the exclusion of nonwhite peoples throughout the history of Australian population policy, and particularly since World War II and the "White Australia Policy." Officially this policy stance underwent revision in the late 1950s, and again in 1966. This gradual modification culminated in the action of the Labor government in 1973 to abolish racial criteria for immigration to Australia: only the guarantee of employment and the assurance of requisite skill-attainment were to be required as immigration criteria. Asians meeting these criteria were even made eligible for passage assistance. This change of policy was consistent with the new government's greater sense of responsibility to the geographical region of southeast Asia and the southern Pacific.

The official position of the government on racial criteria changed, but traditional ethnic preferences are more deeply entrenched. A recent survey conducted by the Department of Demography of the Australian National University among women in Melbourne showed that preferences for the ethnic background of migrants remained very strongly in favor of British and northern Europeans. The least preferred groups were the Arabs, Africans, Turks, Japanese, and black Americans. The Chinese also ranked very low.[7] These preferences are similar to those found in another sample survey conducted in 1971 among the populations of Melbourne and Sydney over the age of eighteen. But there have been long-term changes. A comparison between the 1971 survey and one taken in 1948 suggests that strong opposition in 1948 to southern Europeans had greatly weakened. There had also been a marked softening in attitudes toward the entry of Jews. But the opposition to the acceptance of Chinese had hardened. The British had apparently lost some ground, but they remained by far the most preferred group on the whole. What is common in these surveys is a persistent first preference for British and northern European, a middle (though improving) rating for the other continental Europeans, and the lowest ranking still to Asians. As recently as 1960, Mr. Downer, speaking in Parliament as the Minister for Immigration, commented:

> I believe that both Australia's national growth and our international relations will best be served by continuing our present policies. For they observe well-tried principles: homogeneity, readiness of absorption, familiarity of religion, the same fundamental attitudes to living. Above all, the thought processes of the people we seek to attract are, if not the same, at least in tune with ours.

Some Australian politicians have even gone so far as to argue that there is a positive moral duty to remove the conditions in which racial discrimination grows, that is, the presence of nonwhite immigrants. Yet an increased influx of Oriental people into Australia may lead to a lessening of prejudice against them, as has been the case with similar feelings toward southern Europeans.

Because of the internally inconsistent direction of trends influencing population projections, Australian immigration policy for the rest of this century will require subtle modifications of past practices. Environmental factors will not dominate decisions taken over the next two decades: even with the relatively high immigration rate of 100,000 net settlers annually, the total population will be only roughly 19.5 million by the year 2001, assuming NRR = 1 by 1975-76 (a net immigration rate of 50,000 would produce a population of 15.9 million). Either figure could easily be supported by Australia's resources, including the critical water factor. There will probably be localized problems of resource supply, especially in the larger metropolitan areas, accompanied by environmental deterioration in the form of pollution and overcrowding. But these short run considerations are already being integrated into the policy considerations at local levels.

The policy-influencing pressure of environmentalist groups will favor decentralization rather than an official "fertility policy." They will press for an internal migration policy of incentives for regional settlement according to local ecological potentials and regional carrying capacities. The case will be easy to demonstrate: in 1971 the five mainland state capitals (Sydney, Melbourne, Brisbane, Adelaide, and Perth) contained more than 60 percent of the country's population and during 1966-71 they absorbed 80 percent of Australia's total population increase. Related to this increasing dominance of the largest cities is the clustering of settlement into a few restricted coastal regions.

This pattern of primate city and coastal settlement growth has been the subject of official concern, but as yet there has been no imposition of residential restrictions on unassisted immigrants. The only response to the disproportionate settlement has been the stimulation of regional "growth centers" to draw off some of the anticipated population increase from the major cities. Such centers were not to be satellite towns near existing metropolitan areas, but new cities that would eventually have populations of 200,000 or more.

Unfortunately this effort has had little effect. The new projections incorporating the expected lower levels of fertility and migration predict relatively slow city growth in coming years, even without any effort at decentralization: with a declining birth rate and an already nearly depopulated rural sector, there are fewer people to redistribute without actually drawing in immigrants or draining the large cities themselves.

The National Population Inquiry therefore recommends the simpler policy of limiting immigration to Sydney and Melbourne, the largest cities, leaving unaffected the continued growth of the other capitals. It suggests encouraging the sponsorship of settlers by residents and firms in the smaller cities and massive investment (unspecified) in development in the frontier states of Queensland and Western Australia. It concludes that population growth by itself does not necessarily threaten the environment, but rather that location, technology, the industrial base, and transportation are the sources of appropriate policy concern.

While economic growth and expansion are expected to continue in Australia at roughly the same rate as in the past, high levels of immigration will not be required in the future. The labor pool appears well-stocked for at least the next fifteen years, at which time it appears that relatively minimal levels of immigration will be required to prevent labor shortages. A level of immigration of 50,000 per year is not inconsistent with the present government's policy of maintaining high levels of employment and job security.

The character of the labor force vis-à-vis the composition of economic development in the Australian context is a more important consideration. At least in the short run a prime factor in the selection of new immigrants will be the skills needed by the economy; economic criteria will play a large part in the selection of immigrants to receive passage assistance. The type of immigrant in demand will remain the category of "tradesman, production-process workers, and laborers," the most significant groups in the past and the ones most likely to be required in a rapidly expanding economy emphasizing the industrial sector. Such a selection process is consistent with both the concern over unemployment and the idea of an annual target.

Irrespective of the official government position on racial criteria for immigration assistance, Australian public opinion will continue to oppose the entry of nonwhite peoples. The new standards requiring immigrants to have needed skills will produce indirect discrimination against the entry of certain groups. The fact that over the next twenty-five to thirty years there will not be a high demand for immigrant manpower could mediate against a loosening of overall restrictions on immigrants and make a high level of skill-attainment critical to the acceptance of applicants for permanent settlement.

The current racial policy of "nondiscrimination" may widen the areas from which skilled workers and their families can be drawn, but the ethnic and geographic composition of past immigration will tend to favor a continued flow from Europe for some time. The search for new settlers to reach targets in the past was extended throughout almost all Europe, and the substantial ethnic groups already in Australia have established "chains" that will continue to draw in relatives for at least the next decade, given Australian immigration policy preferences favoring the reunion of families.

The most likely prediction for future immigration policy is a high degree of flexibility in determining desirable immigration targets, with decisions changing on an annual basis. The use of a fixed number of immigrants annually, or a certain required annual percentage of growth in population will fail to provide the needed flexibility in meeting manpower requirements on a year-by-year basis. Flexibility will replace previous rigidities in immigration policy, a condition that should certainly be desirable in a young and vigorous country that is just beginning to realize its potentialities and responsibilities in a rapidly changing world.

NOTES

1. Australian Treasury Economic Paper No. 2, "Economic Growth: Is it Worth Having?" (Canberra, Australia: Australian Government Publishing Service, 1973), p. 46.
2. Frank J. Fenner, "The Environment," in *How Many Australians: Immigration and Growth*, (ed.) Australian Institute of Political Science (Sydney, Australia: Australian Institute of Political Science, 1971), pp. 40-41.
3. Harry F. Recher, "Ecological Aspects of Planning," in *Australia as*

Human Setting: Approaches to the Designed Environment, (ed.) Amos Rapoport (Sydney, Australia: Angus and Robertson, 1972), p. 176.

4. Ibid., pp. 176-177.

5. Institute of Australian Geographers, "Submission to the Public Hearings of the National Population Inquiry" (Canberra, Australia: Australian Government Publishing Service, 1973), pp. 2-3.

6. Preston Cloud, "Resources, Population, and the Quality of Life," in *Is There an Optimum Population?*, (ed.) S. Fred Singer (New York: McGraw-Hill for the population Council, 1971), p. 9.

7. M.E. Buchanan, "Attitudes Towards Immigrants in Australia" (Canberra, Australia: Commissioned Paper No. 17 of the National Population Inquiry, 1974).

10

THE IMPACT OF LONGEVITY THERAPY AND INCREASED LIFE SPAN ON POPULATION PROJECTIONS AND POLICY PLANNING

Gaither D. Bynum

Theoretically, to age does not necessarily mean progressive debility or even death. Though normal human cells appear to undergo a "programmed" demise, multiple examples exist of single-cell organisms and even human tissue cultures which do not seem subject to "death" given a favorable environment.[1] Mankind has labored with some success to increase human lifespan and emulate simpler organisms. The life expectancy at birth of a classical Roman citizen is estimated to have been twenty to thirty years. The average life expectance at birth of a U.S. citizen in the mid-1800s was forty years with only 18 percent of the population surviving sixty or more years. By the 1960s life expectancy rose to 70.4 years.[2] But analysis of trends in survival data indicate that this increase in life expectancy is not the result of a mean increase in lifespan per se but rather of an increased control of a hostile environment (in particular, control of infant mortality) which allows each individual a reasonable chance to maximize his "inherent" lifespan.[3] There are accordingly more individuals than ever before, and a larger percentage of them survive to be the age of seventy, only to succumb to a complex array of age-related disease processes. Increasingly, the clinical and the research arms of the life sciences are being called upon not to prevent disease but rather to support the end product of seventy years of gradual decompensation and accumulated debilities, manifested frequently by heart disease, cancer, hypertension, cerebral disorders, or by a myriad of "minor" dysfunctions such as loss of mobility, taste, sight, hearing, muscle strength, and appetite.

The eradication of many of these processes such as heart disease or cancer would result in one one- and three-year increases respectively in life expectancy at birth; the eradication of all common disease processes would increase the projected life expectancy of a person aged sixty by only an estimated fifteen years.[4] Yet even if these age-related diseases were eradicated, the aged would still be faced with the prospect of progressive debility as attrition continued among the cells of individual organ systems until, their numbers falling beneath a critical mass necessary for function, organs fail and death ensues. Consequently researchers are becoming interested in developing techniques which will expand the life span by deferring or preventing the aging process itself rather than attacking senility-related diseases individually. The probable success of such research has been addressed by two major studies: one by the Rand Corporation[5] which predicted a fifty-year increase in life span by 2020; the other by Smith, Kline, and French,[6] which predicted fifty-year increase in life span by 1990. These predictions are based on rapidly increasing data accumulations related to the process of aging. The data are knit together by a variety of theories.[7] These theories revolve around the concept of genetically programmed and cumulative molecular errors in DNA, RNA, and protein synthesis, with subsequent disruption of cell processes. This process is modulated by such factors as diet, stress, and metabolic rate. A variety of drugs have been evaluated for their effect on survival and life span in attempts to address one or another of the proposed theories of aging, with increases in the life span of mice ranging up to 50 percent.[8]

This paper will consider the impact that the success of this research might have on population dynamics and policy planning. Such an analysis of the possible impact of successful therapeutic intervention in the aging process must be based on an understanding of the concept of aging.

Age is not simply a measure of elapsed time. The assessed age of an object is the result of a complex calculus operating on three factors: chronologic age, functional age, and psychosocial age.

Chronologic age is simply the elapsed time of existence; how old one is in terms of years, for example. No inferences concerning the character of existence can be drawn from chronologic age alone.

The second factor, functional age, measures the character of physical existence relative to some idealized concept of optimum. The functional age of humans, for example, is based upon an estimate of deviation in physiologic status from an idealized optimum. The human functional optimum is considered to be the physiologic status currently associated with the third decade of life. This relationship is ill-defined, however, and may shift with the variable measured. For example, the physiologic ideal for work capacity, as measured by muscle strength, optimizes at around twenty-eight years of age.[9] The chronologic age associated with optimum intellectual function is more nebulous. Intelligence as measured by information stores and vocabulary continues to rise gradually into the sixth decade, while intelligence as measured by performance and reasoning is highest among young adults.[10]

The third factor reflects the human or psychosocial interpretation given to chronologic and functional age. Psychosocial age consists of a number of variables which are associated loosely with chronologic and functional age. These variables can be considered to be arranged in clusters, examples of which would be chronologic and functional age, social status, and relative position in work-retirement and family role sequences. (Social status is a qualitative composite of a variety of age-related variables such as dependency, authority, socioeconomic level, role activity, life goals, friendship interaction, political dealings, and mobility.[11] Work retirement sequence is a qualitative description of whether an individual is retired or working. If working, it is an assessment of the age-related level of contribution to and competitiveness in the job market. For example, the proportion of notable contributions produced in each decade of life for individuals living 70-74 years is:[12] under 20, 2 percent; 20-29, 15 percent; 30-39, 36 percent; 40-49, 28 percent; 50-59, 13 percent; 60-69, 10 percent; 70-79, 4 percent.) The integration of these variables into an expression of psychosocial age is an ill-defined, complex process. The result of the integration is a series of categories or labels which qualitatively describe psychosocial age. The simplest examples are infancy, childhood, adolescence, adulthood (youth and middle aged), and the elderly. The current approximate relationship between these categories of psychosocial age and chronologic age in U.S. society is:

1. Infant   (0– 2 years)
2. Child   (3–12 years)
3. Adolescent   (13–17 years)
4. Young Adult   (18–35 years)
5. Middle-Aged Adult   (36–64 years)
6. Elderly   (over 65 years)

For example, adolescence as a psychosocial label of age might be succinctly defined by the above variables as follows: chronologic age—thirteen to seventeen years; physiologic status—entering sexual maturity, all organ systems functional but at less than maximum potential, growth curve not yet complete; social status—dependent, lacking certain social privileges necessary for full participation; family status—child (as opposed to spouse, parent, grandparent, spinster, or divorcee); work status—not a significant contributor in the work-retirement sequence.

Appraising the consequences of longevity therapy requires consideration of at least two aspects of age; chronologic and functional, or physiologic, age. This generates four conditions for modeling population projections.

A. No intervention in the aging process occurs.
B. Intervention in the aging process occurs which alters both chronologic and functional aging (prolonged lifespan and functional capacity).
C. Intervention in the aging process occurs which alters only chronologic aging (prolonged lifespan).
D. Intervention in the aging process occurs which alters only functional aging (prolonged functional capacity).

Each of these conditions must then be evaluated within the context of human interpretation or psychosocial aging. To provide a framework for the analysis, a simple cohort model of population trends, is now presented based upon conditions A, B, C, and D. For modeling pruposes, a fifty-year increase in life expectancy is assumed, in keeping with the Rand Corporation, Smith, Kline, and French studies.

These projections were accomplished by creating a functional or physiologic age scale which utilizes as a standard the current relationship between physiologic status and chronologic age. Ths scale was then utilized to generate age-specific survival curves for conditions A, B, and C assuming a mean increase in life span of fifty years, as seen in Figure 1. (A graph of condition D cohort survival rate is in essence a square wave with x, y intercepts of (109, 1). Circumstances

Figure 1

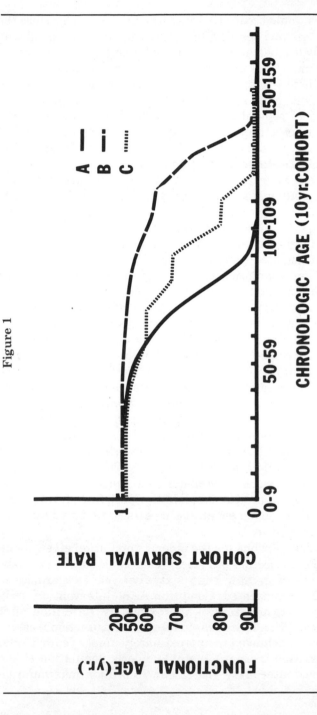

Cohort survival rates for the U.S. population (1960) are presented (A). Additionally, cohort survival is extended by fifty years between the chronologic ages thirty to sixty (B), and above seventy (C). These extensions ars made to simulate the effect of therapeutic interventions in the aging process affecting chronologic and functional aging (B) and chronologic aging alone. (C)

under which this would occur are difficult to envision. Therefore the cohort survival rate and population trends will not be graphed, and will undergo only limited discussion.) Based upon these hypothetical curves, a cohort model was used for population trends. This model is extremely simplistic and at best describes an envelope within which an array of possible, more sophisticated projections might occur.

The projection of population trends in the United States under conditions A (no intervention) suggest that a stable population of 284 million is achieved in sixty years. For B (prolonged lifespan and functional capacity) a stable population of 414 million is achieved in one-hundred years. This represents a 20 to 46 percent larger stable population than anticipated under condition A. For C (prolonged lifespan), a stable population of 325 million is achieved in ninety years. This projection indicates that the previously predicted maximum population (condition A) would be achieved in 30 to 50 percent of the anticipated time.

Alteration of key population elements of society accompany the above alterations in general population projections. Two elements currently receiving much attention are the elderly and work force populations. In Figure 2, work force projections are based upon conditions A, B, and C. The projections rest upon the simplistic assumption that the work force consists potentially of all individuals with functional ages of twenty to sixty years regardless of the associated chronologic age. The prediction for work forces under conditions A (no intervention) and C (prolonged lifespan) are identical, predicting a gradual rise in the potential working population which stabilizes at approximately 125 million after thirty years. For condition B (prolonged lifespan and functional capacity), the work force increases to approximately 280 million in sixty-five years. The level is approximately 2.25 times the work force under conditions A and C. Under condition B, the current projected maximum work force level (condition A) of 125 million is achieved at six times the anticipated rate; i.e., in five versus thirty years.

In Figure 3 are projections for the elderly population given condition A, B, or C. For projection purposes, "elderly" is considered to be the functional age of greater than sixty-five years regardless of chronologic years accumulated. Condition A (no intervention) projects a stable elderly population of approximately 70 million after sixty years. For condition B (increased lifespan and functional capacity) a similar level is achieved in approximately ninety years. Under condition C (increased lifespan), a stable elderly population of 100 million is achieved after sixty years. The 70 million maximum el-

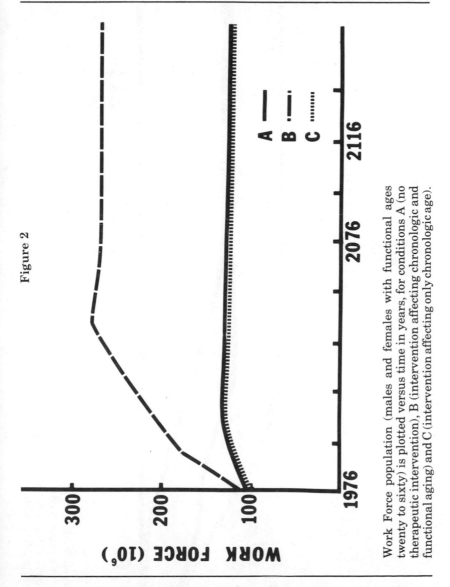

Figure 2

Work Force population (males and females with functional ages twenty to sixty) is plotted versus time in years, for conditions A (no therapeutic intervention), B (intervention affecting chronologic and functional aging) and C (intervention affecting only chronologic age).

derly population, predicted after sixty years without intervention (condition A), is achieved in twenty-five years under condition C (increased lifespan).

A superficial portrait of the total populations under conditions A, B, and C is presented in Figure 4. Projection A (no intervention)

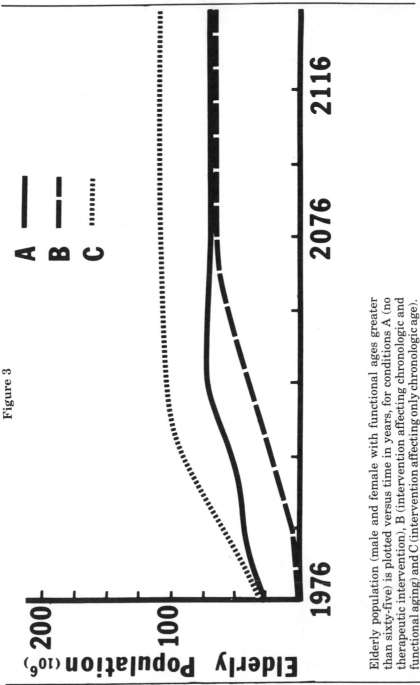

Figure 3

Elderly population (male and female with functional ages greater than sixty-five) is plotted versus time in years, for conditions A (no therapeutic intervention), B (intervention affecting chronologic and functional aging) and C (intervention affecting only chronologic age).

suggests that 49 percent of the population will be eligible for the working force and 25 percent will be elderly. Projection B (increased lifespan and functional capacity) suggests that 65 percent will be eligible for the work force and 18 percent of the population will be elderly. Projection C (increased lifespan) suggests that 43 percent of the population will be eligible for the work force and 35 percent will be elderly. Condition D (increased functional capacity only) would consist almost entirely of a population eligible for the work force. There would be no elderly.

DISCUSSION

These projections will now provide a focus for a discussion of the implications of the abrupt introduction of longevity therapy into the U.S. population. This discussion is intentionally eclectic rather than exhaustive. It is offered in the hopes of stimulating further research into the population dynamics, politics, and public policy arising from gerontologic research.

Projections for conditions A, C, and D are discussed only briefly and will therefore be presented first.

Condition A (no intervention in basic aging processes):

Academic, private, and government centers are devoting considerable energy to analysis of trends given that no major alteration of the aging process occurs. Therefore condition A will not be explored in this paper except as needed for comparison with conditions B, C. and D.

Condition C (intervention in the aging process occurs which increases chronologic age without meaningful alteration in the rate of decline in functional capacity):

It is questionable whether society would feel that a major extension of chronologic age is worthwhile if the functional capacity is not expanded also. This concern is illustrated by the current interest in "the right to die" and the "living will." Under condition C there is a modest increase (155 percent) above the current total anticipated population (see population projections, condition A). The entire increase is composed of individuals with chronologic and functional ages greater than sixty-five. The result is a relative decline from 49 percent (condition A) to 43 percent in the work force which could support an elderly population. This is accompanied by a relative increase from 25 percent (condition A) to 35 percent in the elderly population in need of such support.

Given current concern over the integrity of programs for the elderly (such as Social Security) and popular concern over prolongation of life in an elderly and debilitated state, it would seem that the major practicable policy options for planners would be: (1) to anticipate and discourage the development of interventions such as that described in condition C; (2) to accelerate and expand current efforts to meet the needs of an increasing dependent elderly population.

Condition D (intervention in the aging process which significantly decreases the rate of functional aging; chronologic life expectancy remains stable):

In the event that a condition D type intervention did occur the same problems which are obtained under condition B (prolonged lifespan and functional capacity) would occur; i.e., a large increase in the potential work force with a secondary conflict over a chronologic versus functional definition of elderly. These issues will be discussed under condition B. It is difficult to conceptualize circumstances under which condition D might occur since significant increases in functional capacity would almost certainly result in increased lifespan.

Condition B (intervention is basic aging processes occurs which prolongs both chronologic lifespan and functional capacity):

It is the purpose of this section to discuss population trends, assuming that therapeutic intervention in the aging process occurs which alters the rates of chronologic and functional aging. The assumption is that such intervention will not only produce a mean increase in chronologic lifespan, but also increase the number of years in which individuals are functionally competent. The condition B is based upon the assumption that under therapy, the portion of the population with chronologic ages of thirty to 110 years will be the functional equivalent of thirty to sixty years old by current physiologic standards. It also assumes there is no increase in the number of years spent at functional ages greater than sixty. This is a simple extension of broadly accepted intuitive notions. Each of us, for example, is familiar with someone who, though eighty-five years old, has a cardiovascular system functionally equivalent to that of an average fifty-year-old. For that one physiologic variable, the octogenerian will have expanded the number of chronologic years spent in a functional age of thirty-sixty years as judged by current physiologic standards.

Scientists have long been aware that differences may occur between apparent physiologic age and chronologic age[13], and several efforts are being made to obtain a quantitative index relating the two.[14]

Discussion of condition B will be presented in three sections: Work-Retirement Sequence, Authority and Wealth, and General Considerations.

Work-Retirement Sequence

The hypothetical population projections of condition B suggest a minimum of two sources for social stress. The first will be the general burden of increased population. This consequence follows increases in chronologic life expectancy and an increase in the number of years that the population remains functionally at a thirty to sixty-five-year age level by today's standards. The second stress follows from a necessary reassessment of psychosocial age categories. Society will have to decide, for example, whether people should be defined as elderly based upon chronologic or functional ages. This is not a trivial distinction. To be defined as elderly implies, among other things, a high chance of exclusion from the work force, and inclusion in retirement status. It can be seen (Figure 1) that if current trends are maintained and the elderly condition is defined as a chronologic age of sixty-five or greater, then individuals would be eligible for compulsory retirement at functional ages of thirty-five to forty under condition B. But if the psychosocial age category "elderly" is defined by a functional age of sixty-five, then individuals would be eligible for work up to a chronologic age of 110. Those current policies supporting compulsory retirement at chronologic ages of sixty-five would be subject to change.

The problems surrounding the psychosocial assessment of the elderly are to some extent felt today. It is already true, for example, that fewer men now retire than ever before because of ill health, and more men now survive until retirement age. Thus an increasing percentage of the U.S. work force remains physiologically employable beyond retirement age. At the same time, the labor force participation of American males over the age of sixty-five has declined from 68.3 percent in 1890 to 27.8 percent in 1965,[15] while the rate of compulsory retirement at age sixty-five has doubled (1951-63).[16] This may be interpreted to mean that chronologic lifespan and functional capacity are increasing and the psychosocial definition of "elderly" is rigidifying at a specific chronologic age. The regulations based upon a chronologic definition of a psychosocial age category "elderly" are coming in conflict with physiologic ages. This issue in a work ethic society is emotion-laden. In an effort to absorb this disparity and others like it, attempts are being made to legislate an age discrimination clause within the proposed Equal Rights Amendment. (Though less dramatic, other examples exist of variation in psychosocial age relative to chronologic or physiologic age. "Young adult" changes with time when measured by age of entrance into the work force. In 1900, 63.6 percent of males aged fourteen to seventeen entered the work force. In 1960, 32.1 percent of males aged fourteen to seventeen entered the work force.[17] Between 1900 and 1960, the boundary between "adolescent" and "young adult" psychosocial age categories can be construed as increasing in chronologic age. The chronologic age associated with the psychosocial age category "elderly" changes with time when measured by work and retirement life expectancies at birth. The work and retirement life expectancies at birth in 1900 were 32.1 years and 1.7 years respectively. In 1960, work and retirement life expectancies at birth were 41.4 and 5.6 years respectively.[18] The popular conflict over shifts in legal drinking ages between eighteen and twenty-one provide yet another example of shifts in the boundary between "adolescent" and "young adult.")

Under condition B, society would be faced with an unanticipated maximum population. Moreover, a larger proportion—65 percent as opposed to a previously anticipated 49 percent (condition A)—will be between the functional ages of twenty to sixty-five years. This change represents a 188 percent increase in the number of people anticipated as being eligible for the work force. Moreover, of the 65 percent of the total projected population that are between the functional ages of twenty and sixty-five, 31 percent will be above the chronologic age of sixty-five. A dilemma appears. If society adjusts the calculus by which it derives the psychosocial age "elderly" there will be a work force population 188 percent in excess of the previously anticipated maximum (condition A). If society does not make this adjustment, two new problems will immediately arise. Thirty-one percent of the population will be functionally middle aged, i.e., between the ages of thirty and sixty-five, but they will have chronologic ages of greater than sixty-five, and might be excluded from the work force. The potential for discontent under such circumstances has been discussed. In addition, this population, if excluded from the middle-age category and the work force, automatically falls into the psychosocial age category of "elderly." If the psychosocial age category "elderly" under condition B consists of those with functional ages above sixty-five, then the elderly population will be 18 percent of the total popula-

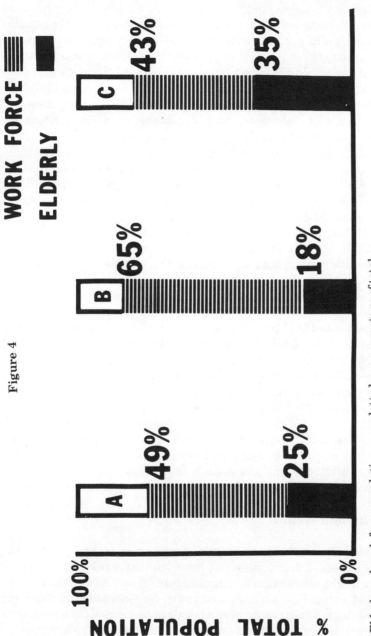

Figure 4

Elderly and work force populations are plotted as a percentage of total population for conditions A (no therapeutic intervention), B (intervention affecting chronologic and functional aging), and C (intervention affecting only chronologic aging).

tion. If the "elderly" category includes those with chronologic ages of greater than sixty-five, then an additional 31 percent of the total population is included. This result will increase the elderly population approximately 200 percent above the previously anticipated maximum (condition A). The implications in terms of increased demands on social benefit structures such as Social Security are obvious. Should condition B occur, those concerned with policy planning will be faced with complex questions. Basically these are: is it best to attempt to modify psychosocial age categories, by legislation for example, and obtain an inflated work force population and an uninflated elderly population? Or, is it better to conserve current psychosocial age categories and accept an inflated elderly population? Under this assumption, approximately two-thirds of the elderly population would have functional ages of less than sixty-five years and therefore might, as discussed earlier, feel unfairly and prematurely excluded from the job market in addition to providing an additional burden on the social benefit structure.

The question regarding an inflated work force population is a particularly appropriate one. Current trends suggest that the work force population exceeds the job market even without the added population resulting from a hypothetical longevity therapy. (John Snyder, president of U.S. Industries, in his 1971 testimony before the U.S. Senate Subcommittee on Employment and Manpower, suggested that automation would be a major factor in the loss of 40,000 jobs a week. The Department of Labor's more conservative estimate is 4,000 jobs per week lost.[19] Such estimates contribute to projections by some futurists who foresee fifteen percent of the population providing all necessary goods and services.) Perhaps in response to current job market trends more than seven hundred U.S. companies are scheduling four-day work weeks and one thousand more contemplate such a shift. The inflated work force population possible under condition B may enhance a current trend toward a leisure society.

Authority and Wealth

Given condition B, an increased competition in the job market might be expected. In addition to a more limited access to jobs, policy planners might also anticipate limited lateral and upward job mobility. If past experience serves as an indicator, increased chronologic and physiologic life expectancy can result in decreased personnel flow through positions of relative power and authority. A current popular example would be U.S. congressional committee chairmanships. In the eighteenth and nineteenth centuries, architects of the U.S. system of government constructed congressional committee chairmanships based upon lifespan expectations of approximately forty years. The resulting disparity which has developed in the twentieth century secondary in part to the increases in life expectancy is manifested by accusations of fossilization and destructive accumulation of power with congressional committee chairmen. This disparity may not resolve quickly or with ease, if current revisionist debates in Congress are any indication. Currently, between 50 and 75 percent of men in some vocations maintain expectations of upward and lateral mobility between the chronologic ages of twenty-five and fifty.[20] This expectation is maintained, although at decreasing levels up through the chronologic age of fifty-nine. These expectations may be frustrated as increases in physiologic life expectancy result in a stabilization of personnel at the higher job levels. Given a potential for frustration of such expectations, policy planners might consider alternatives to the current work-retirement sequence. The current sequence emphasizes vocational achievement as the major goal of middle age, followed by a short period of decreasing vocational aspiration in preparation for retirement. In a society with a work ethic perhaps policies encouraging separation of the concept of work and job are worth pursuing.[21] The individual ego then could perhaps be maintained by avocational work. Society could be maintained by periodic vocational inputs from individuals eligible for the work force, however that may be defined. Particular emphasis could be placed on policies which would limit the time spent in positions of authority. Such postures would also relieve to some degree the frustration of those individuals who could be excluded from the job market at a chronologic age of sixty-five by a psychosocial age category "elderly" even though they maintain a functional age of less than sixty-five since the new norm for all functional ages would be an avocational work state punctuated by periods of vocational endeavor to meet society's needs.

At a different level the question is not one of satisfying vocational expectations or preventing age-related stagnation of management positions. The question arises as to whether there is a potential for disadvantageous accumulation of wealth. Certainly with increased life expectancy, the frequency with which family wealth is subject to inheritance taxation decreases and the potential for accumulation is greater.

In general, the method for controlling such accumulations is geared to decrementing resources as they are acquired or as they pass from one individual to another usually at or near death. If functional life is extended substantially, then the points of vulnerability at which those resources may be attached decrease. Policy planners are then left with the alternative of decrementing stable, established personal or family resources while they are still the property of the living. Defining mechanisms for maintaining an equitable distribution and turnover of wealth in the private sector (assuming that it is desirable) without violating personal rights is an exceedingly delicate undertaking that deserves the most careful consideration.

General Considerations

All of these projections and specific models point out the need for gerontologically related policy planning, especially involving issues that are already of much public and academic concern, such as employment, the elderly, and control of destructive accumulations of authority and wealth. The occurrence of therapy interventions such as condition B will affect almost all aspects of our existence since our lives are governed in important ways by age-related regulations and expectations. These regulations and expectations affect at what age and for how long we go to school, when we are politically mature, when we may have means of independent transportation, when we may have sexual relations without committing statutory rape, when we may fully join the job market, etc. All of these psychosocial judgments are based on expectations of chronologic and physiological life span. With intervention which increases chronologic life span and functional capacities, the psychosocial judgments and categories will shift and increase in subtlety. For example, we have a series of expectations and social markers against which we measure the ascendancy of individuals in a competitive job field. We have only one honorable expectation once an individual reaches his highest level of achievement: retirement. As people live longer and remain functionally competent we will also have to provide a graded downslope of vocational responsibility and authority that is socially expected, accepted, and honorable. Given a shift in emphasis from vocational to avocational work one may have to consider changes in the whole character of education. What consideration should be given to the nature of marriage under condition B? With increasing life expectancies we are already experiencing (not necessarily causally) a trend from the extended to the nuclear family in which partners may change repeatedly. If this trend continues, married life could become a relatively small percent of the total life span, a small segment intentionally, transiently, and contractually set aside for the rearing of children.

An iteration of potential points at which therapeutic intervention in the aging process might impact on our lives would be long. The potential social disruption of our life styles at each of these points could be lessened if subjected to prospective analysis. If the quest of Ponce de Leon is, in the end, successful, the need for prospective philosophic governmental action will greatly rise.

POLICY OVERVIEW

The discussion just presented has been superficial and based upon a large number of assumptions which, for brevity's sake, were left unstated. The discussion has had four goals:

1. To point out that therapeutic intervention in the aging process represents a possible future.
2. To demonstrate that the consequences of therapeutic intervention must be as complex as the aging process itself.
3. To illustrate possible changes in population trends if intervention in the aging process succeeds.
4. To illustrate briefly the potential nature of changes which policy planners must anticipate.

The potential magnitude of changes resulting from longevity therapy suggests that resources might be allocated to monitor and prepare for the advent of such therapy. Broadly stated, the measures needed would be:

1. To generate support for intelligence functions geared primarily to assessing trends in gerontological research. This is necessary since the model demonstrated that trend shifts are a function of the nature of longevity therapy. The relatively free flow of government and academic research information can be tapped with modest effort from the open literature and grant reviews. The development of intelligence from private research conducted by pharmaceutical houses might require government intervention since large resources are invested in these highly competitive research ventures. The policy clusters supporting accumulation of necessary intelligence from the private sector could involve the generation of guaranteed secure and anonymous data repositories

and fiscal incentives for the release of unpublished private research.

2. From intelligence gathered, to generate population projections for each trend in gerontological therapy assuming a variety of implementation techniques.

3. Using multidimensional impact analysis (economic, social, etc.) on projected trends, to discern the most probable outcome of the array of longevity therapies considered for instrumentation.

4. To generate policy clusters designed to optimize the most probable population futures associated with the most probable array of longevity therapy.

NOTES

1. V. Cristofalo, "Animal Cell Cultures as a Model System for the Study of Aging in Adv.," in *Gerontological Research*, ed. B.L. Strehler (New York: Academic Press, 1972), pp. 45-79.

2. B.L. Strehler, Implications of aging research for society, *Fed. Proc.*, 34 (1975): 5-8; A. Comfort, *The Biology of Senescence*, (Boston: Routledge and Kegan Paul, 1964), pp. 268-282; and M. Spiegelman, *Significant Mortality and Morbidity Trends in the United States since 1900*, (Bryn Mawr: The American College of Life Underwriters, 1964) p. 8.

3. See Sources in note 2.

4. L. Hayflick, "The cell biology of human aging," *N.E.J.M.*, 295 (1976): 1302-1308.

5. T.J. Gordon and D. Helmer, *Report on a Long Range Forecasting Study* (Santa Monica: Rand Corporation, 1964) pp. 1-45.

6. A. Bender, et al., "Delphic Study Examines Developments in Medicine," *Futures*, 1 (1969): 284-303.

7. L. Orgel, "Aging of Clones of Mammalian Cells," *Nature*, 243 (1973): 241-245; and L. Hayflick, "The cell biology of human aging" *N.E.J.M.* 295 (1976): 1302-1308.

8. D. Harman, "Free Radical Theory of Aging: Effect of Free Radical Reaction Inhibitors on the mortality Rate of Male LA7 Mice," *J. Gerontol*, 23 (1968): 476-482.

9. M. Riley and A. Foner, *Ageing and Society* (New York: Russell Sage Foundation, 1968), p. 250.

10. Ibid., p. 255.

11. Ibid., pp. 341-436.

12. Ibid., p. 437.

13. B.S. Linn, "Chronologic vs. Biologic Age in Geriatric Patients," in *The Physiology and Pathology of Human Aging*, ed. R. Goldman and M. Rockstein (New York: Academic Press, 1975), pp. 9-18.

14. J. Hollingsworth et al., "Correlation Between Tests of Ageing, Hiroshima. An attempt to Define Physiologic Age," *Yale J. Biol. Med.*, 38 (1965): 11-26; and T. Furokawa et al., "Assessment of Biologic Age by Multiple Regression Analysis," *J. Gerontol.*, 30 (1975): 422-434.

15. C. Odell, "The Trend Toward Earlier Retirement," *Interdiscipl. Topics Geront.*, 6 (1970): 33-42.

16. E. Palmore, *Social Security Bulletin*, 27 (1964): 3.

17. Riley and Foner, p. 42.

18. Ibid., p. 422.

19. Palmore, op. cit.

20. Riley and Foner, p. 411.

21. Ibid., p. 422.

11

CULTURAL VALUES AND POPULATION POLICIES: CASES AND CONTEXTS

Donald P. Warwick

Systematic analysis of population policy has been hampered by the lack of conceptual frameworks which (1) give due recognition to the role of contextual factors in shaping national policies and programs, and (2) take account of the intimate connection between policy formulation and program implementation. Using case materials from four developing countries, this paper will develop and illustrate a conceptual scheme which attempts to meet both specifications. As is true in most writings on population policy in the developing countries, the dominant emphasis will be on policies relating to fertility and demographic growth. Despite frequent and often ritualistic protestations to the contrary, this remains the operational focus of most policy discussions.

GUIDING PROPOSITIONS

The central arguments of this essay can be summarized in four propositions:

1. The sociohistorical and political environment of a country will

condition the very possibility of overt discussions about population matters. International conflicts or severe internal ethnic tensions, for example, may cast a political shadow over every aspect of demographic policy, including public debates, data-gathering activities, legislation, and even private family planning programs.

2. The sociohistorical and political context will also shape both the contents and the process of policy formulation. With regard to process, environmental factors will make a difference for *whether* a government perceives a population problem, *when* this perception occurs, *who* participates in policy deliberations, and *how* these deliberations are conducted. At the level of contents, the same forces may affect the specific definition of a population problem which underlies governmental actions, the policy options chosen and avoided, and the language in which policies are presented to the public.

3. Policy formulation, in conjunction with the sociohistorical and political environment, will greatly influence the implementation of population programs, including: (a) the sensitivity of the population issue for the public at large; (b) the visibility given to the program and the efforts made to mobilize public support; (c) the organizational structure and location of the program; (d) the extent to which the government commits national resources; (e) the limits of political support by the governmental leadership—how far it is prepared to go in support of the program when faced with concerted opposition; (f) the choice of target populations; and (g) the commitment of program workers to implementation.

4. The implementation of population programs will feed back into and often modify the sociocultural and political environment. A family planning program, for instance, may achieve short-term statistical success through an all-out sales campaign, but at the same time touch off political controversies in the environment. The resulting turbulence might then force the government to close down, curtail, or deemphasize the population effort. The environment, in other words, should be viewed as an unstable equilibrium of forces open to alteration by the effects and side-effects of population policies.

COUNTRY CASES

Stated in slightly different fashion, these four propositions served as the point of departure for the Project on Cultural Values and Population Policy.[1] Begun in 1974, the project involves a coordinated series of major case studies in Egypt, Kenya, Mexico, and the Philippines, with smaller studies elsewhere. The following discussion draws upon the preliminary results of the major studies to construct and exemplify a partial analytic framework for population policy in the developing countries.[2] A brief review of each national situation will be helpful as a backdrop to the analytic discussion.

Egypt

Although various observers had warned about the dangers posed by rapid population growth, it was not until the 1952 revolution that the government sensed a problem in this area. Responding to persuasive figures in the country's rate of demographic growth, Nasser and his fellow leaders often expressed concern about Egypt's ability to feed more mouths. At first they were quite confident that the development begotten by a fresh revolution would raise the standard of living and create other conditions favorable to a decline in fertility. But when the population growth rate continued unabated into the 1960s and the country's overall economic situation worsened, Nasser shifted his stance. In 1962 he declared that "population increase constitutes the most dangerous obstacle of production" and that "attempts at family planning deserve the most sincere efforts supported by modern scientific methods."[3] With full benediction from Nasser, the Egyptian government in 1966 initiated its National Family Planning Program.

The story of the Egyptian program since that time is one of organizational confusion, inadequate funding, discontinuous leadership, and fluctuating commitment by the heads of government. The family planning effort was launched on a massive scale with maximum speed and minimal expenditure. Basically run as an overtime activity in existing health centers, it attracted few takers, especially in the rural areas. Part of the difficulty was organizational (poorly trained personnel, limited hours for service, shortage of supplies, etc.), but also at work was Egypt's preoccupation with international questions, which became acute after the 1967 war with Israel. In the early 1970s, the senior population administrators became highly frustrated with the existing model and gradually shifted to a developmentalist strategy. At present the Egyptian policy is one of promoting population-oriented development through such means as education, women's employment, industrialization, the reduction of infant mortality, and social security. The integrated program also includes population education and the provision of family planning services.

To date there is no evidence that the new approach has been implemented, or that it has had any greater success than its less complex predecessor.

Kenya

During the colonial period, the British government showed some ambivalence toward population growth in Kenya, but on balance leaned toward pronatalism. There was also a strong current of opinion favoring "benign neglect" of the population question. The reasons were essentially political. In the period immediately preceding independence to argue that Kenya had too many people for its resources would lead the nationalists to gesture toward the vast, rich, underutilized farm areas of the "white highlands." The problem, they were wont to say, is not an excess of people but a shortage of land created by colonial greed. Another reason for caution was the need for cheap African labor to help the white farmers compete in world markets. A successful effort to curtail population growth might well diminish this labor supply and drive up wages. The more optimistic of the settlers also believed that increased agricultural and industrial output would amply justify a larger population. Although there was only faint interest in controlling population for economic or political reasons, the planned parenthood movement did enter Kenya during this period with some nominal African participation. But its services were aimed at promoting freedom of choice about family size, maternal health, the emancipation of women, and related individual and family values.

The advent of independence in 1963 touched off a crisis of confidence for the nascent government. The Mau Mau uprisings before independence were linked in the Western press to the subsequent exodus of the former settlers. The Kenyatta regime was thus faced with a frightfully poor image in Europe and North America, one which could be a fatal deterrent to foreign investment. To offset this liability, it made generous concessions toward business and took other steps to improve its credit rating in the international community. In the view of some, it was this desire, much more than a self-generated concern about population growth, which explained Kenya's subsequent adoption of a national population policy.

The proximate origins of this policy lie in two related developments: population projections prepared by J.G.C. Blacker, the government demographer, and a mission sent to Kenya by the Population Council. Using data from the 1948 and 1962 censuses, Blacker developed projections purporting to show that Kenya would face economic disaster if existing rates of population growth continued. These anlayses were picked up by foreign advisors to the government's planning unit and used to convince Tom Mboya, minister of economic planning and development, of the need for external assistance. With Mboya's consent the advisors drafted the basic specifications for a mission from the Population Council. After a visit of three weeks in 1965 the council mission prepared a report that was subsequently adopted in its entirety by the Kenyan government. Its key recommendation was that Kenya adopt an explicit policy favoring reduced demographic growth and toward that end institute an official family planning program. An observer close to the mission reports that there was never any doubt about what its conclusion would be. The country visit appears to have been window-dressing for a policy recommendation that had already been drafted by the foreign advisors.

Both the contents of the population policy and the process by which it was adopted touched off vigorous protest. The Catholic archbishop argued that there was no population problem in Kenya, with vast lands yet to be inhabited. Odinga Odinga, the opposition leader, decried Kenya's capitulation to foreign genocidal interests. Yusuf Eraj, a gynecologist who had helped to establish the private family planning program, charged that entirely too much attention was being directed to the population issue when the real problem was a maldistribution of resources. Others criticized the speed with which the Population Council report became national policy, especially the lack of public hearings and parliamentary debates about birth control. The reactions among members of Parliament ranged from hostile to tepid.

In the face of this unexpected opposition, official enthusiasm for family planning soon cooled. Mboya, the key figure involved in calling attention to the "population problem" later played down its seriousness and in the end, according to some, became completely disenchanted with the stated policy. The family planning program itself was assigned to the Ministry of Health, where emphasis was placed on birth-spacing and health rather than on the socioeconomic consequences of demographic growth. Top officials, including several ministers of health, gave out signals that population and family planning were not high on their lists of priorities. As a result, a program was mounted but with heavy staffing by expatriate medical personnel and little commitment at higher levels. Although reliable statistics are difficult to obtain, the consensus among most knowledgeable observers is that Kenyan family planning effort has attained little success. In many quarters one hears the view that this was ultimately a foreign idea imported through the government's back door and sustained only by the abundant availability of international aid. Whatever the validity of this perception, its widespread diffusion throughout the country has had a significant impact on program implementation.

Philippines

If the evolution of population policy in Kenya was marked by a sharp spurt followed by a jagged plateau, the process in the Philippines was more incremental and undulating. Long before the Commission on Population was established in 1969, private individuals and organizations had been active in promoting family planning. The initial impetus came from physicians concerned about the health and welfare of their patients. In the 1960s their involvement meshed with the burgeoning interest and funding of several international organizations, most notably the U.S. Agency for International Development (USAID), the Pathfinder Fund, and the International Planned Parenthood Federation. The creation of the Family Planning Association of the Philippines in 1965 added to the momentum. Also significant during this period were the efforts of a few local governments, such as the Manila City Health Department, to initiate small-scale family planning programs.

The first sign of formal governmental endorsement of population control was seen in 1967 when President Marcos signed the world leaders' statement on population and human rights. Two years later he issued an executive order instituting a commission on population "to recommend policy, make program recommendations, and undertake research." Recognizing the sensitivity of the population question in the Philippines, Marcos tried to forestall opposition by appointing commission members from almost every major interest group, including the Roman Catholic church. During much of 1969 the government's concern with population matters was subordinated to the more pressing issue of reelection. Having won a new term, Marcos became more energetic in his support of fertility control. In his State of the Nation message in January 1970, he proposed legislation making family planning programs a part of governmental services, and shortly thereafter created the new Commission on Population to implement this policy. Although there was some popular and congressional criticism of the population bill, it passed with no opposition, though with numerous absentees, on July 17, 1971. The law set forth the structure and functions of the Commission on Population and laid down guidelines for family planning and other aspects of population policy.

With the advent of martial law in 1972, the Marcos government became more aggressive in its approach. The Revised Population Act (P.D. 79) of that year had a less elevated tone than its predecessor and placed much more emphasis on effective means of fertility reduction. Since 1972 the population program has moved ahead in many areas, but it has also suffered from a complex and cumbersome organizational structure centered in the Commission on Population. While family planning services have spread across the country, the effort has been plagued by interagency rivalries, high discontinuation rates, rumors about the side-effects of contraceptive methods, and other administrative difficulties. Further, despite frequent affirmations of support by President Marcos and other key officials, there is a lingering doubt about the government's willingness to finance the program should the present heavy influx of foreign funds be withdrawn. A key question, to be pursued shortly, is why the government adopted the organizational forms and policy emphases now found in the program. The answer will require careful attention to two actors: USAID and the Roman Catholic church.

Mexico

The most striking feature of Mexican population policy is the abruptness with which it changed in 1972. Throughout its history Mexico, like most Latin American countries, had shown a marked preference for pronatalism. The usual conditons favoring high fertility, such as labor intensive agriculture and high infant mortality, were augmented by several unique, population-related events in Mexican history. Notable among these were the country's loss of half its territories to the United States in 1848 and the heavy casualties of the 1910 revolution. In the postrevolutionary period, the notion of an expanding population was woven into the complicated fabric of nationalist populism. As late as the 1970 presidential campaign, the ruling party's candidate, Luis Echeverria Alvarez, declared himself in favor of more Mexicans and opposed to birth-control programs. It was this same Echeverria who, two years later, shifted the policy level into "Reverse."

Even now the precise reasons for this shift can only be inferred. The decision was apparently made in the highest councils of the Institutional Revolutionary party, or perhaps even by the president himself. Both because of the customary secrecy of decision making in Mexico and the sensitivity of the population issue, the true rationale for this change has never been made public. Nevertheless, most observers agree that a concern about the detrimental impact of population growth on Mexican development was a major factor.[5] Demographic research during the 1960s produced convincing evidence that the country's economic expansion was not keeping pace with the demands for employment arising from rapid population growth. Also at work was a concern about urban deterioration in Mexico City, the large number of illegal abortions throughout the country, and a fear of the political consequences of a swelling population of young people.

Although the reversal of the stated population policy was almost instantaneous, there were, in retrospect, premonitory signs of change over the previous decade. Starting around 1960, informed observers of the Mexican scene began to comment that the country's development problems were not being solved. Job opportunities, housing, schools, and other public services were not being provided to the growing population. It was not until around 1967, however, that serious sociodemographic studies on these questions were carried out. Over the next three years, both these studies and research on abortion aroused official interest in exploratory action programs. In 1969 and 1970, the Institute of Social Security took the first steps to develop a postabortive family planning program in this institution. For political reasons no action was taken during the period surrounding the presidential campaign of 1970. Faced with internal economic difficulties and the prospect of rampant international inflation, Echeverria officially reversed his position at the end of 1972. Shortly afterward family planning services began to be offered as part of governmental programs in maternal and child health. In 1973 the existing population law was changed in an antinatalist direction, with a great deal of publicity in the media. This change was followed in 1974 by the creation of the National Population Council (CONAPO) and the government's active participation in World Population Year. In 1974 and 1975 CONAPO vigorously promoted the expansion of family planning services, as well as educational, training, research, and other supporting activities. Throughout this last period the government's population policies became entwined with the politics of the presidential succession.

The remainder of this paper presents a tentative analytic framework for relating the sociohistorical and political environment to the formulation of population policy. The aim is less to offer a series of precise, all-embracing hypotheses than to propose a strategy for

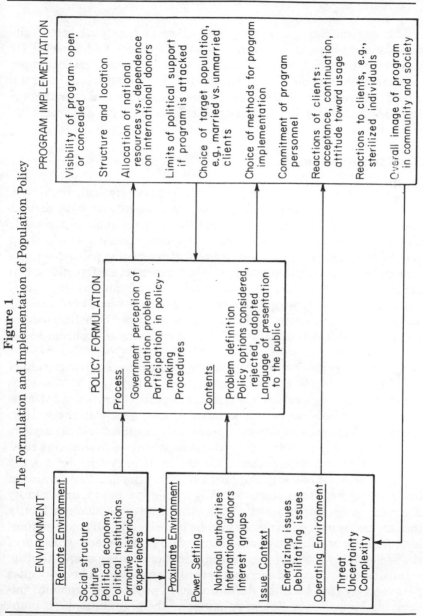

Figure 1

The Formulation and Implementation of Population Policy

conceptualizing the complex interactions arising in national population efforts. The central elements in the framework are presented
schematically in Figure 1. The first challenge is to inject content into
the serviceable but rather hollow concept of "environment."

ENVIRONMENT[6]

The environment of population policy is the total set of circumstances affecting its evolution at all stages. To be useful for
analytic purposes, this broad notion must be translated into more
circumscribed and observable categories. The first distinction in the
model, one reflecting differences in the immediacy and directness of
environmental impacts, is between the *remote* and the *proximate*
environment.

Remote Environment

The remote environment consists of those physical, historical,
sociocultural, ecological, and technological conditions with distant
effects on the policy process. Because the range of such influences is
almost without limit, the analyst must quickly determine which set
of conditions holds the greatest promise of explaining policy formulation and program implementation. While the exact configuration will
necessarily flow from the unique situation of each country or culture,
four components of the remote environment have broad applicability
across diverse situations: social structure, culture, the political economy, political institutions, and formative historical experiences.

Social structure and culture Prominent in the remote environment of
population policy is the social structure and culture of the total
society as well as its subgroups. Social structure refers to the patterns
of interaction between or among members and groups in the society.
From the standpoint of demographic policy, its most critical aspects
are often kinship patterns, the class structure, and interethnic relations. In most developing countries, the kinship system defines the
family to include not only the husband, the wife, and their children
but a variety of other relatives. Where this sytem is found, family
planning programs beamed at the American-style nuclear family
(not an uncommon occurrence) may be perceived locally as meaningless, foreign, or subversive of cultural values. The class structure of
the society may also have serious implications for the shape, timing,
intensity, direction, and success of population policies. Leñero argues
persuasively that both the definition of a "population problem" underlying Mexico's population policies and the programmatic content
of these policies are decidely middle class in inspiration.[7] This situation, in his view, grows out of the class structure created in the wake
of the 1910 revolution. Ethnic conflicts also play a significant role in

many countries, including Kenya, Ruanda, Burundi, Lebanon, and Malaysia. In Kenya the presence of forty-two diverse and often competing tribal groups kindles constant suspicion about the "true" purpose of the government's family planning program.

Culture, in turn, embraces the norms, values, beliefs, and symbols guiding the choices made by members of the society and shaping their interactions with each other. The ways in which a nation's culture and subcultures can impinge on population policy are legion. The economic and social value placed on children, conceptions of right and wrong in the area of sexuality and contraception, definitions of proper sex role behaviors, abiding notions of obligations to kinsmen, conceptions of magic and the supernatural, and beliefs about the efficacy of any kind of planning are only a few of the cultural elements with direct relevance to family planning programs.

Political economy The political economy of a nation is a component of the remote environment with far-reaching, if sometimes invisible, implications for population policy. This term refers to the total structure of a country's economic relations and decision making, domestic as well as international. The adjective "political" underscores the inherent power dimension in economic transactions.

Two aspects of political economy are especially significant for population policy and programs. The first is the degree of the country's dependency on export markets, foreign investment, and foreign aid. In general, the greater the dependency on external sources of income, the weaker the country's bargaining position on population issues. There is persuasive, if indirect, evidence that donor agencies have put pressure on recipient countries to undertake or increase population activities. The main effect of dependency is to strengthen the leverage which such organizations can exert. This point has particular relevance for Kenya and the Philippines. Secondly, the internal structure of ownership and economic decision making, which are inseparable from the class structure, largely determine which domestic interest groups enter the proximate environment and the amount of influence they can bring to bear on policy decisions. For example, despite the heavy participation of the state in Mexico's economy, the structure of ownership makes the industrial group of Monterrey a force to contend with in many areas of policymaking, including population.

Political institutions The formulation and implementation of governmental population policies are also tied to the country's political institutions. Both the formal and the informal structure of power within the government help to determine who will be in the proximate environment of policy setting, what weight each actor will have, where the policymaking will be enacted, the political connotations a given strategy will evoke, and the overall chances of implementation. The present research suggest two basic questions about a country's institutions.

First, what is the *formal* structure of authority and decision making? Is there a legislature, and does this body have to be consulted on matters of population policy? While both the frequency and the influence of independent legislatures seems to be shrinking, even a rubber-stamp institution can affect the timing, if not the substance, of population policy. Committees must be struck, hearings held, and perhaps accommodations made in the interests of muting opposition. The enactment of the first population law in the Philippines, for example, was a considerably more protracted process than a successor decree issued under martial law. The presence of an independent judiciary also leaves open the possibility that certain policy provisions, such as compulsory sterilization or mandatory courses on birth control before marriage, will be struck down as unconstitutional. In general, the greater the diffusion of power across formal institutions and the greater the number of groups with a legal right to consultation, the more likely a country is to endorse voluntarism and eschew coercion. Conversely, the more authority is concentrated in a few hands, such as a military leader or a strong chief executive, the greater the opportunities for rapid action and coercive measures of population control. In Egypt the highly centralized Nasser government was able to move almost overnight to add family planning to the normal responsibilities of the country's health clinics. This opportunity was not available to President Marcos of the Philippines before martial law.

Second, what is the *informal* or de facto decision-making structure in the government? By law, custom, or force, who are really the key figures in determining population policy? Whatever the formal provisions of Mexico's constitution, a potent legacy of centralization and paternalism makes the presidency the commanding institution in public policy. It is also inconceivable that any major decision would be taken in Kenya without the approval of President Jomo Kenyatta and, just as importantly, that any program would be vigorously implemented if he were skeptical about its worth. Although Kenya has a parliament and a nominal opposition, Kenyatta's position as the nation's founding father, bolstered by tight political control in many spheres, makes him an overriding institution himself. This point has a direct bearing on the present population effort in Kenya. Beyond the presidents or chief executives who have been crucial actors in all of the countries under consideration, it is essential to know the other actors comprising the institutional setting for a given decision arena, such as population. The main role of the remote environment in this respect is to select those who will form the immediate power setting for policy formulation and implementation.

Formative historical experience One of the most challenging tasks in policy analysis is to determine the relative influence of distant historical experiences. Two extremes on this point seem equally misguided. One is exaggerated historicism, the view that nothing in the present can be properly understood without minute analysis of the country's distinctive heritage. This approach can easily degenerate into a ritualistic quest for a nonexistent continuity or, if there is continuity, into a romantic historical determinism. Rigid ahistoricism, on the other hand, runs the risk of missing the true wellsprings of policy development and of overstating the potency of contemporaneous forces.

The Project on Cultural Values and Population Policy sought to avoid both extremes by focusing on *formative* historical trends and events—those circumstances in the past with significant transference to the immediate environment of population policy.[8] The touchstone of assaying history became reasonable evidence that a given conflict, issue, attitude, or event produced reverberations carrying over to the present. This is scarcely an exact criterion, but it has served well in defining the limits of historical analysis. Even so, there have been sharp disagreements among the country directors on the weight to be assigned to the past. These differences arise in part from genuine dissimilarities in national experiences and in part from varying definitions of the proper role of history as an explanatory factor.

From the beginning, students of the Mexican experience have found that it is impossible to grasp the dynamics of that country's present population policy without careful attention to historical antecedents. The final report lists several factors which, in the eyes of the author, had a crucial impact on the current policy environment.

First, throughout Mexican history, even in the prehispanic period, population growth was seen as an essential element in the struggle for survival. Among the tribes who populated the area before the arrival of Cortes, large numbers were needed for both conquest and defense. The Spanish, for their part, had even greater reasons to support abundant reproduction. Growing numbers of Indians and mixed breeds (*mestizos*) would provide the extensive labor required by the hacienda system as well as the large mining industry, manual laborers for construction, and an abundant servant class. Also favoring pronatalism was the uncontested belief that open lands should be filled with people, and that "to govern is to populate."

Second, at specific points in Mexico's past, this deep-rooted pronatalism was given a sharp boost by heavy losses of people and territories. Whatever the predilections of the Spaniards, the massacres, disease, and exploitation of the conquest produced an absolute decline in population. Leñero estimates that some 250 years after the beginning of Spanish rule the population had dropped from 7.3 to 5.2 million.[9] The war of independence (1810-1821) produced additional casualties. To make matters worse, in 1848 Mexico lost about half of its total land area to the United States. The fact that the conquered territories were only sparsely settled reinforced the belief that low population density encourages expansionism from the North. As subsequent efforts to attract European migrants bore little fruit, the policymakers of the day concluded that high fertility was the sole answer. A final wave of losses, amounting to about 10 percent of the population, came with the Revolution of 1910. The nationalism born of this uprising set limits on foreign immigration, so that fertility remained the only viable option for growth.

Third, the evolution of church-state relations over the last century produced a tacit division of influence with clear implications for population policy. During the colonial period the church had great authority in all spheres, but its main focus of interest and power was in matters of culture and the family. The traditional precept of "increase and multiply" and the doctrine of natural law as applied to procreation became accepted moral teachings in Mexico. The liberal reforms of Juarez (1859-1861) stripped the church of much of its secular power but, ironically, bolstered its influence over religion and ethics. It soon became apparent that the humanistic ideology of the reformers was not a substitute for the more systematic and robust ethics of Catholicism. As a result, the church was given de facto hegemony in the area of mortality, particularly the family and procreation. The same pattern was repeated after the Revolution of 1910, which saw extensive anticlericalism and repeated attacks on the church. Anxious to heal the wounds of this conflict, the government once again came to terms with the hierarchy. Speaking of this period, Leñero comments:

The fear of re-opening new conflicts and frictions means that the government allows the Church to form an elite in Catholic schools—despite the fact that they are illegal—and to establish religious organizations. The government keeps out of the normative field of individual ethics, which continues to be the Church's domain. Within this field fall reproductive behavior and the integrity of the traditional family. In turn, the Church withdraws from the political and economic area so as not to inconvenience the government .... Therefore, a demographic policy with implications for changing family behavior is not seen as a strategic objective by post-revolutionary governments.[10]

It was precisely on these terms that the church entered the proximate environment of population policy in the 1960s.

Fourth, between 1910 and 1972 a commitment to population growth became an accepted ingredient of the populist nationalism espoused by the Institutional Revolutionary party. The longer the revolutionary government was in place, the more it made sense to exalt the growth of its political offspring. At the same time, for deeply felt historical reasons, the nationalist ideology reacted strongly against anything North American, particularly a culture-laden export such as birth control.

To judge from the preliminary results of the Project on Cultural Values and Population Policy, distant historical experiences had less of an impact on current population policy in Kenya, Egypt, and the Philippines than in Mexico. For Kenya a paramount and still unresolved question concerns the demographic consequences of colonial land policy. At the very least the British preoccupation with safeguarding the rich "white highlands" seems to have worked against overt action on population control. Even to have raised the population question in the immediate preindependence period would have provoked charges that the issue was not overpopulation but excessive concentration of land among the white settlers. Also salient in Kenya and much of sub-Saharan Africa is a lingering fear that birth control is a latter-day outcropping of the genocide wrought by slavery. The genocide issue continues to hover, like a contaminating cloud, over many aspects of program implementation.

Research to date suggests relatively few formative historical experiences in either Egypt or the Philippines. The Egyptian research team maintains, in effect, that the true history of population policy in that country begins with Nasser in 1952. Policymakers do not feel constrained by a compelling legacy of pronatalism nor obligated to justify family planning on the grounds of consistency with historical values. In the Philippines, as in Mexico, a crucial survivor of the past is an intricate pattern of conflict and cooperation between church and state.

Proximate Environment

The proximate environment includes those actors, issues, and conditions with an immediate and/or direct influence on the policy process. Immediacy and directness are related but not identical concepts. The essence of immediacy is being close at hand, while directness implies action without intervening persons, conditions, or agencies. The minister of health in a developing country often has an immediate as well as a direct influence on population policy by being a live participant in policy formulation and implementation. A politician, on the other hand, would have immediate but indirect influence if he had the ear of the minister on all population matters but took no formal part in policy deliberations.

The distinction between remote and proximate environments is not water-tight, but it can be useful in ranking the impact of external influences and in winnowing out those with a trivial effect on population policy. The proximate environment is analogous to the frontstage of a dramatic production and the remote environment to the backstage. On the frontstage are the performers with assigned parts in the play as well as those conditions, such as sets, lighting, props, and costumes, which shape audience response and the flow of action onstage. On the backstage and in the wings are the individuals and conditions affecting the frontstage performance, including the producer, director, set designers, and lighting technicians. In the population drama one would want to add a category of unchartered actors who, with slight provocation, can leap uninvited onto the stage and coopt the lead roles. This group might include traditional religious leaders, disgruntled members of the opposition, and others eager to jump in should the scheduled production falter. The point to be emphasized is that the remote environment sets the stage for population policy, while the drama is enacted in the proximate environment.

The proximate environment includes three overlapping subparts: the power setting, the issue context, and the operating environment. The first embraces individuals, groups or organizations; the second matters of public concern; and the third environmental conditions.

The Power Setting

The power setting consists in those individuals, groups, or organizations with an immediate and/or direct influence on population policy. In the developing countries the main actors usually include national authorities; international donors; and national, international, or mixed interest groups.

National authorities. The first question to be asked in determining the power setting is who has formal authority to direct, restrain, supervise, investigate, audit, or otherwise participate in the policy process. The most common participants are the chief executive, ministers, and other key individuals in the executive branch; legislative bodies, which may both authorize action on policy and establish the administrative structures and arrangements to be followed; monitors, particularly auditing agencies which can demand accountability on expenditures, program efficiency and related matters; and formal collaborators, or the agencies which must work together in designing or carrying out population policies. The fragmentation of authority common to many governments combined with competition for scarce resources often makes policy actions at once diffuse and inherently political. The critical role of national authorities is evident in the findings from Mexico, Kenya, Egypt, and the Philippines.

The presidency looms very large on the Mexican political scene, as does the rite of presidential succession held every six years. The adoption of a formal population policy in 1972 immediately became interlaced with the politics of choosing a successor to Echeverria. Although the formal unveiling of the leading party's candidate was not scheduled until September 1975; by 1973 the contest was well underway. The heir apparent was then widely thought to be Mario Moya Palencia who, like Echeverria before him, headed the Ministry of the Interior (Secretaría de Gobernación). Moya not only came out enthusiastically in favor of the new population policy, but took the lead role in adapting it to the cultural values and political realities of the country. Almost inevitably, however, his unannounced but generally accepted candidacy for the presidency became inseparable from the population effort. Moya adroitly maneuvered to insure that the policies and programs formulated by the government would be preeminently Mexican and would generate as little domestic political opposition as possible. Before long aspirants to lesser power also saw paydirt in population.

> Hundreds of persons and personalities who a few years before were indifferent to the population problem or even spoke against family planning on the grounds of basic value principles, now became enthusiastic promoters of the new programs. Some even found themselves suddenly directing these programs . . . .
>
> People who until then had no background in the field became, from one day to the next, *animadores* and activists for creating an awareness of population programs throughout the country. At root there was a dynamic of political action cells linked to the fortunes of the very possible candidacy . . .of Lic. Moya Palencia.[11]

The linkage between population policy and presidential politics had both short and long term implications. Between 1973 and 1975 the development of specific population strategies became very much a political endeavor. Politics entered into the policy options chosen and rejected, the language adopted in presenting the new concepts to the public, Mexico's prominent espousal of the "population and development" position at the World Population Conference in 1974, decisions about which regions to select for pilot projects, and a concerted effort to mobilize constituency support among state governors, union leaders, academic researchers, and other opinion leaders. On more than one occasion Moya's staff also made it clear to population researchers that controversy in this area was to be avoided. As it happened, in September 1975, the candidate of the Institutional Revolutionary party was not Mario Moya Palencia but José López Portillo. There is some speculation, in fact, that Moya's keeness for family planning, however hedged in Mexican phraseology, may have impaired his candidacy by linking him too closely to a position regarded as American. As this juncture it appears that the new government will be inclined to treat family planning in a technical rather than a political manner. Those who were originally attracted to this area for political reasons have left and are seeking greener pastures elsewhere.

In Kenya the sway of the president over population matters is so overwhelming that it cannot be discussed openly.[12] Jomo Kenyatta seems caught between the tensions created by ethnic rivalries, which could argue against active involvement in family planning, and contrary pressures from international donors. The solution seems to be a compromise calculated to produce the greatest benefits and the least harm for Kenya. On the one hand the government accepts funds from international agencies and mounts a national, if feeble, family planning effort. On the other hand the president refrains from comment on the issue, while those close to him, including the relevant ministers, show few signs of enthusiasm. So far as can be determined, at no time has Kenyatta ever spoken openly in favor of family planning or allowed his name to be used in promoting this program. The resulting situation, as we shall see, has critical implications for the level of commitment to program implementation.

The situation in the Philippines illustrates a point which also seemed to apply to India under Indira Gandhi: the greater the centralization of executive power, the greater the opportunities for vigorous action on population control. Lopez and Nemenzo contrast the tone and content of Philippine population legislation before and after the martial law of 1972:

> Within less than three months after the declaration of martial law on 21 September 1972, a more aggressive population policy was put into effect. Unlike the earlier documents, the Revised Population Act (P.D. 79) emphasizes service strategies and incorporates such untested outreach innovations as the commercial distribution of contraceptives and the utilization of paramedics in dispensing family planning methods. Sterilization, previously allowed but not encouraged, is included . . . .
>
> Comparatively, the 1969 statement was loft in conception; it reflected the influence of the commission's subcommittee on Religion and Culture in stressing education for responsible parenthood. Presidential Degree 79, on the other hand, is more pragmatic in orientation. It provides for family planning as part of a long-range educational program, but given greater concern to means for the immediate adoption of family planning.[13]

The authors' conclusion underscores the importance of the total context of executive power: "Needless to say, the political situation left no opposition to the innovative programs—at least at the formulative stage."[14]

International donors. Across the developing world, with the notable exception of China, international assistance agencies have had an incalculable effect on the formulation and implementation of national population policies. The precise influence of given agencies is difficult to assess, for it is often merged with that of other organizations, national and international, mediated through training activities, or obscured by national pride and diplomatic delicacy. The manner in which such influence is exercised ranges from direct pressures to indirect consciousness-raising activities.

Whatever the truth of the matter, there is a widespread perception in Kenya that international donors put the government under pressure to accept aid for a national family planning program. According to Ndeti, the Dutch government threatened to withdraw its assistance unless action was taken on population.[15] Other donors, including the World Bank, apparently sent out signals indicating that requests for other projects would be viewed more favorably if set in a development context including family planning. The government's strong need for foreign aid and outside capital meant that such guidance could not be scorned. But the cost may have been formal compliance with the donor's wishes but inward dissent leading to minimal commitment and temporizing at the implementation stage.

USAID was and is a decisive force in the evolution of population policy in the Philippines. While it, too, may have put direct pressure on the government, its main strategy seems to have involved the creation and support of a variety of domestic organizations. These, in turn, were able to generate a critical mass of family planning activities which lent credence to the notion of a larger, coordinated national program. Lopez and Nemenzo describe the USAID approach in these terms:

> Technically, the USAID should have channeled its funds through the NEC (National Economic Council) but with a chairman opposed to family planning programs, a means was devised to circumvent this obstruction. In 1968 USAID signed a contract with the Department of Health (DOH) to create a Project on Maternal and Child Health (POMCH); through the project, USAID was able to mask its support of family planning programs. Because one of the functions of POMCH was to coordinate USAID-assisted health projects that included family planning, the latter was given the opportunity to work with and thereby influence a number of Filipino private organizations ....
>
> The strategy employed by USAID in establishing a population program is known to have violated a few of the agency's canons. While the normal operating procedures call for institution-building in carrying out programs, a family planning program was launched among a number of private organizations competing with one another for donor agency funding. The programs did not involve extensive host government administration, and

United States support was not conditioned on traditional self-help financing. In fact, the USAID consciously offered near total financing for projects it deemed promising.[16]

USAID as well as other donors have used similar strategies elsewhere.

The role of the Ford Foundation in Mexico, by contrast, illustrates the effect of low-key, indirect foreign assistance. Except for India, where it mounted a highly visible program of direct assistance, the foundation's preference has been for research, institution-building, training, conferences, and similar activities. In Mexico Ford worked in the population field primarily through grants to institutions, such as the Colegio de Mexico and the Instituto Mexicano de Estudios Sociales, which were concerned with demographic issues. The foundation staff also brought the research directors together with other interested parties at meetings and cocktail parties. According to Leñero, who was one of the first participants, the resulting exchanges stimulated an awareness of demographic trends and their implications for Mexico. The Ford Foundation carried out comparable activities in many other countries, including Egypt, and was also a prime mover in establishing centers for international demographic training and research in the United States.

Interest groups. Population policies and programs usually impinge on the interests and self-definitions of various organized groups in the society, including political parties; religious organizations, racial and ethnic groups; medicine, nursing, social work, and allied professions; family planning associations; teachers; and parent-teacher associations. Most often these groups are national in origin and inspiration but sometimes, as in the case of the Roman Catholic church and family planning associations, they may represent a mingling of foreign and domestic influences. In any given case the challenge for policy analysis is to identify those groups with a frontstage role. The precise configuration will differ from country to country, but research to date suggests a remarkable consistency among the lead actors in the population field.

In Roman Catholic countries, such as Mexico and the Philippines, the church will almost inevitably enter the policy equation. In earlier days the government was often put on the defensive by fulminations from the cardinal archbishop or minatory declarations from the papal nuncio. Even now, when Catholic leaders are less inclined to public edicts, the church is very much a presence on the policy stage. In the search for acceptable strategies policymakers and program implementers alike must steer around the reefs of doctrinal orthodoxy and the shoals of intractable issues. Examples from Mexico and the Philippines later will show that defensive reactions to anticipated church opposition can have a marked effect on national policies and programs. Religious leaders have also played a significant role in Kenya and, to a lesser extent, in Egypt.

The other key interest groups emerging from the present research are political parties, family planning associations, professional organizations, and ethnic groups. Leaders of the Institutional Revolutionary party in Mexico, especially legislators, apparently made a deliberate effort to ensure that the government's new population policies would mirror the populist nationalism which was its hallmark. The aim was in part to present an appearance of internal ideological consistency and in part to ward off charges by political adversaries that Mexico had "sold out to U.S. imperialism" or otherwise sullied national values. Local family planning associations, usually with the backing of private physicians, lent momentum to the development of explicit population policies in all four of the countries studied. Their impact seems to have been greatest in the Philippines, next in Mexico, and least in Kenya, where the family planning movement had only tenuous roots in the society. Medical associations in these countries have also been influential in opposing the nonclinical distribution of contraceptives or other changes in the traditional doctor-patient relationship. Ethnic rivalries have had the greatest impact on population programs in Kenya, where tribal tensions are pervasive. Although there is considerable cultural heterogeneity in the Philippines, ethnicity has emerged as a serious issue only in the Moslem region of Mindanao, where the familiar charges of genocide are heard. Racial and cultural cleavages thus far have spawned no significant conflicts in either Mexico or Egypt, but the potential exists among indigenous groups in Mexico.

Issue Context

The issue context is that aspect of the proximate environment comprising matters or points in question, under discussion, or in dispute. Issues are neither actors, as in the power setting, nor conditions, as in the operating environment, but rather questions serving as the focal point of controversy in the society. They might be compared to the nerves of the human body which both energize its organs and signal pain in the system. Some issues, such as maternal and child health, economic development, and a fear of overcrowding, can transmit the positive impulse of political legitimation to population policy. Divorced from broader programs of political and social development, this impulse will usually be weak. Other questions, such as those raised in charges of tribalism, genocide, or imperialism, may be so heated that they cause instant pain or distress when linked to population policy. By instinct as well as design government politicians usually seek to associate population efforts with positive, energizing issues and to avoid those with debilitating effects. Opposition parties and other adversaries commonly try to reverse the process.

The issues most closely tied to population policy are usually the direct legacy of a country's social structure and culture, political economy, and formative historical experiences. The question of tribalism in Kenya, an issue growing out of the nation's colonial experience as well as its present social and political structure, can scorch, sear, or char any policy which it touches. For both historical and contemporary reasons anti-Americanism stands out as an inflammatory issue for policy setting in Mexico. With an eye to the past and the present the policy analyst must uncover the precise bundle of issues, latent and manifest, which stretch across the proximate environment of population policy in a given country at a given time. These are often elusive, tangled, and subterranean. For practical purposes once the issues are mapped the analyst can turn to the power setting and the operating environment, for it is there that they come into play. Issues with no actors to seize upon them can safely be relegated to political paleontology.

Operating Environment

The operating environment is the set of conditions immediately impinging on the processes of policy formulation and implementation. As used here, a condition refers to a pattern of impersonal circumstances affecting the operations of individual decision makers or policy-related organizations. Three kinds of conditions seem especially relevant for understanding population policy in the developing countries: threat, uncertainty, and complexity.

Threat. A state of threat exists when the environment is viewed as a real source of harm, loss, or other severe form of deprivation. For nation-states threat may arise from external as well as internal sources. As Gadalla notes, Egypt's loss to Israel in 1967 eclipsed the government's concern with stemming population growth:

The widespread recognition and serious attention which family planning received from the political leadership and top government officials in 1965 and 1966 declined very rapidly after the 1967 war with Israel. The prime concern and commitment of Egypt was directed to the necessity of rebuilding its armed forces and introducing rapid changes in its political system and external relationships in order to pull the country out of the humiliating state of defeat. Consequently, family planning was one of the programs which faded out of the focus of attention and was seldom mentioned or commented upon in the speeches of political leaders.[17]

After its success in the 1973 war, by contrast, Egypt seemed more ready to turn its attention to the population question.

In both Mexico and the Philippines perceived threats to internal political stability galvanized concern about population growth. During congressional debates on population policy in the Philippines, O.D. Corpuz, then secretary of education and chairman of the Population Commission, "argued publicly that radical movements and violent student unrest could be blamed on the population explosion."[18] Similarly, the 1968 student uprisings in Mexico, joined to the massacre that followed, provoked a severe crisis throughout the country. Leñero argues that this chain of events shattered the triumphalism of the ruling party and dealt a fatal blow to the concept of a growing but united "revolutionary family."[19] As a consequence, Mexico "had to recognize that there were serious problems with no solution in sight, and that demographic growth made these increasingly difficult."[20] The sense of threat was accentuated by the growing number of land invasions in urban as well as rural areas, a disorder even more easily traceable to population growth. In Kenya, as we have seen, the country's adverse image in Western nations jeopardized its chances of obtaining badly needed foreign capital. The government's willingness to be the first African nation with an explicit population policy may have sprung from a desire to remove the threat by creating an image of "responsible government."

Uncertainty. The degree of uncertainty or unpredictability in the environment will also affect both policy formulation and program implementation. Two hypotheses already have solid support from case studies of national programs. First, the greater the degree of political uncertainty in the country, the less likely is the government to adopt explicit antinatalist policies. Within the spectrum of development programs, population activities, and especially family planning programs, are among the most volatile. Particularly when plagued by ethnic and religious tensions, as was the case with Lebanon for many years, political leaders will hesitate to embark on ventures which could further endanger political stability. Second, the larger the measure of uncertainty about the future of the government, the greater the reluctance of senior program implementers to commit themselves wholeheartedly to program implementation. They may well fear that if the political winds shift, their association with a tainted program would prove to be a severe liability. J.C. Caldwell writes of Africa:

> However, a fact of life in most of tropical continental Africa is the instability of governments and the ever present possibility of their replacement by a new regime ... which may single out the policies of the previous regime as having been wrong or evil. This ... makes officials, both in government and private organizations, reluctant to become too fully committed to one policy or to be too conspicuous in pushing the development of a programme. Where the programme may be contentious in terms of the society's value system, as family planning programmes still are in most African countries, the officials may hedge their bets by letting it be known that their enthusiasm is qualified or they may proceed faster with the paper work ... than with the build-ups of clinics and personnel.[21]

Despite the tendency of some to view population policies as largely a technical matter, the experience of many countries leaves little doubt that they are inextricably bound up with the uncertainties of the larger political system.

Complexity. The concept of complexity refers to the number of elements found in the policy environment and the intricacy of their connections. The central elements for population policy include the number and diversity of international donors operating in the country; the variety of interest groups with a stake in population matters; the range of domestic organizations which must be consulted in policy formulation or which take part in program implementation; the geographic dispersion of the country and the adequacy of communication facilities from one region to the next; and the number of sensitive issues touched by the contemplated policies and programs. While the environment for population policy is never simple, the range of complexity varies enormously. Some countries, such as Indonesia, must contend with large numbers of people, ethnic and linguistic heterogeneity, a plurality of religions, far-flung and sometimes inaccessible regions, and a profusion of international agencies which may be in competition with each other. South Korea, by contrast, offers a far less labyrinthine operating environment for population programs.

Although the precise effects of complexity will hinge on many other circumstances, research to date suggests several hypotheses. First, the greater the political complexity, the greater the need for extensive consultation during policy formulation, and the slower the process of developing explicitly formulated policies. Second, the greater the number of organizations, national or international, involved in program implementation, the greater the problems of coordination and the greater the chances of bureaucratic rivalries. This point is well illustrated in the Philippines. Partly because of the proliferation of competing agencies resulting from the early USAID involvement, the Commission on Population faces extraordinary difficulties in coordinating the disparate units falling within its mandate. Third, the greater the complexity, the greater the pressures to develop a centralized bureaucracy to impose order on a seemingly chaotic environment. The larger the bureaucracy, the greater the chances of complaints about rigidity and the more insistent the demands for new organizations to provide "innovative responses" without the shackles of hierarchy and rules.

The foregoing discussion points to a variety of ways in which the remote and proximate environments can affect population policy, and vice versa. We now offer a more systematic presentation of the dimensions and interrelationships of policy formulation and program implementation. Although policy formulation is the first topic to be treated, it should be remembered that in some cases program implementation, often in the form of quiet experiments and pilot projects, actually precedes and sometimes legitimates explicit statements on the policy which it implies. The relationship between these two processes is thus best viewed as interactive rather than linear.

POLICY FORMULATION

The policy environment as well as the existing state of program implementation will shape both the *process* and *contents* of policy formulation. Process and contents are interconnected in the sense that different forms of policy formulation will yield different options, while initial statements on the goals of policy setting will affect who participates and how the deliberations are conducted.

Process

The central questions about the policy-setting process are the following:

Does the government perceive a population problem, and when does this perception occur? Some countries, especially in Africa and Latin America, report that they experience no problems with respect to demographic growth or other policy variables. In this case explicit policy formulation never begins or is quickly terminated. In other countries national leaders may perceive a problem of excessive growth, but refrain from initiating formal discussions because of the cultural or political sensitivity of the population question. The timing of problem perception is also related to the policymaking process. A government may state that it has no problem of excess population, but as part of its deliberations authorize a series of demographic studies. As the results become available they may create or reinforce a need for more explicit policy action. USAID, among other donors, has often supported demographic research with the hope that it would lead to national consciousness of a population problem.

Who participates in policy formulation? The range of participants involved in policy setting will affect not only the options chosen and rejected but the legitimacy of the results in the surrounding society. Policies perceived to be the creation of a narrow elite, a specific interest group, or some other potentially biased source will be open to attack on the grounds of nonrepresentativeness. Excluded groups may also, as a matter of principle or political retribution, mount a minor crusade against both process and contents. For this reason governments sometimes take pains to coopt potential opponents by giving them formal roles in the policy deliberations. Such was the case with the Roman Catholic church in the Philippines:

> The Catholic Bishops Conference of the Philippines (CBCP) had been made a member of the Commission on Population during the first years of its existence as an advisory body to the Executive Office. This was a strategic political move as it brought a threatening force to collaborate with government in formulating policy on a sensitive issue. Certain themes espoused by the hierarchy, like the emphasis on responsible parenthood and examination of macro-measures for fertility control, were reflected in the 1969 Statement on Population Policy and Program. The commission, however, upheld integration of family planning in the health care system, and the acceptability of foreign assistance. While most bishops remained firm in their

support of official Catholic teaching, theologians in the commission's Committee on Culture and Religion recognized the primacy of the couple's freedom of choice to select the type of contraceptive to be adopted. This paved the way for the cafeteria approach of service delivery rather than a purely rhythm program, which some Church leaders had hoped for.[22]

The attempt to coopt potential adversaries can backfire, however, if they discover the true purpose of the participation or have a change of heart. At their annual meeting in 1971 the Philippine bishops voted to withdraw their representative from the Population Commission.

One theologian interpreted the move, supported by the papal nuncio to the Philippines, as being in line with the alleged general Vatican policy against artificial birth control. The main reason given by the CBCP was that its presence on the commission was being used by some field workers to support the claim that the Church approved all methods.[23]

In a decision arena enmeshed in value conflicts, participation may help to forestall procedural objections, but it is unlikely to resolve the deeper divergencies of belief. Process can elude but rarely vanquish substance.

How are the deliberations conducted? The reception accorded to population policies also depends on the manner in which policy deliberations were carried out. One issue is the degree of their secrecy or openness. There is still a feeling in Kenya that the government's family planning program was whisked past the parliament as well as ordinary citizens. This feeling, added to the fact that the policies adopted were almost identical to those recommended by the U.S.-based Population Council, has left a foreign taint on Kenyan program. Completely open deliberations, on the other hand, increase the opportunities for political sniping and organized counteroffensives by the government's adversaries. The speed with which policies are adopted may also reflect environmental pressures as well as condition subsequent acceptance. Hastily enacted legislation, for example, may satisfy internal or donor demands for "action" but leave the resulting programs with very shallow emotional and political roots.

Contents

The remote and proximate environments, as well as ongoing programs, will further affect three aspects of the contents of population policy: the definition of a "population problem" underlying policy formulation; the specific policy options chosen, rejected, and never considered; and the language used in formulating policies and presenting them to the public.

Problem definition. Government population policies invariably address themselves to the solution of some problem. In the 1960s the most common justification for policies to limit fertility was that demographic growth is an obstacle to economic development. For many countries the immediate source of this problem definition was less a careful analysis of the national situation than a ready acceptance of theories and data developed elsewhere. Adding to this impetus was pressure from international donors to accept the conventional wisdom as the basis for national programs. As time went on, both the evidence supporting this problem definition and its appropriateness to certain national situations were increasingly called into question.[24] Thus in its first stages of policy formulation the Kenyan government accepted without question the thesis that population growth harmed economic growth. When this thesis was severely challenged by domestic critics, however, the rationale began to shift to health and welfare considerations. Government spokesmen now say that Kenya is not interested in controling population, but rather in increasing the freedom of couples to choose family size and to enhance the welfare of mothers and children. After the World Population Conference of 1974, which cast further doubt upon facile economic correlations, even hard-core advocates such as USAID added other rationales to their armamentarium, particularly maternal health and the freedom to choose. The fact that these shifts have produced little change in either population aid or national programs suggests that they often serve as window dressing for predetermined conclusions.

Policy options. The decision-making environment is a preponderant factor in determining which policy options will never come up for formal consideration, which will be considered and rejected, and which will finally enter into official policy. For most Roman Catholic countries abortion is such a delicate moral and political issue that it will not be presented as a live option. Such seems to have been the case in both Mexico and the Philippines, as well as in Egypt and Kenya for different reasons. Sterilization, on the other hand, is often considered, but its handling is highly sensitive to environmental pressures. In the Philippines before 1972 and in Mexico, the governments decided that this method could be made available but that it should not be actively promoted. According to Leñero, the Mexican government feared that any conspicuous emphasis on sterilization would touch off the charges that it was violating the natural right to bear children—a tender nerve in the issue context then and now.[25] Finally, the power setting, the issue context, and the participation process can affect the definition and ordering of the alternatives selected. A pivotal issue in the Philippines, one championed by the Catholic hierarchy, was freedom in the choice of contraceptive methods. A decisive requisite for church acquiescience was agreement that the national program would offer the rhythm method. The Commission on Population has nominally acceded to the church's wishes on this point with its policy of a "cafeteria" approach to family planning, with the choice of methods left to the client. Whether this policy accords with clinical reality is another question.

Language of presentation. The manner in which a policy is presented to the public often tempers its reception as much as does its operational content. In most Catholic countries a family planning program billed as "responsible parenthood" would set off more harmonious vibrations than one called "birth control" or "fertility regulation." The resonances evoked by a given phraseology depend in part on the society's cultural traditions but also on the immediate issue context. It is scarcely accidental that both of the Catholic countries in the present study, Mexico and the Philippines, adopted the language of "responsible parenthood" in their formal policies. By borrowing a phrase from the papal encyclicals the policy officials sought to avert charges that family planning was un-Catholic or against the natural law.

Mexico has probably gone further than any country in choosing language to generate a maximum of support and a minimum of opposition. In a detailed analysis of the present Population Law, Leñero shows that the government legitimated its policy in a thoroughly eclectic manner, drawing values from all the prevailing ideologies.[26] The following are among the law's stated objectives:

1. "To pursue economic and social development and not substitute for it." This phrase, which echoes the World Population Plan of Action, not only reflects the widely shared value of developmentalism but could ward off the usual charges from the socialist wing.
2. "A policy based on the sovereign self-determination of the nation, rejecting neocolonial attitudes." This objective reaffirms tradi-

tional Mexican nationalism and, by implication, states that the new policy was not imposed by the United States.

3. "Absolute respect for human rights and our national cultural values." A further certification of Mexican identity together with language designed to satisfy Catholic critics and those suspicious of the government's strongly centralized authority.

4. "A national character with the collaboration of *all* the social sectors, public as well as private." The added endorsement of the law's Mexican credentials seems designed to allay lingering fears of foreign inspiration. The emphasis on cooperation seems a concession to the populist values of the PRI as well as a promise of negotiation with potential critics, such as the church.

5. "Equality of the sexes." In this and related actions the government seeks the support of women by linking responsible parenthood to feminine liberation. By implication, the government suggests that family planning could be an instrument of reducing male dominance (machismo) in Mexican society.

Mexican population policy, in other words, is purely Mexican in origin, reflects Mexican values and traditions, is designed to solve pressing national problems, and will serve the interests of all sectors of the society. This carefully tailored language, together with adroit publicity for the new law, had their desired effect. Public acceptance ran high, while attacks from the government's traditional critics, including the church and the Marxists, were not vociferous.

PROGRAM IMPLEMENTATION

The combined forces of the environment and policy formulation will be of crucial importance as policies move from the drawing board into action. Unfortunately, in the literature on population planning this point has often been obscured by unfounded assumptions of rationality in programming and by a machine theory of organizations. Planners commonly assume that the essential ingredient for effective population programs is a coherent and sharply formulated plan. Such rationalism is usually coupled to an unstated organization theory which views program implementers as unthinking, unfeeling, driven cogs on the wheels of administjation. Guided by lucid plans and propelled by the engine of authority, program officials need little more than adequate pay, tight supervision, and decent working conditions to ensure compliance with orders from above. Politics, conflicts, inertia, and stupidity can, of course, cause bureaucratic "foul ups," but these can easily be remedied by tightening up the machine and applying the time-honored solvents of remonstrance and persuasion.

Both organizational research in general and specific studies on population programs point up the absurdity of a rational, machine model of implementation.[27] Quite clearly partisan politics, religion, cultural traditions, and other extrarational influences can impinge on every aspect of program execution. If officials do not believe in what they are doing or find themselves caught in impossible value dilemmas, they will make adjustments that are adaptive for themselves, including the oft-encountered response of doing nothing. The present research suggests ten areas in which the environment and prior policy formulation can influence program implementation.

Visibility

The sociopolitical context will make a difference, first of all, for whether programs are openly identified or buried under other organizational rubrics. In many countries, including Kenya, population questions are so highly charged that family planning programs cannot be allowed to stand naked before the public. Hence they are typically merged with maternal and child health (MCH) and postpartum programs or placed under other umbrellas. The fact that there may be sound medical and administrative reasons for such combinations does not negate the political motives for "integration." What applies to the overall family planning program may also apply to specific methods. Where abortion is a volatile issue, pressures will be strong to play down its existence and to mask it with terms such as "menstrual regulation." Rogers, in fact, provides operating instructions on how to construct salable euphemisms for troublesome items.[28]

Structure and Location of Program

How a population program is organized and where it is placed within the government bureaucracy will also reflect contextual influences. Where government commitment is strong and birth control is not an overly sensitive issue the family planning program may form a single, strong, independent organization with its own mandate and its own budget. Where, on the other hand, public opinion is polarized and the government itself is ambivalent, family planning is more likely to be a subsidiary of some other agency, such as the

Ministry of Health, or an independent but relatively weak coordinating body. Those familiar with Mexico would also not be surprised to learn that the National Commission on Population (CONAPO) is closely tied to the Secretaría de Gobernación, a portfolio which handles inter alia questions of domestic politics.

The Philippines illustrates how the cumulative impact of foreign donors can merge with national conditions to create a distinctive organizational structure. As noted earlier, USAID's entering wedge was a strategy of buying into a series of national organizations in order to mobilize domestic support for family planning. Once on stage these agencies wanted, of course, to remain active. Philippine politics in 1969 augmented the pressures for widespread consultation and participation in formulating population policies. As a result, when the government reached the point of establishing an organizational superstructure, it had to deal with a balkanized environment of competing agencies. The body which emerged, the Commission on Population, was assigned the task of coordinating this heterogeneous mass, rather than beginning de novo with fresh programs. Lopez and Nemenzo describe the continuing tensions produced by this arrangement:

> The progeny of USAID in the form of numerous organizations competing for donor agency funding is also problematic. At the field level, rivalry between agencies is not an infrequent occurrence. When one agency's program does not reach expectations it is sometimes easier to continue the existing operations rather than call the attention of the agency's representative, especially if that agency is a member of the governing board of the commission. This is not surprising when one considers that social acceptance, smooth interpersonal relations, and sensitivity to personal affront are characteristic Filipino values.[29]

Beyond such indirect influences, donors may take a direct hand in specifying or negotiating organizational structures as part of a project agreement. The World Bank is especially known for its concern with organization and management structure.

Allocation of National Resources

History, politics, and culture will also affect the government's willingness to commit its own funds, personnel, buildings, and other resources to population programs. In general, when population is controversial within the society and the government itself does not rank it as a high priority, it will not be inclined to allocate more than a minimum of resources. In these situations donors are often more than willing to fill the gap in the interest of overcoming resistances to family planning. Kenya seems to be a case in which the government, despite official affirmations of support, is reluctant to provide substantial financing to the population effort. The donors have responded by making more money available than the country will take or can usefully spend. This very eagerness to dispense foreign funds reinforces suspicions that the program is not in the national interest. In Mexico, by contrast, the government has taken pains to demonstrate that its population program is of national origin, inspiration, and funding. Although it does receive assistance from the United Nations and other donors, the bulk of the funds provided are indeed from Mexican sources. From 1972 to 1976 one overriding reason for both the image and the reality was Mexico's desire to avoid any impression that the program was an American import.

Limits of Political Support

Under heavy criticism or attack, to what lengths is the government willing to go in backing a population program? Typically, the extent of support will be directly correlated with the degree to which the program reflects national values and aspirations, accords with the government's own priorities, avoids the snares of partisan politics, and provides services which are genuinely desired by the country's citizens. The program is most likely to be jettisoned in battle if it is the creation of a single leader or a small, controversial elite group; if it was established largely as a concession to foreign donors; if in its contents, staffing or products it conveys the image of foreign goods; if it touches tender nerves of politics, religion, or ethnic relations; and if its services are pressed upon a disinterested public through coercion, manipulation, or propaganda. Perceptions about the limits of support, in turn, will mediate the degree of commitment to the program at all levels. To the extent that program officials sense that the government will abandon the population effort under slight to moderate attack, they will take protective cover under rules, regulations, memoranda, clearances, interunit concurrence, and other disguises for interaction. The vehemence of the attacks launched against the Pakistan government's population program in the immediate post-Ayub period, and the speed with which it was closed down, suggest that such defensive reactions are scarcely irrational. This writer has the distinct impression that fears of limited support are pervasive in the higher echelons of the Kenyan government's family planning program.

The Choice of Target Populations

Foreign donors, national traditions, and domestic actors in the power setting often interact in shaping policy decisions about the target for population programs. In the case of family planning programs, the pivotal question in many countries is whether services should be offered to all takers, or only to married persons. Donor organizations, particularly USAID and the International Planned Parenthood Federation, invariably press for unlimited distribution of family planning services. The Roman Catholic church, on the other hand, has been vehement in its opposition to services for the unmarried. In both Mexico and the Philippines it would have been political suicide for the government to propose unrestricted services. Official policies in both countries explicitly restrict services to married couples. In Kenya, by contrast, contraceptives are freely available, and national authorities estimate that about 50 percent of the clients are unmarried women. This policy, as we shall see, has had significant repercussions on the program's image in the country.

The Choice of Methods

Local traditions and interest groups also influence the methods chosen and avoided in population programs. In predominantly Islamic and Roman Catholic countries the religious heritage will usually preclude abortion and raise serious moral doubts about sterilization. Largely for religious reasons abortion has been banned in all four of the countries reviewed here. There is clear evidence, at the same time, that some donor organizations, particularly the International Planned Parenthood Federation and the Pathfinder Fund, are quietly lobbying for changes. Abandoning its traditional strategy of opposing all forms of artificial birth control, the church in the Philippines has focused on the issue of freedom in the choice of methods, and implementation issue.

If the church in general has appeared silent or neutral with regard to the family planning program, it has nevertheless been vocal about the manner in which the program has been implemented. A year after the Revised Population Act was issued the hierarchy came out with a pastoral letter criticizing the content of the program (e.g., the bias for pills and IUD, adoption of the quota system of acceptors) and the proposed innovative strategies of the Commission (e.g., the utilization of paramedics for pill dispensing and IUD insertion) on the grounds that they militated against freedom of choice and the exercise of moral integrity.[30]

The church appears to exercise similar tutelage in Mexico and other Latin American countries. Whether or not its leaders issue pastoral letters or speak out openly on the subject, the very fact that they are known to be concerned will typically breed caution among policymakers.

Commitment of Program Personnel

No matter how clear and direct government policies may be and how strong the statements of support from political leaders, no population program will succeed without the commitment of those who carry it out. Serious studies on the sources and correlates of commitment are still in their infancy. Still, there is mounting evidence from many countries that staff willingness to observe and execute formal policies is highly sensitive to political, cultural, and other environmental influences. The Project on Cultural Values and Population Policy is exploring several questions in this area.

First what is the effect on lower program levels of commitment at the top? Although complete data are not yet in, the Kenya case suggests a mixed and somewhat counterintuitive pattern. From all indications politicians and high-level administrators are, at best, ambivalent about the family planning program. No one, Kenyan or other, has accused the government of pulling all administrative stops to produce rapid results. But interviews with attendants and field workers in local clinics reveal a high degree of stated belief in the program—higher than that manifested by their superiors. The reason may be that many of these workers have relatively little formal education, but receive salaries roughly one-third higher than comparable health personnel with greater education. It is also highly doubtful that their stated belief in the program translates into all-out effort to win new converts to family planning. Nevertheless, the Kenyan example suggests that while high-level commitment is of crucial importance, its effects may be felt more in the middle than in the lower echelons of program administration.

Second, what is the impact of the immediate political context on program implementation? What happens, for instance, when local staff are seriously committed to a family planning program, but encounter strong opposition from local politicians and opinion leaders? One could hypothesize that where workers come from the same ethnic group as their critics and judge that they will need their support for promotions or other types of career advancement, the pressures will be strong to hold back on vigorous action.

Third, what is the effect of value conflicts experienced by staff members themselves? What are the implications for commitment when a nurse does not believe in sterilization or the IUD, but is still expected to dispense this service or commodity as part of the clinic's program? Dilemmas of this sort have arisen for family planning workers in the Philippines. Similarly, what will result when a staff member sees conflicts between the family planning effort and professional or ethnic identifications? S.U. Kodikara points up this problem in Ceylon:

> At an organizational level, much depended on the Medical Officer of Health who was manager of the family planning team in his district.... Though he had training in family planning work, he might give it low priority in relation to other aspects of preventive medicine entrusted to him. Or he might be concerned with the ethnic implications of family planning. In such cases the progress of family planning in his district was bound to suffer.[31]

Feeble commitment may reveal itself in attention to other priorities, inaction, absenteeism, hostility or indifference toward clients, preoccupation with bureaucratic details, slipshod work leading to complaints or rumors, direct subversion by starting or abetting rumors, and in other ways.

Reactions of Clients

All of the influences noted thus far can bear upon client reactions to a population program. In the case of family planning programs there are three critical dimensions of client response. The first concerns *initial acceptance* of the program, commonly measured by acceptor rates. Despite the sweeping and inflated statements sometimes made about the universality of demand for family planning services, the experience of Kenya and other countries shows many instances in which clients, especially in rural areas, do not come forth when these services are offered. The reasons are many: high infant mortality, low literacy and education, the social and economic value placed upon children, the image created by the program itself, and so on. A second dimension is *continuation*, usually reflected in continuation rates for contraceptive usage. In some cases initial acceptance is high, but it is followed by high levels of complete discontinuation or a shift to "less effective" methods, such as the condom. The experience of the Philippines suggests that cultural factors, including rumors about the side effects of the pill and the IUD and pressures from mothers or mothers-in-law, are related to continuation. A third and more subtle issue lies in *attitudes toward usage or adoption*. A priest reports, for example, that some Mexican women, faced with overwhelming economic pressures to restrict childbearing, decide to take the pill. At the same time they feel that what they are doing is sinful.[32] Similarly, Elder reports that Indian men who have undergone sterilization later experience guilt feelings for having sexual relations with no possibility of conception.[33] Such feelings are often written off as irrational, but they may well contribute to an environment of ambivalence about family planning, even among users. Should the pendulum swing toward opposition, even adopters may temporarily join the ranks of the antagonists to assuage their own guilt.

Reactions to Clients

How the community and the larger society respond to program clients will affect their willingness to continue as users, their disposition to praise or condemn the program before others and, ultimately, the program's overall image in the society. Community reactions to sterilized males are a case in point. While the operation is usually billed as safe, quick and simple, research in India indicates that it can produce quite varied reactions according to local cultural conditions. In Gujarat state, vasectomy is linked in the popular mind to a semireligious group of castrated or impotent males who are incapable of intercourse.[34] A man returning to this environment would undoubtedly elicit different reactions and develop a different self-image from one residing in an urban area where the operation was not a particular focus of attention. The cumulative impact of such "sleeper effects" once again might be to contaminate the environment for subsequent program interventions in the area.

Overall Image of the Program .

The sociocultural context, the process by which policies were developed, the contents of the policies, the choice of target populations, client response or nonresponse, and other conditions already mentioned will shape the population program's image in the society. This, in turn, will feed back into and often change the proximate environment. For example, a widespread perception that the family planning program is a source of immorality and corruption or a manifestation of colonialism can affect the society's image of itself. Beyond a certain threshold these changes can set off homeostatic mechanisms designed to protect the system against further alteration. The protective devices could include dismantling the entire effort, closing down certain controversial operations, such as propaganda campaigns, or a quiet decision to deemphasize and decelerate but still maintain the program.

The Kenya study provides several examples of negative images begotten by the activities or staff of the family planning program. A major complaint emerging from interviews with national opinion leaders was that the program is a prime source of immorality in Kenya. The reason most often cited was the policy of distributing contraceptives to the unmarried. When asked about the effects of the program on national morality, the executive director of a welfare organization replied:

> Yes, the young people have been made more flexible and have lost the moral values of the African people. Most of them have abused the objectives of the programme. The single unmarried were not intended to use the programme, but today they are the ones using these methods.[35]

In response to a question about whether anyone should be discouraged from using family planning, a tribal chief stated:

> School girls, because ... their morality will be wrecked. This will impair future family stability when these girls marry and still think they are free to have sex with anybody.

Other opinion leaders drew an explicit connection between supplying contraceptives to the unmarried and moral decay in Kenyan society.

A related issue has to do with the characteristics of the family planning program's staff. Several commentators said that by hiring single and especially divorced women the program gave off an image of disrespectability. This was reinforced by the practice of paying poorly educated field workers at rates higher than for those around them. The impression left was that family planning workers are morally dubious people who have to be given special benefits to compensate for "dirty" work.

A third contaminant is the perception that by paying "lavish" salaries and providing special equipment the family planning program is overshadowing more basic development activities. A nutritionist at a health center commented:

> These days there are only mobile family planning clinics; other medical services are not there in mobile form. So people think this is washing over medical services.

For some critics the very copiousness of funds for family planning, coupled with their scarcity for other health services, fortifies the perception that population programs are an offshoot of imperialism and a genocidal attempt to reduce the number of Africans.

CONCLUSION

In conclusion, a thorough understanding of population policies and programs requires a complex, dynamic, and interactive conceptual model. At one level it is instructive to consider the effects of the sociopolitical and historical environment on policy formulation, and the joint impact of the environment and policy formulation on program implementation. While helpful, this unidirectional approach may overlook two sets of questions: (1) the ways in which antecedent program implementation legitimates and sets the stage for explicit policy formulation; and (2) the ways in which both policy formulation and program implementation feed back into and change the environment, with implications for later policies and programs. This paper presents a preliminary model which allows the policy analyst to address both questions. As next steps it would be useful to develop a set of hypotheses about the various kinds of relationships and to test them with a broader range of case studies than those explored here.

NOTES

This paper grows out of the Project on Cultural Values and Population Policy coordinated by the Institute of Society, Ethics, and the Life Sciences in Hastings-on-Hudson, New York. It is a partial summary of the first findings of this project. The author is indebted to the authors of preliminary reports on country situations: Luis Leñero Otero of Mexico; Maria Elena Lopez and Ana Maria Nemenzo of the Philippines; Saad Gadalla of Egypt; and Kivuto Ndeti of Kenya. Although the discussion borrows from their analyses, the author accepts ultimate responsibility for the interpretations made here. Present plans call for a book-length treatment of the questions raised in this chapter when the country studies are completed.

1. The project is a cross-national investigation coordinated by the Institute of Society, Ethics, and the Life Sciences with support from the United Nations Fund for Population Activities (UNFPA). The coparticipants in the major country studies are the Instituto Mexicano de Estudios Sociales of Mexico City; the Social Research Center of the American University in Cairo, Egypt; the Institute of Philippine Culture of the Ateneo de Manila University in the Philippines; and Dr. Kivuto Ndeti and his associates at the Center for African Family Studies at Egerton College, Njoro, Kenya. The author has been project manager of the investigation since its inception. The views expressed here should be interpreted as those of the author alone, rather than of the UNFPA or any of the other participating institutions and individuals.

2. The following discussion is based on five reports prepared for the Project on Cultural Values and Population Policy:

> Luis Leñero, *Investigación Sobre Valores Culturales y Políticas de Población en Mexico* (Mexico City: Instituto Mexicano de Estudios Sociales, A.C., 1976).

> Luis Leñero, *Values and Population Policies in Mexico: Preliminary Study* (Mexico City: Instituto Mexicano de Estudios Sociales, A.C., 1975).

> Maria Elena Lopez and Ana Maria R. Nemenzo, "The Formulation of Philippine Population Policy," *Philippine Studies*, 24 (1976): 417-38.

> Saad Gadalla, *Development and Prospects of Egypt's Population Policy and Family Planning Program* (Cairo: Social Research Center, the American University in Cairo, 1976).

> Kivuto Ndeti, *Preliminary Report for the Project on Cultural Values and Population Policy*, 1976.

In addition to these reports, the paper will also draw on oral presentations made by the country directors at several project meetings, and on the author's own interviews and conversations in Mexico (where he resided in 1974-1975), Kenya, and the Philippines.

3. Gadalla, p. 5.

4. *Family Planning in Kenya: A Report Submitted to the Government of the Republic of Kenya by an Advisory Mission of the Population Council of the United States of America* (Nairobi, Kenya: The Ministry of Economic Planning and Development, 1965).

5. Leñero, 1976. See also Frederick C. Turner, *Responsible Parenthood: The Politics of Mexico's New Population Policies* (Washington, D.C.: American Enterprise Institute for Public Policy Research, 1974), pp. 2-12.

6. The conceptual framework developed in the following pages draws on Donald P. Warwick, in collaboration with Marvin Meade and Theodore Reed,

A Theory of Public Bureaucracy: Politics, Personality, and Organization in the State Department (Cambridge: Harvard University Press, 1975), especially chapter 4.

7. Leñero, 1976, pp. 43-47.

8. The concept of formative historical experiences has been developed by Seymour Martin Lipset, *Revolution and Counterrevolution: Change and Persistence in Social Structures* (Garden City, New York: Doubleday, 1970).

9. Leñero, 1975, p. 12.

10. Ibid., pp. 16-17.

11. Leñero, 1976, p. 73. Translation by author.

12. This interpretation of Kenya is entirely that of the author rather than of the Kenyan research team. It is basically an inference from the preliminary findings on Kenya as well as from interviews which he conducted with various persons knowledgeable about the country.

13. Lopez and Nemenzo, pp. 432-433.

14. Ibid., p. 433.

15. Ndeti.

16. Lopez and Nemenzo, p. 423.

17. Gadalla, p. 16.

18. Lopez and Nemenzo, p. 427.

19. Leñero, 1976, p. 31.

20. Ibid.

21. J.C. Caldwell, "Family Planning in Continental Sub-Sahara Africa," in *The Politics of Family Planning in the Third World*, edited by T.E. Smith (London: George Allen and Unwin, Ltd., 1973), p. 61.

22. Lopez and Nemenzo, pp. 428-29.

23. Ibid., p. 429.

24. For a careful critique of the data linking population growth to economic development, see Michael Conroy and Nancy Folbre, *Population Growth as a Deterrent to Economic Growth: A Reappraisal of the Evidence* (Hastings-on-Hudson, New York: Institute of Society, Ethics, and the Life Sciences, 1976).

25. Leñero, 1976, p. 62.

26. Ibid., pp. 80-83.

27. The machine theory of organizations has been widely criticized in the literature on organization theory. For a concise statement of the limitations of this position, see J. March and H. Simon, *Organizations* (New York: John Wiley, 1958).

28. E. Rogers, *Communication Strategies for Family Planning* (New York: Free Press, 1973).

29. Lopez and Nemenzo, p. 438.

30. Ibid., p. 18.

31. S.U. Kodikara, "Family Planning in Ceylon," in *The Politics of Family Planning in the Third World*, p. 333.

32. Arnaldo Zenteno, S.J., "It is Good. But a Sin." *Boletin Documental Sobre Las Mujeres*, Special Issue: An Anthology on Women in Latin America (CIDAL, Cuernavaca, Mexico), October 1974.

33. R.E. Elder, Jr., *Development Administration in a North Indian State: The Family Planning Program in Uttar Pradesh* (Chapel Hill, North Carolina: Carolina Population Center, Monograph 18, 1972).

34. T. Poffenberger and H. Patel, "The Effect of Local Beliefs on Attitudes Toward Vasectomy in Two Indian Villages in Gujarat State," *Population Review*, 8, 1974, 37-44.

35. This and the following two quotations are based on interviews conducted under the direction of Dr. Kivuto Ndeti in Kenya.

Contributors

HAROLD D. LASSWELL is Ford Foundation Professor Emeritus of Law and Social Sciences at Yale University Law School, and co-chairman of the Policy Sciences Center in New York City. He is a fellow at the Center for Population Studies, Harvard University. His most recent book is a preview of the policy sciences.

JOHN D. MONTGOMERY is Professor of Public Administration at Harvard University. His most recent book is *Technology and Civic Life: Making and Implementing Development Decisions.*

JOEL S. MIGDAL is Associate Professor of Government and research fellow at the Center for International Affairs at Harvard University. His most recent book is *Peasants, Politics and Revolution* (Princeton University Press); his forthcoming book is *Palestinian Society and Politics* which will be published by Princeton University Press in 1979.

JOHN C. ICKIS, formerly Assistant Professor, The Graduate School of Business, Harvard University, is currently consultant on population policies to governments and regional centers in Latin America.

DAVID C. KORTEN is Visiting Lecturer on Population Studies, Department of Population Sciences, Harvard School of Public Health. He is currently serving as project advisor in development administration at the Ford Foundation Office in the Philippines.

FRANCES F. KORTEN is Visiting Lecturer on Population Studies, Department of Population Sciences, Harvard School of Public

Health. She is currently serving as program officer for development planning and management at the Ford Foundation Office in the Philippines.

FARRUKH IQBAL is formerly population specialist and economic planning advisor at the International Bank for Reconstruction and Development and is currently doing research in the Department of Economics at Yale University.

MYRON WEINER is Ford International Professor of Political Science at the Massachusetts Institute of Technology and a member of the Center for Population Studies at Harvard University. His most recent book is *Sons of the Soil: Migration and Ethnic Conflict in India.*

NANCY LUBIN, a former student in government at Harvard University, has completed advanced studies at Oxford University and is currently on a research assignment in the Soviet Union.

ELEANOR E. GLAESSEL-BROWN is a doctoral student in the Department of Political Science at the Massachusetts Institute of Technology. She is currently doing research on the effect of labor migration from Latin America on New England industry.

PHILLIP G. CLARK is an affiliate of the Harvard Center for Population Studies and consultant for international programs at the Institute of Society, Ethics and Life Sciences (The Hastings Center) in New York.

GAITHER D. BYNUM, M.D. has been engaged in biomedical research at the Quartermaster Research Laboratory, Natick, Massachusetts. He is currently staff physician at the National Institute on Aging, Gerontology Research Center, Department of Health, Education and Welfare, Baltimore City Hospitals, Baltimore, Maryland.

DONALD P. WARWICK, institute fellow at the Harvard Institute for International Development and lecturer on education and on sociology at Harvard University, has been manager of the project on cultural values and population policy of the Hastings Center. His most recent book is *A Theory of Public Bureaucracy* (Harvard University Press).

Index